National Trauma and Collective Memory

National Trauma and Collective Memory

Major Events in the American Century

Arthur G. Neal

M.E. Sharpe
Armonk, New York
London, England

Library of Congress Cataloging-in-Publication Data

Neal, Arthur G.
National trauma and collective memory : major events in the American century /
Arthur G. Neal.
p. cm.
Includes bibliographical references and index.
ISBN 0–7656–0286–5 (hardcover : alk. paper) — ISBN 0–7656–0287–3 (pbk. : alk. paper)
1. United States—History—20th century—Case studies.   2. United States—Social
conditions—1933–1945—Case studies.   3. United States—Social conditions—1945—
Case studies.   4. Crises—Psychological aspects—United States—History—20th
century.   5. Memory—Social aspects—United States—History—20th century.
6. National characteristics, American. I. Title.
E741.N43   1998
973.9—dc21   97–46625
CIP
Printed in the United States of America

The paper used in this publication meets the minimum requirements of
American National Standard for Information Sciences—
Permanence of Paper for Printed Library Materials,
ANSI Z 39.48-1984.

∞

BM (c)   10   9   8   7   6   5   4   3   2   1
BM (p)   10   9   8   7   6   5   4   3   2   1

Dedicated with deepest love and affection to my wife, Helen Youngelson-Neal. She made my personal life much less traumatic than it otherwise would have been.

Contents

Preface

The present book was designed to develop narratives on the major traumas of the twentieth century. There are many stories that have been told and retold about the extraordinary events of concern. Indeed, the many nuances of each of these episodes permit telling the story in a variety of ways. The present emphasis is limited to the trauma aspects of these events. Efforts were directed toward taking the concept of trauma as it has been elaborated for dealing with crises in the personal lives of individuals and giving it a collective reference. Thus, attention has been directed toward comparison and contrast with traumas in the lives of individuals and traumas as they were experienced collectively. My own perspective is that of a social psychologist who is interested in both the individual and collective responses of Americans to some of the more memorable events of their time and place.

Each case study focused on individual and collective reactions to a volcano-like event that shook the foundations of the social order. Conditions of national trauma called for examining the qualities and attributes of social life, how they had changed, and what they were likely to become. An attempt was made to capture the shock and disbelief associated with the disruptions of everyday life. The newsworthy events of concern became disturbing to all major subgroups of the population. An emphasis was placed upon both the emotional and the cognitive aspects of collective responses. The many ways in which plausible explanations of how and why the tragedies occurred were also of concern. Additionally, an emphasis was placed on the enduring effects of these traumas as they become embedded in the collective memories of the nation.

The narratives of these traumatic events can never be told once and for all. As historical circumstances change, the stories must be told and retold by each succeeding generation. The retelling of stories is in part based upon the excavation of new data about them with the passing of time. But, more important, the stories take on new meanings for subsequent generations as they rework their social heritage and confront new sets of challenges. Further, the accounts of our past are being selectively retold by those who see themselves as disadvantaged by the social heritage from the past. The uncertainty surrounding national traumas permit drawing upon them as raw materials for forging new identities, for setting the record straight, and for shaping new sets of opportunities.

We may ask, why select the traumas of the twentieth century? Certainly, the American Revolution, the institution of slavery, and the Civil War were major traumas that are deeply embedded in the American conscience. However, with the passing of time, these aspects of our past more appropriately belong to the domain of professional historians. The more recent traumas are a part of the memories of Americans now living. There are millions of Americans alive today who still vividly remember their direct encounters with the Great Depression of the 1930s, the Japanese attack on Pearl Harbor, the Cuban Missile Crisis, the assassination of President Kennedy, and the Vietnam War. The recency of these events conveys implications for data collection and analysis that are not available for those events that are frozen in a more distant past. It is the reflections of those now living that will have the more immediate impact on the linkage of historical encounters with hopes and aspirations for the future.

This book is intended to serve as a stimulus for conversation across generational lines. New generations have surfaced that had no direct experiences with the traumas that had such a serious impact upon the lives of their parents and grandparents. There is a tendency for the older generations to avoid talking about experiences that were painful, while many members of the younger generations have little interest in events that are now frozen in the past. Yet, the more consequential events of the twentieth century have a direct bearing on the personal and collective identities of Americans. Traumatic events of the recent past are important ingredients of our social heritage and continue to convey implications for the prospects and limits of the world in which we live.

What is or is not a national trauma? Certainly there is room for disagreement on the conceptual boundaries for what to include and what to exclude. Students in my graduate seminar suggested that the death of Elvis Presley was a national trauma, while others claimed that the AIDS epidemic qualifies as a national trauma. The news media promoted the Tanya Harding case and the O.J. Simpson murder trial as national traumas. The present study, however, is limited to those events that had a major impact on the institutional structure of society and fed into overriding forms of collective fear and anxiety.

National traumas are not necessarily traumas for all individuals within a society. Because of the size and complexity of modern society, many people respond to national events with cynical indifference, while most who read newspapers or watch the nightly news respond as concerned citizens. National traumas enter into the personal sphere of individual lives in a selective process. The trauma of war, for example, has a direct impact upon the military personnel assigned to combat units and upon their families. The trauma of the Great Depression had a severe impact on those who lost their life savings through bank failures and upon those who found themselves among the ranks of the chronically unemployed. In the final analysis, however, the test for a national trauma is that of the disruptive effects of an extraordinary event on the institutional underpinnings of the social order.

There are many people to whom I am indebted for many of the ideas incorporated into this book. I am particularly indebted to Jan Hajda and Helen Youngelson-Neal for reading all of the early drafts and making helpful suggestions for revision. I am also indebted to several colleagues at Bowling Green and Portland State University for suggesting references or making critical comments on specific chapters. These include Bernard Sternsher, Gary Hess, Ray Browne, Phil Terry, Joe Perry, Lorna Gonsalves-Pinto, Harold Vatter, Joy Spaulding, Jack Fried, David Wrench, Morton Paglin, and Richard Brinkman. Many useful suggestions came from several of my students in social psychology, American culture, and mass communication. Finally, I would like to express my appreciation to the many strangers in airports, coffee shops, and other places who shared with me their personal experiences with one or more of the traumas involved.

Part I

Introduction

1 • Collective Sadness, Fear, and Anger

The concept of trauma is applied primarily to extraordinary experiences in the personal lives of individuals. Trauma involves an element of shock, such as the shock of being stung by a bee, touching a live electrical wire, undergoing surgery, or being in a serious automobile accident. These examples represent the essence of the trauma experience in the sense that an ongoing activity has been interrupted by an adverse happening that is unexpected, painful, extraordinary, and shocking. A trauma has an explosive quality about it because of the radical change that occurs within a short period of time.

Many of the more severe personal traumas grow out of abrupt changes in the qualities of social relationships. Previous feelings of safety and security are replaced by perceptions of danger, chaos, and a crisis of meaning. Such traumas include, for example, having to confront the sudden death of a child or a spouse, being raped by a friend or an acquaintance, or being diagnosed as having the AIDS virus. These are traumatic events in the sense that a fracture has occurred in the lives that men and women have built. The rape victim becomes traumatized through a diminished sense of social value and personal integrity. The person diagnosed as having the AIDS virus is traumatized by the isolating effects of the disease and by the reduced opportunity for living a normal life. Such traumas are frequently of a sufficient magnitude that the individual feels that he or she has become "damaged" or permanently changed.

The psychiatric components of trauma involve the many maladaptive responses that follow an encounter with a deplorable event. These include such symptoms as intrusive recollections of the event, recurrent nightmares and other sleep disturbances, eating disorders, feelings of detachment and estrangement from others, impaired memory, difficulty in concentrating on everyday tasks, a sense of emptiness, and psychological numbing. In effect,

3

the psychological and physiological responses to traumatic events add up to feelings of helplessness and a crisis of meaning in the personal lives of individuals. Restructuring a self-identity and reestablishing one's place in the broader scheme of human affairs becomes necessary.

The concept of trauma may also be applied collectively to the experiences of an entire group of people. Here conditions of trauma grow out of an injury, a wound, or an assault on social life as it is known and understood. Something terrible, deplorable, or abnormal has happened, and social life has lost its predictability. Initial responses to a traumatic event are those of shock, disbelief, and incredulity. Chaos prevails, and people become uncertain about what they should or ought to believe. Individuals lose confidence in their abilities to see the interrelatedness of events, and disturbing questions are raised about the linkage of personal lives with historical circumstances.

A national trauma differs from a personal trauma in the sense that it is shared with others. A rape victim or a person diagnosed as having the AIDS virus experiences some degree of stigma and is thrown back on his or her own resources. The trauma of the victim is an individualized experience that occurs within a context of otherwise normal and happy people. The victim runs the risk of being rejected, developing a sense of estrangement from others, and losing the support of significant others. In contrast, a national trauma is shared collectively and frequently has a cohesive effect as individuals gather in small and intimate groups to reflect on the tragedy and its consequences. Personal feelings of sadness, fear, and anger are confirmed as appropriate when similar emotions are expressed by others.

The enduring effects of a trauma in the memories of an individual resemble the enduring effects of a national trauma in collective consciousness. Dismissing or ignoring the traumatic experience is not a reasonable option. The conditions surrounding a trauma are played and replayed in consciousness through an attempt to extract some sense of coherence from a meaningless experience. When the event is dismissed from consciousness, it resurfaces in feelings of anxiety and despair. Just as the rape victim becomes permanently changed as a result of the trauma, the nation becomes permanently changed as a result of a trauma in the social realm.

Responses to national trauma involve elements of fear and a sense of vulnerability. The fear response reflects a sense of danger and feelings of personal insecurity. For example, the Japanese surprise attack on Pearl Harbor evoked intense levels of fear that the attack was simply a forerunner of a planned invasion of California. People living on the West Coast conjured up images of living in an occupied country. The Cuban Missile Crisis was accompanied by a fear of nuclear war. Mass destruction and death were seen as possible outcomes. Thus, national trauma evokes imagery of living in a dangerous world that is unresponsive to personal needs and interests.

Under conditions of national trauma, the borders and boundaries between order and chaos, between the sacred and the profane, between good and evil, between life and death become fragile. People both individually and collectively see themselves as moving into uncharted territory. The central hopes and aspirations of personal lives are temporarily put on hold and replaced by the darkest of fears and anxieties. Symbolically, ordinary time has stopped: the sun does not shine, the birds do not sing, and the flowers do not bloom.

When collective sadness is accompanied by anger, a volatile situation frequently develops. For example, following the Japanese attack on Pearl Harbor, collective anger was directed toward Japanese Americans living on the West Coast. The Japanese Americans were the most readily available target for venting a collective sense of rage and hostility toward the Empire of Japan. Following the assassination of Martin Luther King Jr., collective anger took the form of widespread destruction and looting in American cities. The actual sources of the stress were not clearly identifiable, while at the same time there seemed to be a need for some kind of action in response to a sense of outrage. Proximate symbols were substituted for venting the aggressive impulse. The facades of harmony and tranquillity in the social realm broke down as collective resentments became expressed in violent action.

A national trauma involves sufficient damage to the social system that discourse throughout the nation is directed toward the repair work that needs to be done. The integrity of the social order has been called into question, and shared values are threatened. The disruption may take the form of a threat of foreign invasion, a collapse of the economic system, a technological catastrophe, or the emergence of rancorous conflicts over values, practices, and priorities. Whatever form the trauma takes, a significant and deplorable departure from the normality of everyday life is in process.

While traumas become transitional events in the life of a nation, some traumas have more lasting effects than others. Permanent changes were introduced into the nation as a result of the Civil War, the Great Depression, and the trauma of World War II. The shock of these events touched the entire fabric of the nation. Other traumas have intense emotional effects at the time of the crisis, but tend to have less lasting effects on the social system. For example, the trauma of President John F. Kennedy's assassination elicited one of the more intense emotional responses in the history of the nation, but very few changes in national priorities or public policies grew out of the event.

The degree to which a nation dwells upon a trauma depends on the degree of closure that is achieved. For example, a few days in October of 1962 were the most terrifying moments in the history of the nation. We were on the brink of nuclear war. However, the Cuban Missile Crisis subsided with the removal of the Soviet missiles from Cuba. The case was closed, and most people were able to put the episode behind them. In contrast, the lack of closure to the conditions surrounding the assassination of President Kennedy resulted in continued preoccupation with what happened in Dallas on November 22, 1963. Although this date is alive in the memories of many Americans, it was not an event that was associated with any clear policy implications or any line of action other than the quest for setting the historical record straight.

The emotions that are tapped by a national trauma grow out of what it means to be human. Universally, the ingredients of trauma include some form of bafflement, some level of suffering, and perceptions of evil in human affairs. The bafflement grows out of an encounter with chaos and an attendant loss of a sense of coherence. Perceptions of evil reflect the frustrations of human effort and an awareness that one's own sense of morality and decency is not shared by others. Because of the suffering associated with trauma, individuals are unable to remain emotionally detached or indifferent. Experiences suggest that to be human is to be vulnerable and that efforts directed toward mastery and control over the outcome of events are limited in their effectiveness.

A national trauma frequently has enduring personal consequences of a highly disturbing nature for those who experienced the event directly. For example, psychiatric studies have revealed that those who had direct experiences with the Japanese attack on Pearl Harbor continued to suffer from flashback memories and recurrent nightmares. While the Japanese attack lasted less than two hours, the experiences of fear, terror, and helplessness were of sufficient intensity to persist and to reoccur sporadically throughout the lifetime of the survivors.

On the fiftieth anniversary of the D-Day invasion of Europe, interviews with survivors received a great deal of attention in the news media. Personal stories were told in a variety of ways about confronting the probability of one's own death, the sadness of seeing comrades killed, the feelings of survivor guilt, and the moral conflicts growing out of being required to kill others. The trauma of the event had a permanent impact on the thousands of men who participated in the heroic undertaking.

The traumas of the past become ingrained in collective memories and provide reference points to draw upon when the need arises. Hearing or reading about an event does not have the same implications as experiencing an event directly. However, as parts of the social heritage, events from the past become selectively embedded in collective memories. For example, following the opening of the U.S. Holocaust Memorial Museum in Washington, D.C., an extraordinary number of people came. Museum officials found it necessary to request that people stay away or postpone their visit to a later date. The people came because of the importance of drawing upon the traumas of the past for reflections on the human condition. The horrors and atrocities inflicted upon human beings by other human beings in Nazi Germany became ingrained in historical memories as one of the major traumas of all times. In reflections on the holocaust it becomes clear that the range of worlds that humans are capable of creating is very vast indeed.

Social Disruption

An event becomes a collective trauma when it appears to threaten or seriously invalidate our usual assessments of social reality. Under such conditions, doubts emerge about the future as an extension of the present, and social events are perceived as discontinuous. Forces are operating that can neither be clearly understood nor controlled. It becomes difficult to integrate the problematic event with perceptions of the orderliness of social life. A deplorable condition has surfaced in the social realm that requires some form of remedial action. The integrity of the social fabric is under attack, and some form of repair work is needed to promote the continuity of social life.

The crises precipitating a national trauma are of two types. One consists of an acute crisis that impinges upon the normal course of events in an abrupt and dramatic fashion. The acute crisis is an unscheduled event in the sense that it falls outside the range of harmony and order within the social system. Acute crises include such events as the firing on Fort Sumter by Confederate forces at the beginning of the Civil War, the assassination of President Abraham Lincoln, the Japanese attack on Pearl Harbor, and the assassination of President Kennedy. While these were abrupt disruptions of the social order, they were not isolated events. A great deal of collective stress and tension preceded each of them. However, they were generally perceived as resembling "a bolt from the blue."

The second type of crisis is chronic, enduring, and long lasting. A chronic crisis lacks the dramatic beginning of an acute crisis, but builds in intensity with the passing of time. This is the type of crisis that grows out of persisting contradictions within a social system. Conditions become deplorable, and problems emerge that require the attention of the nation. Rather than a volcano-like intrusion into an otherwise orderly system, a chronic crisis grows out of enduring conflicts within a social system and the emergence of a crisis of authority. The Great Depression and the Vietnam War are each prime examples of a chronic crisis in the social realm.

While the stock market crash of 1929 is typically regarded as the beginning of the Great Depression, it was not in and of itself a national trauma. Certainly the collapse in the price of stocks was traumatic to many investors, but not to the entire nation. The stock market has a volatile quality to it, and the fluctuation of prices was widely recognized as a market characteristic. What was different about the early 1930s, however, was the scope and severity of the economic decline that ensued. As banks began to fail with increasing frequency and as levels of unemployment escalated, the nation confronted one of the more severe traumas in its history. Economic hardship took its toll on all major sectors of the economy. Capitalism was in a state of crisis, and the free enterprise system failed to work. Economic hardships translated into fear, vulnerability, and a sense of despair. The trauma of economic failure had an indelible imprint upon the consciousness of the entire society.

The trauma of the Vietnam War grew out of conflicts over American foreign policy. The nation became more highly divided than at any time since the Civil War. We were committing troops and resources to a war that a significant number of Americans regarded as immoral and unjust. The combat veterans in Vietnam became unclear about the purposes of the war and what we were trying to accomplish. Before the war was over, several million American men and women served in Vietnam but failed to yield any major victory. It became increasingly evident that it was a war we could not win. Following the fall of Saigon, most Americans wanted to forget about the war and put the nightmare behind us. The veterans returning from Vietnam were unable to make a smooth reentry into civilian life and continued to suffer from post-traumatic stress disorders. The enduring pain and suffering experienced by the veterans commanded the attention of the nation.

It is not the scope of human injuries, deaths, and suffering alone, however, that makes an event a national trauma. For example, the American fatalities in the Korean War exceeded 50,000, only slightly less than those we suffered in Vietnam or in all of the Pacific during World War II. Much of the fighting for the hills in Korea was fierce, and many American lives were lost. The war in Korea was certainly traumatic for the men who fought in it, but we do not think of the Korean War as a national trauma in the same way we think of the Vietnam War as a national trauma. Public opinion was polarized over our involvement in Vietnam in ways in which it was not regarding our commitment of troops to Korea. We did not win the Korean War in the usual sense of winning a war, yet it did result in a stalemate that succeeded in stopping the spread of communism. Our national objectives had been achieved. It was never officially designated as a war, but only as "a police action" under the auspices of the United Nations. The military engagement was perceived as proper and just not only by the policy makers but also by the American public more generally.

Several of the major collective traumas of the 1960s and 1970s grew out of the problems of political and criminal violence. Attention came to be focused on the causes, conditions, and consequences of violence in American life. The fear of personal victimization and the rhetoric of law and order were evident in public discourse and debate. Many Americans were shocked at the violence directed toward participants in the civil rights movement. Others were shocked at the scope of violence in urban riots and looting following the assassination of Martin Luther King Jr. One of the more intense emotional experiences in the history of the nation followed the assassination of President Kennedy. Concerns for violence in the public sphere were subsequently extended to include concerns with such intimate forms of violence as rape, child abuse, and spouse abuse.

The major traumas of the twentieth century lead to a recognition that the orderliness of society is a human creation. But regardless of how well a society is organized, serious and unexpected problems emerge. For example, the spectacular technological achievements of the twentieth century have also been accompanied by extraordinary tragedies. The ingredients of trauma were embedded in the sinking of the *Titanic* in 1912, in the explosion of the *Hindenburg* in 1937, and more recently in the Buffalo Creek flood in West Virginia, the "nuclear accident" at Three Mile Island, the collapse of an interstate bridge in Connecticut, and the explosion of the space shuttle *Challenger*. Each of these events dramatize the dangers inherent in the modern world. To adequately understand the place of trauma in the human experience, it is necessary to examine the conditions that give rise to catastrophes that no one actually intended or wanted.

A collective trauma grows out of shared experiences with a deplorable event that falls outside the range of ordinary human experiences. This form of trauma is evident in such natural disasters as earthquakes, volcanoes, hurricanes, floods, and tornadoes. Such natural disasters result in the loss of human life, demolished homes and property, and the destruction of community. Humans are reminded that their life plans are subjected to disruptions in unintended ways when the forces of the physical world become hostile and unfriendly. Yet, natural disasters are less the subject for analysis in studies of national trauma than those disruptive events that grow out of the social worlds that humans have created.

An extraordinary event becomes a national trauma under circumstances in which the social system is disrupted to such a magnitude that it commands the attention of all major subgroups of the population. Even those who are usually apathetic and indifferent to national affairs are drawn into the public arena of discussion and debate. The social fabric is under attack, and people pay attention because the consequences appear to be so great that they cannot be ignored. Holding an attitude of benign neglect or cynical indifference is not a reasonable option.

Newsworthy Events

Calamities and tragedies in the social realm provide the core ingredients of a newsworthy event. Extraordinary disruptions become attention-getting and arouse widespread public responses. The news that is reported on a daily basis tends to emphasize dramatic events, unusual happenings, and moral disorders. The activities of ordinary people are seldom reported unless they are engaging in social protest or acting in opposition to some established institution. Rather, it is the disruption of everyday life that constitutes the newsworthy event. Something unexpected has occurred and adjustments are required to changing circumstances.

Disruptions of the social order become prominent in conversations throughout the country. Such shocking developments as the Manson murders, the mass suicides at the People's Temple in Jonestown, and the confrontation between the FBI and the Branch Davidian Cult at Waco, Texas, commanded the attention of the nation for an extended period of time. Such episodes, however, are limited in their long-range effects on the social system. They primarily serve to define the moral boundaries of society and convey the message that people make serious mistakes and suffer from them. These events are significant primarily because of the large number of people that respond to them and because of the opportunities they provide for examining selected aspects of social life.

A unique feature of news in modern society derives from the fact that the activities of a small number of people are observed selectively by millions of spectators. Messages that originate at some central location are disseminated over a large geographical area. People pay attention to news events because of their need for living in a meaningful cosmos. The millions of people who watch the evening news and read a daily newspaper are seeking information for linking personal lives with an ultimate set of values. In this process, news events provide stimulants for reflecting on social norms and deviancy, on public attitudes and behavior, and on social trends and unusual developments. Awareness of societal happenings serves to modify and clarify everyday assumptions and thus establish a firmer link between oneself and the broader scheme of human affairs.

The selective task of individuals in responding to the news is that of separating the genuine from the spurious, the illusion from the reality, and the authentic from the inauthentic. Routinely, the pronouncements of government officials are disproportionately reported as newsworthy events. Both the Red Scare of the 1920s and the fear of communism during the McCarthy era were intensified by the credibility the news media gave to statements by public officials. Outrageous claims about communist subversion in American life were embellished by the appearance of authenticity through reports in newspapers, news magazines, and television coverage. Public officials are thought of as the caretakers of the nation, and their actions and decisions symbolically represent the agenda of the nation. When public officials and the news media misinform the general public, it is often because of incomplete information about the area of concern. Yet, misinformation may also stem from the ideological and economic conditions under which the news media operate.

Audiences respond not only to the basic facts being transmitted by the news media, but also to the special meanings that are given to events. Such happenings as a presidential resignation, a nuclear accident, an oil embargo, or a sharp increase in the cost of living may generally be understood as newsworthy events. However, the specific meanings of these events are shaped by the life circumstances of individuals. The millions who constitute a television or a movie audience face different kinds of personal problems and concerns, differ in their social characteristics, and they differ in their hopes and aspirations for the future.

The construction of reality is a continuous process in our everyday lives, and in this respect we are all newsmakers. Through reading or listening to the news we extend our awareness beyond the range of experiences available in our immediate environment. Remote events become a part of our general understanding of the organization of social life. Events in the broader society are of practical importance to us in establishing reference points for orienting our lives. One illustration of this process is the social "game" in which individuals recall the routine activities of their lives when they were interrupted by some major event of societal importance. This game takes the form of a question such as "Where were you when you heard about the Japanese attack on Pearl Harbor?" This question could easily be asked about the death of President Roosevelt, the assassination of President Kennedy, and the resignation of President Nixon. Such games reveal more than interesting topics of conversation. We tend to draw on news events as benchmarks for linking the past with the present in our personal lives. Important occurrences are useful in marking social time in much the same way that birthdays, anniversaries, getting married, getting a job, becoming a parent, changing place of residence, and attending a funeral are used by individuals as reference points for assessing the overall quality of their lives. Such events are used creatively for constructing the meaningfulness of past experiences and anticipating the future.

Twenty-nine years after the assassination of President Kennedy, Abigail Van Buren invited the readers of her newspaper column to send in a postcard describing what they were doing when their activities were interrupted by the news of the president's death. To her surprise, about 300,000 people responded. It was apparently a moment that became frozen in the memories of Americans and was thus unforgettable. Ordinary time was put on hold as millions of Americans stopped what they were doing and went home to turn on their television sets. Continuing business as usual did not seem like a reasonable option in view of the extraordinary events that were happening.

When a trauma intrudes into our lives, ordinary time seems to stop, and our everyday pursuits are put on hold. Our equilibrium has been upset and our engagement in a continuous flow of events has become problematic. The tragic occurrence is replayed over and over in our minds as we seek to understand what has happened and why it happened. Through becoming a marker in the lives of individuals, it provides a framework similar to the ways in which primitive peoples measured time without clocks or watches. Events that occurred in the personal lives of individuals prior to a trauma became mentally separated from the events that occurred after the trauma. This is especially the case when the trauma is of the magnitude of the Japanese attack on Pearl Harbor or the assassination of President Kennedy. Turning points occurred in the social life of the nation and in the personal lives of individuals.

Under conditions of serious social disruptions, individuals frequently desire more information than the news-gathering agencies can make available. This especially occurs during times of crisis and may be noted in reactions to urban riots, natural disasters, or unsolved mass murders. Social life becomes disrupted, and people make a collective attempt to arrive at an adequate understanding of the event in question. Individuals verify and modify their assessments of events through engaging in conversations with others. Because of the pervasive ambiguity surrounding a national trauma, individuals reach out to others for social support and reinforcement. The major task, individually and collectively, is that of integrating the traumatic event into the fabric of social life in order to make it less threatening.

If the official news sources are perceived to be inadequate or if the news coverage is regarded as untrustworthy, individuals pool their intellectual resources in an attempt to make events coherent. Imagine, for example, the Japanese Americans living in the San Francisco Bay area on December 7, 1941, who suddenly found themselves suspected of being enemy agents, or the confusion among residents of Hiroshima on August 6, 1945, in the world's first encounter with the atomic bomb. These are examples of dramatic events that cannot be understood in terms of past experiences. Under these conditions, individuals react not as separate entities but in collaboration with others in the quest for understanding and action. By deliberating on the events in question, a pattern of agreement tends to emerge for the construction of plausible explanations of events and their implications.

The communication patterns associated with trauma at the individual level differ from the communication patterns associated with trauma at the national level. At the individual level, there is particularly a reluctance to communicate negative information to the persons that are affected by it. The uncertain outcome of transmitting undesirable information was evident long ago in ancient Sparta, where the messenger who brought bad news was sometimes put to death. The stigma associated with such forms of trauma as rape or being diagnosed with the AIDS virus leads to withholding information from friends, relatives, and coworkers. Through this tendency to keep bad news of a personal nature to oneself, individuals are frequently cut off from the social supports that otherwise may be available.

In contrast, news of a national trauma tends to be communicated very rapidly, not only by the news media but also by the exchange of information at the interpersonal level. Telephone lines frequently become overloaded with the large number of calls that individuals make as they reach out for support and interpersonal reinforcements. Serious disruptions of the social order are shared collectively and become associated with the need to talk about their meanings and implications. In this respect, national traumas tend to have cohesive effects within interpersonal networks in ways in which trauma of a highly personal nature do not.

Causal Explanations

It is through causal explanations that the dynamics of the social world are constructed into coherent patterns. We make assumptions about cause and effect because we must if we are to live in a world that is understandable. Without the assumption of causality, events would appear to be random, haphazard, and chaotic. In this respect, we construct the world through our perceptions of it. Especially important in constructing a predictable world are notions about how human intentions, decisions, and actions are linked in shaping the course of events. Causal explanations promote an understanding, even if erroneous, of the social world and reinforce a sense of management both in the social realm and in personal lives.

Beneath the appearances and facades of everyday life, there are necessarily plans, strategies, and plots that are not available for public scrutiny. Sociologists describe this aspect of modern life in theatrical terms by observing that there is "a backstage" and "a front stage" to public performances. Under conditions of national trauma, the mystery and secrecy surrounding backstage areas results in perceptions of devious plots and conspiracies. Through conspiracy theory it is assumed that most of the news that is reported reflects only the tip of an iceberg. Only a small part of what is happening is made visible through the news of the day. When the news media are defined as untrustworthy, or when the news is regarded as incomplete, people fill in the information gaps by imposing their own structure on the situation. Meaning is attributed to senseless events: order is imposed upon chaos; and simplistic explanations are constructed from complex and contradictory information.

For example, at the time of Lincoln's assassination, it was widely assumed that the presidential slaying was the result of a Confederate plot. The South had lost the war, but resentments and hostility were still running high. The assassination of President Lincoln was seen as a form of revenge. While the South had been defeated, it was still possible to retaliate through an assault on a major national symbol. A crisis of meaning occurred with Lincoln's death, and individuals became unclear about what they ought to believe. Much more was assumed to be involved in Lincoln's death than had been brought out into the open. Many believed that the Civil War had not really ended. While no supportive evidence was ever found, conspiracy theories persisted for several decades after the war was over.

While those individuals located at the periphery of modern society are ready-made targets for suspicion and distrust during times of crisis, there is also a tendency among Americans to impute conspiratorial motives to those at the center of power and influence. Throughout American history there has been a clamor for strong and effective leadership at the same time there has been a fear of too much concentration of power at the center. The ambivalence about power is reflected in both admiration for political leaders and the belief that politics is a dirty business. Schemes, plots, and underhanded dealings are perceived by many Americans as the way the system works.

The negative images of public officials go beyond seeing them as involved in devious plots surrounded by secrecy. The more pervasive form of political negativism grows out of perceptions of inefficiency, waste, and mismanagement. Here, the view is held that public officials are not so much evil men and women as they are incompetent. Why were we so disastrously unprepared for the Japanese attack on Pearl Harbor? Why did the space shuttle *Challenger* explode shortly after launching? Ready-made responses to such questions draw upon perceptions of incompetence and a dereliction of duty. Those in positions of power and authority were seen as having failed to do the things that should have been done under the circumstances.

Fear of religious conspiracies have also been present throughout American history. The early witchcraft trials were based on the notion that human beings had entered into an alliance with the devil and that a conspiratorial demonic order had been organized to shape the course of events. In colonial America, each of the thirteen colonies had enacted laws defining the practice of witchcraft as criminal conduct. The linkage of religion with evil frequently occurs in public perceptions of those groups whose beliefs and practices stand in opposition to the dominant values of a society. Such dramatic episodes as the Manson murders, the mass suicides at the People's Temple at Guyana, and the tragedy at Waco, Texas, generated a fear of new religions as satanic cults or demonic groups. National trauma is frequently associated with evil in human affairs, and perceptions of demonic conspiracies are regarded by some as plausible explanations.

Encounters with the tragedy and sadness of traumatic events prevents most people from remaining indifferent. The quest for news is great and the amount of information that can be made available is limited. It is for these reasons that plausible explanations are offered individually and collectively. The psychological tensions of national trauma require individuals to try to separate the authentic from the inauthentic, the facade from the substance, the appearance from the reality. Concerns are directed toward the implications of the traumatic event for the personal lives of individuals and for the future of their country.

Vague perceptions of personal vulnerability and the dangers of the world in which we live were evident in 1938 when Orson Welles's broadcast on the fictitious invasion from Mars precipitated a mass panic. The radio broadcast was structured to have interludes of music interrupted by news reports from New Jersey on the landing of the Martians. As on-the-scene reports of "the invasion" came in, the level of hysteria mounted in the New York City area. Approximately 6 million people panicked in response to the broadcast. Some engaged in flight, got into their automobiles and drove away from the area. One man drove all the way to Cleveland before he discovered the broadcast was a hoax. It was a time in which it was difficult for the individual to know what should be believed. Anything and everything seemed possible.

Psychological Modernity

Through mass communications, the millions of people comprising large viewing and listening audiences become aware of much more than they could experience directly. Happenings in faraway places are brought into the homes and lives of millions of people. In this respect, local areas are not isolated, self-contained units of meaning but instead are influenced by decisions and events occurring in society at large. Through developing an awareness of broader events, the individual seeks a firmer link with the totality of modern social life.

Most people hold some set of beliefs about how the conditions that prevail in the later part of the twentieth century differ from those of any previous century. Such beliefs are notions about psychological modernity and include perceptions by individuals of the historical uniqueness of their time and place. The concept embraces notions about the dominant types of men and women who prevail, the defining characteristics of society, the primary agencies of social change, and the direction in which history is moving. Such conceptions are typically held by all adults and represent constructions of the social world from the individual's vantage point. It is the content of such ideas that shape the moods and motivations of the general population.

Within this context, responses to national traumas have meaning for individuals through the creation of links between personal thought and action and the historical dimensions of their time and place. Accordingly, the time dimension of psychological modernity is reflected in perceiving how we got to where we are now, where we are now, and where we are headed as we move into the future. Coping with changing conditions in society, responding to the changes that are occurring within ourselves, and elaborating on the meaning of social events are among the many aspects of modern awareness. In effect, modernity is the social setting in which we enact the drama of freedom and control as we seek to invent our futures.

Traumatic events are symbolic in the sense that they represent much more than is immediately visible. They grow out of the ambiguous forces and remote dimensions of a social system. In any given case, reflection is required in order for an extraordinary event to be understood and made coherent. The consequences as well as the causes of the trauma must be evaluated. Is the event in question an advanced indicator of additional calamities that are to follow? Or, is the event simply an ephemeral occurrence that will pass in significance as the general population returns to business as usual? Immediate responses are oriented toward juxtaposing the abnormal event against the normality of everyday life.

Several variations in styles of thought surface as individuals assign meaning to traumatic events. The least complicated style of thought is reflected in strong moralistic judgments in terms of right or wrong, good or bad, true or false. Such simplicity overlooks the intricacies and complications of human tragedy, while providing for an immediate resolution of an encounter with chaos. Such a response reflects only a superficial awareness of events and a tendency to place extraordinary events within such preexisting frameworks as religious fundamentalism or a political ideology.

The emergence of a crisis in the social realm provides a ready-made framework to justify a social cause among those who perceive the main drift of society to be one of moral decay. Routinely, cherished beliefs and values are challenged by new lifestyles and new moralities. These sentiments frequently develop into what sociologists describe as "a symbolic crusade." Symbolic crusades focus on specific symbols that are selected to indicate the degenerative character of modern social life. Alcoholism, pornography, and abortion are frequently topics of concern and provide a basis for condemning the erosion of traditional values, the loss of patriotic sentiment, and the decline of religious values. Crisis events permit crusaders to wax eloquent about the need to uphold moral mandates, restore traditional values, and restrain the forces of evil. They tend to insist strongly that their own conceptions of right and wrong be accepted and applied by the rest of society.

Others recognize the complexities of a national trauma but tend to be overwhelmed by it. These individuals respond to the counterpressures of the many explanations that are being offered and take on the role of neutral observer. This perspective essentially holds that we must wait for more information or that we must wait until the event can be placed into a historical perspective. There is a disinterest or an unwillingness on the part of a segment of the population to probe beneath the surface of public events. The emergence of a national trauma confirms ready-made notions about living in a chaotic and unpredictable world. Such views are reflected in the failure to become informed about the consequential happenings in one's society. Unfortunate events just happen, and there is nothing we can do about it.

A more rational response to complex events consists of a high degree of receptiveness to available information and accepting the challenge of integrating information into a coherent position for oneself. Alternative explanations are weighed and evaluated. The feasibility of different points of view are examined and synthesized. This is the rational decision-making model growing out of scientific, technological, and economic approaches. This approach also reflects the ideals of court proceedings and investigative committees. The ideals of official reports, however, can seldom be met under conditions of incomplete information, high levels of emotional involvement, and competing constraints and demands on time and energy.

The appointment of commissions to investigate the conditions surrounding national traumas (such as the assassination of President Kennedy, the lack of preparedness at Pearl Harbor, and the explosion of the space shuttle *Challenger*) serves multiple purposes. Making such appointments gives recognition to the importance and to the complexity of the issues involved. Through seeking authoritative explanations, a great deal of time and effort goes into the fact-finding process. However, appointing an investigative committee also becomes a way of buying time to take pressure off of public officials for some immediate line of action. Given the complexity surrounding a national trauma, an investigative committee is frequently unable to bring closure to the case. The causes, conditions, and consequences of most national traumas become topics for debate and argumentation for many years to come.

A national trauma frequently has liberating effects on a social system. Older ways of doing things are called into question, and new opportunities for change and innovation surface. The very fact that a disruptive event has occurred opens up the possibility that the social system will be perceived as defective in some way or another. In confronting the danger implied in a crisis event, new opportunities emerge for innovation and change. For example, the Great Depression provided new opportunities for governmental involvement in solving problems that previously had been neglected. The Japanese attack on Pearl Harbor provided opportunities for elaborating military institutions and developing new forms of technology. Such crises as those growing out of economic failure, the threat of a foreign attack, or the breakdown of law and order generate a need for new forms of public policy initiatives.

Social order is always a fragile creation. Regardless of how men and women construct their world, it cannot endure for long. Changes are always occurring within ourselves and in the world outside. A great deal of repair work is required in the maintenance of social order because both societies and individuals always remain unfinished products: People pursue self-interests at the expense of the group's well-being, human efforts lead to frustration and failure, people sometimes make mistakes and do stupid things. In that fragile structure called civilization it sometimes seems that hardly a brick touches the ground. Under conditions of national trauma, aspects of the foundation seem to be crumbling or to rest on quicksand. If the trauma is of sufficient severity, all things appear possible. A basic human problem is that of imposing order on chaos and making sense out of the conditions of existence. The study of trauma in its collective form has a special relevance for an understanding of our time and place.

Bibliography

Balsiger, David, and Charles E. Sellier Jr. 1977. *The Lincoln Conspiracy.* Los Angeles: Schick Sun Classic Books.

Barber, Bernard. 1983. *The Logic and Limits of Trust.* New Brunswick, NJ: Rutgers University Press.

Becker, Ernest. 1968. *The Structure of Evil.* New York: George Braziller.

Berger, Peter L. 1977. *Facing Up to Modernity.* New York: Basic Books.

Berger, Peter L., Brigitte Berger, and Hansfried Kellner. 1973. *The Homeless Mind: Modernization and Consciousness.* New York: Vintage Books.

Bettelheim, Bruno. 1960. *The Informed Heart: Autonomy in a Mass Age.* Glencoe, IL: Free Press.

Bok, Sissela. 1978. *Lying: Moral Choice in Public and Private Life.* New York: Vintage Books.

Brown, Roger, and James Kulik. 1977. "Flashbulb Memories." *Cognition* 5: 73–99.

Burke, James. 1978. *Connections.* Boston: Little, Brown.

Cantril, Hadley. 1940. *The Invasion from Mars.* Princeton, NJ: Princeton University Press.

Curry, Richard O., and Thomas M. Brown, eds. 1972. *Conspiracy: Fear of Subversion in American History.* New York: Holt, Rinehart, and Winston.

Douglas, Mary, and Aaron Wildavsky. 1982. *Risk and Culture.* Berkeley: University of California Press.

Elliot, Gil. 1972. *The 20th Century Book of the Dead.* New York: Ballantine.

Erikson, Kai. 1994. *A New Species of Trouble: The Human Experience of Modern Disasters.* New York: W.W. Norton.

Fein, Helen. 1993. *Genocide.* Newbury Park, CA: Sage.

Fine, Gary Alan. 1996. "Reputational Entrepreneurs and the Memory of Incompetence: Melting Supporters, Partisan Warriors, and Images of President Harding." *American Journal of Sociology* 101: 1159–1193.

Frankl, Viktor E. 1965. *Man's Search for Meaning.* New York: Washington Square Press.

Gans, Herbert J. 1979. *Deciding What's News.* New York: Pantheon Books.

Goffman, Erving. 1963. *Behavior in Public Places.* New York: Free Press.

Herman, Judith Lewis. 1992. *Trauma and Recovery.* New York: Basic Books.

Janoff-Bulman, Ronnie. 1992. *Shattered Assumptions: Toward a New Psychology of Trauma.* New York: Free Press.

Kennedy, Paul. 1993. *Preparing for the Twenty-First Century.* New York: Random House.

Lifton, Robert Jay. 1973. *Home from the War.* New York: Basic Books.

Lipsky, Michael, and David J. Olson. 1969. "Riot Commission Politics." *Transaction* 6 (July–August): 8–21.

Mirowsky, John, and Catherine E. Ross. 1989. *Social Causes of Psychological Distress.* New York: Aldine de Gruyter.

Neal, Arthur G., ed. 1976. *Violence in Animal and Human Societies.* Chicago: Nelson Hall.

Nisbet, Robert A. 1953. *The Quest for Community.* New York: Oxford University Press.

Parenti, Michael. 1993. *Inventing Reality: The Politics of News Media.* New York: St. Martin's Press.

Shibutani, Tamatsu. 1966. *Improvised News.* Indianapolis: Bobbs-Merrill.

Short, James F. Jr., ed. 1986. *The Social Fabric.* Beverly Hills, CA: Sage.

Slaby, Andrew E. 1989. *Aftershock: Surviving the Delayed Effects of Trauma, Crisis, and Loss.* New York: Villard Books.

Tuchman, Gaye. 1973. "Making News by Doing Work: Routinizing the Unexpected." *American Journal of Sociology* 79: 110–131.

Warner, W. Lloyd. 1962. *American Life: Dream and Reality.* Chicago: University of Chicago Press.

Wilson, John P. 1989. *Trauma: Transformation and Healing.* New York: Brunner/Mazel.

2 • Society as Moral Community

The social edifices that bind men and women together into a system of meaning frequently are thought of as imperishable. Social order, however, is always a fragile entity. Through the unfolding of traumatic events, social landscapes may be disrupted by upheavals of volcanic proportions. Cracks in the system may continue to widen until internal and external pressures can no longer be contained. Under these conditions, the social order is replaced by chaos, and a great deal of repair work is required. Social systems may then be seen as recurrently undergoing a process of collapse and rebuilding. The resolution of crises are replaced by new sacred meanings that seek to restore continuity in the social realm.

While the responses of individuals to national traumas are highly varied, collective responses tend to become standardized through the elaboration of myths and legends for defining the moral boundaries of society. Stories are told about extraordinary events, noteworthy accomplishments, and unusual tragedies. Such accounts provide ingredients for the creation of a sense of moral unity among any given group of people and permit linking personal lives with historical circumstances. Notions about "who we are" and "what we are to become" are shaped to a large degree from the shared identities that grow out of both extraordinary difficulties and extraordinary accomplishments in the social realm.

Perceptions of the greatness of a nation is confirmed by historical memories of how resources were pooled in times of trouble. For example, during the American Civil War a deep fracture threatened the unity of the nation. Whether the United States would continue as one nation or whether it would be divided into two became an issue that could be resolved only through armed conflict. The thousands of books that have been written, and still are being written, about the Civil War serve as a reminder of the epic struggles growing out of the deep divisions within the nation. While the

21

coercive powers of the state had sealed the fracture, the healing process was long and tedious.

The collective suffering, sadness, and anger growing out of social disruptions provide the raw materials for the recreation of society as "moral community." The notion of society as moral community is selectively embellished through the creation of a body of sacred symbols. The role of trauma in the creation of these symbols is evident. Arlington Cemetery, the Vietnam Veterans Memorial, the Washington Monument, the Lincoln Memorial, and the Tomb of the Unknown Soldier are among the more sacred symbols that are drawn upon in shaping the national identity of Americans. Each in its own unique way reflects the personal sacrifices that have been made individually on behalf of the nation.

Under conditions of national trauma, the moral underpinnings of a society are subjected to close scrutiny. Volcano-like disruptions call into question the qualities and attributes of social life. Men and women strive for new ways to relate to each other, and everyday hopes and aspirations are temporarily put on hold. Restoring a sense of order and coherence becomes a necessary societal response to conditions of trauma. Insofar as traumatic events result in a fragmented community, a great deal of repair work may be necessary to discover new forms of social glue for binding people together into a shared form of membership and belonging.

Shaping a National Identity

The cumulative effects of national traumas are of central importance in forging the collective identity of any given group of people. Among Americans, there are three events that stand out above all others in shaping a national identity. The epic struggles of the American Revolution, the trauma of the Civil War, and the heroic undertakings in winning World War II required extensive personal sacrifices and permanently changed the content of what it means to be an American. Taking an active approach toward mastery and control over events through the pooling of collective resources became embedded in national consciousness. The creation of heroic and legendary figures to symbolize the aspirations of the nation provided sources of inspiration for future generations.

The trauma of the American Revolution helped to shape the identity of Americans as separate from the British. The Revolution is remembered as a time in which the colonists were oppressed by the British and in which pleas for the redress of grievances fell on deaf ears. Some of the more militant colonists came to the conclusion that nothing short of a revolution was a viable alternative. Of the many events of the Revolution, few are remembered as vividly as the suffering at Valley Forge and the signing of the Declaration of Independence. Through the Declaration of Independence the moral basis for the Revolution was grounded in the notion that any given group of people have an inalienable right to alter or abolish a government that is perceived to be unjust. Government, it was argued, exists for the benefit of the governed. The revolutionary ideology held that the right to "life, liberty, and the pursuit of happiness" permitted overthrowing an alien and tyrannical government. The suffering at Valley Forge became emblematic of the long and difficult struggle through which our Founding Fathers emerged victoriously.

While the Declaration of Independence established the revolutionary identity of Americans, it was the development of the Constitution that permitted an opportunity for a fresh start in building a new nation. The Constitution built upon collective sentiments about what a government should be like after the revolution was over. Elitist values and social class privileges could be downplayed by guaranteeing certain liberties to all citizens and giving all men the right to vote. The new nation emphasized the personal dignity of the individual, the integrity of the common man, and permitted popular democracy to play a major role in shaping the policies of the nation. The pride of Americans in their new nation provided the foundations for a new national identity built upon revolutionary and democratic principles.

The American Revolution led to the creation of two separate countries in North America, not just one. Canada was created as a country that was separate from the United States. Several thousand colonists who did not share the revolutionary fervor of the day resolved their discontent by moving to Nova Scotia or Ontario. The ideologies surrounding the American Revolution were rejected by those who wished to retain their British heritage. Evolution, rather than revolution, became the preferred way to approach the problems of social change. In the absence of the type of heroic struggles that characterized the Revolution and the American Civil War, Canadian national identity is less sharply defined. It has been said that Canadian national identity is built primarily around the assertion "we are not Americans."

In creating a new system of government, Americans were bent on demonstrating that they were a distinctive group of people separable from the rest of the world. While the Constitution created a new "social contract" by which Americans were to be governed, the Declaration of Independence provided Americans with a clear conception of their genesis as a separate nation. July 4, 1776, is a date deeply etched in American consciousness as the beginning of a new nation that was clearly distinguishable from all other nations of the world. We became independent at the moment that we announced we were, at the moment we developed a clear justification for revolution, at the moment we committed ourselves to overthrowing the yoke of British rule. In the absence of any similar type of historical experience, Canadians do not agree or seem to care when they became a separate and independent nation.

For more than 200 years, the speeches delivered on the Fourth of July have served to rejuvenate the values associated with American society as a moral community. The annual commemorations of the Revolution permit a blending of secular and sacred values, linking personal sacrifices with promoting the collective good and expressing devotion to our Founding Fathers. While the specific content of the speeches vary from year to year, all are directed toward promoting the notion that there is a source of unity to American consciousness that cuts across the multiple groups and vested interests within the nation. In view of the heterogeneity of the United States in terms of race, ethnicity, social class, and religion, many foreign observers have been puzzled by the depth of the American belief that there is a national consensus, almost of a sacred nature, that binds Americans together. In the absence of a similar genesis myth among Canadians, pluralism and cultural differences tend to be given priority over a national consensus. Canadians lack any form of commemoration comparable to the Fourth of July for solidifying a sense of collective identity.

The second major event in shaping the American national identity was the Civil War. The nation became deeply divided over the issues of slavery, state rights, and our revolutionary heritage. The firing on Fort Sumter represented the beginning of an insurrection that would eventually result in one of the bloodiest wars the world had ever known. The emotionality surrounding the issues of the Civil War became so intense that the war became a sacred crusade both for the North and the South. The crosses at Arlington, Gettysburg, Antietam, and many other places serve as a grim reminder of what can happen when mass armies meet on the field of battle. It was the Civil War in its many phases and consequences that constituted the dominant historical experience of Americans during the nineteenth century. It was through the coercive powers of the state that the unity of the nation was confirmed and elaborated.

Following the conclusion of the Civil War, the assassination of President Lincoln provided the nation with one of its major heroic figures for all times. The sanctification of Lincoln placed his image on a par with that of the first president. While Washington had played a major role in shaping the identity of Americans, Lincoln came to symbolize the leadership of a coherent and organic nation that could not be torn asunder by insurrection. Notions of America as "a confederacy of nations," or as "league of na-

tions," were firmly rejected. As a result of the heroic and protracted struggles of the Civil War, Lincoln's presidency came to symbolize heroic sacrifice, emancipation, and military victory in affirming the unity of the nation.
In the creation of Presidents Day as a national holiday, Lincoln stands
alongside Washington as a major president to be remembered. The traumas
and the triumphs of the Revolution and the Civil War remain at the forefront of the collective identity of Americans.

While Canadians never had anything like the American Civil War, internal conflict and fragmentation has persisted historically as a defining characteristic of their society. The development of a unified identity has been
precluded by the sharp divisions between the French Canadians and the
English Canadians. The French were in Canada first and developed a large
population that was geographically based. The position of the French Canadians in the power equation has been sufficiently strong that English Canadians were prevented from imposing their own language and other aspects
of culture on the total population. Attempts to designate Canada as a "bilin-
gual" or "multicultural" society continues to generate considerable controversy and dissension. As a result, the success of developing a national unity
that all Canadians can identify with and draw upon has been limited. Canadians repeatedly remind themselves of the forces that divide them, such as
region and language, while the sources of unity have a much lower profile.

The third major trauma for shaping the national identity of Americans
grew out of the Japanese attack on Pearl Harbor. The integrity of the United
States had been assaulted, and the effects were electrifying in the transformation of American society into a moral community. The collective sharing of a
sense of sadness and a sense of anger produced nationally unprecedented
feelings of cohesion, membership, belonging, and community. Now that we
were at war, we were involved in an historical struggle of epic proportions.
The nation was militarily unprepared and there was widespread uncertainty
over what the outcome would be. Previous opposition to American involvement in World War II vanished, and virtually all Americans reflected on the
part they would play in the national objective of winning the war. Group
differences that had divided the nation disappeared, or were suspended, as all
segments of the population became engrossed in the historical undertaking.
National symbols came to be endowed with special sacred meanings. Chills
ran up the spines of many Americans as Kate Smith sang "God Bless America." The nation became unified with an unprecedented level of intensity.
The war effort had indeed become a moral crusade.

The national identity of Americans became permanently altered from the
trauma of the war experiences. While other countries had suffered greater
fatalities and greater damage to their infrastructure, Americans believed that

it was their contribution to the war effort that resulted in the decisive defeat of Nazi Germany and the Empire of Japan. The United States came out of the war strong militarily and economically. The other countries of the world did not. The United States had been thrust into a position of world leadership. The problems of the world had become our problems. The psychological separation of the United States from the rest of the world went by the wayside. We had provided the resources that were necessary for winning World War II, and we had the resources for rebuilding the postwar world. The world had become more interdependent, and we had found a new place for ourselves among the nations within it. Advances in technology had made all areas of the world accessible, and Americans had come to occupy center stage on the world scene. It was no longer a viable option, nor seen as desirable, for the United States to maintain a position of isolation from the rest of the world.

The effects of World War II have been profound in shaping the national identities of the defeated nations. Both Germany and Japan were required to struggle with the evil and banality of their conduct during the war. In Germany, a separation is frequently made between "the Nazis" and "the Germans" in discussions of the atrocities of the war. Many Germans claimed they were mostly spectators or that their cooperation with the Nazis was primarily based on necessity and coercion. What are seen as the best qualities of the German social heritage were frequently separated from the aberrations of the Nazi regime. Japan was also faced with the problem of dealing with a difficult and traumatic past. The scope of the atrocities committed by the Japanese army in the countries they occupied included not only inhumane medical experiments on thousands of captives, but also the brutal slaying of about 15 million Chinese civilians. At the end of the war, the people of each country drew a sigh of relief as they began the challenge of rebuilding a seriously damaged infrastructure and a seriously damaged national identity.

At the conclusion of the war in Japan, feelings of surprise, relief, and apprehension spread throughout the country when the Emperor went on radio to announce an unconditional surrender to the American forces. The Japanese had been prepared psychologically to give their lives if necessary for the defense of their country. The immediate sense of relief stemmed from the freedom of no longer being obligated to die for a national cause. The level of apprehension was subsequently diminished through the recognition that the Japanese people would not be brutalized by the army of occupation. Through being given the rights of self-determination in building a new social order, the Japanese were provided with an opportunity to reinvent their society. New social institutions were elaborated, and older institutions underwent extensive reforms that were generally recognized by the Japanese people as essential.

The economic and technological development of Japan is one of the major success stories of the twentieth century. The rebuilt society selectively retained positive values from before the war, while discarding those that had resulted during an intense trauma for Japan as a nation. Such traditional values as personal discipline, commitment, and group loyalty facilitated the development of one of the world's strongest economies. Traditional Japanese values were incorporated in a modified form in several institutional areas. For example, the Samurai emphasis upon discipline and loyalty are very much evident among employees in business corporations. The disciplined approach to life is also reflected in the sense of duty among children and young adults to put forth their best efforts in preparing for the competitive examinations that will determine which college or university they will be permitted to attend and in preparing for subsequent entry into the labor force.

The numbing effects of the American bombings of Hiroshima and Nagasaki more than offset any sense of national shame or humiliation resulting from their decisive defeat. While Hiroshima became permanently ingrained in the collective memories of the entire world, it had a special salience for the national consciousness of the Japanese.

There are wide gaps between the Japanese and American perceptions of the meaning of Hiroshima. Americans saw the use of the atomic bomb as a necessary and expedient means for ending the war. Many Japanese place the bombing of Hiroshima and Nagasaki alongside the holocaust as two of the major crimes against humanity during the twentieth century. In their view, avoiding the deaths of a few American military personnel did not justify the sacrifice of 200,000 guiltless civilians. The bomb indiscriminately killed old men, women, and children, rather than military combatants. The Japanese believe that the Americans used the bomb to test out their weapon on a human population, to justify the expenditure of $2 billion on the Manhattan Project, and to intimidate the Russians.

Both the United States and Japan had difficulties with the question of how to properly remember Hiroshima on the fiftieth anniversary of the bombing. The event had such a lasting impact on each of the countries, indeed upon the rest of the world, that some form of historical recognition seemed necessary. The trauma of the nuclear holocaust for Japan became ingrained in collective memories and superseded any feelings of humiliation or shame that may have otherwise resulted from losing the war. Americans had their revenge for the surprise attack on Pearl Harbor, while the Japanese were made keenly aware of the negative consequences of permitting the military to gain control over their society.

A storm of protest emerged in Japan in response to plans by the U.S. Post Office to issue a stamp portraying the mushroom cloud over Hiroshima. The stamp had disturbing implications and was regarded as an insult to modern Japan. It commemorated a glorious American victory without raising serious moral questions about the appropriateness of using such a weapon of destruction on a civilian population. Many Americans agreed with the Japanese, and the Post Office canceled plans to issue the stamp.

Plans at the Smithsonian for commemorating the fiftieth anniversary of the bombing of Hiroshima were designed to develop a reflective attitude on the atomic bomb and the uses of nuclear devices as instruments of war. The planned exhibit was to include an emphasis on the decision to drop the bomb, the story of the crew that delivered the bomb, photographs of the victims at Hiroshima and Nagasaki, and the implications of the bomb for the cold war. Members of Congress and veteran groups protested vehemently against the planned exhibit, and as a result the Smithsonian canceled their plans. The objections came from the emphasis on Japanese victims and on the moral issues that were involved. Veterans maintained that it detracted from the heroic sacrifices of Americans in the war. Older Americans still have vivid memories of the war and believe that the actions of Americans in vaporizing the two Japanese cities were both appropriate and necessary. A national survey, however, indicated that the majority of Americans under fifty years of age now believe that it was morally wrong to drop the atom bomb on the Japanese cities.

While the relationships between Japan and the United States have been positive ones over the past several decades, residual elements of the trauma of the war remain. The destinies of the two countries became linked not only through the conduct of the war but also in the process of building a new world order once the war was over. The critical battles of the war became too firmly etched into the living memories of older Americans to be completely swept aside. The Japanese, however, have a special sensitivity to the ways in which Americans publicize the historical events of the war. As a result, the recognition Americans now give to decisive battles at such places as Iwo Jima, Guadalcanal, and Okinawa have been tempered by a reluctance to intensify any latent sentiments of humiliation and shame in Japan over their conduct during the war. The younger generations in contemporary Japan feel that they bear no direct responsibility for the atrocities of the past.

Japanese officials, however, have issued many apologies over the years for the atrocities that were committed by the Japanese during World War II. The apologies have had a dramatic impact on the modern national identity of Japan. The serious mistakes that were made in the past have served as a major referent for what to avoid in the future. The dominance of their society by the military had calamitous effects for both the Japanese people and the peoples of the Pacific Rim nations. Through renouncing war as a means for resolving international disputes, Japan built a new national identity around economic development. A stratified view of the nations of the world, which was deeply embedded in the social heritage of Japan, took the form of striving for excellence in technological development and becoming a major force in international trade and commerce. The repair work in developing a new national identity provided the Japanese people with a new source of pride in themselves and in their place among the nations of the world. Compensations for the mistakes of the past were achieved through building a new position of respect in the economic sphere among the nations of the world.

National identity has been much more problematic for Germany in the postwar years. The place of the atrocities of the holocaust in national consciousness continues to be surrounded with controversy and uncertainty. What happened at such places as Auschwitz, Dachau, Buchenwald, and Treblinka still defies adequate explanation. How was it possible for a nation that produced some of the world's finest contributions to philosophy, music, and literature to also produce Adolph Hitler? Why did the German people comply with the mandates of the Nazi Party when it was not in their own best interest to do so? Most Germans would prefer to forget about their recent past, to just move on, and to leave explanations of what happened to professional historians. The lessons of the holocaust are of such a magnitude, however, that selectively forgetting is not a reasonable option. The issue continues to surface and resurface in intellectual discourse both in Germany and in the rest of the world.

When the news was released that President Ronald Reagan planned to celebrate the fortieth anniversary of V-E Day by placing a wreath to honor the German military cemetery at Bitburg, an unanticipated storm of protest surfaced. Reagan had intended the ritual as an act of reconciliation. Instead, it tapped into continuing resentments over the traumatic events of the Third Reich and World War II. Recriminations were clearly evident in the United States and elsewhere. Veteran groups, Jewish organizations, and several other constituencies expressed indignation at Reagan's ceremonial act. The holocaust had such a dramatic impact that the world is ready neither to forgive nor to forget. Instead, in the absence of other more pressing issues, the ending of the cold war has provided a time for serious reflections on the recent social heritages of many nations of the world.

The debates over the holocaust frequently center around whether this event was unique among the atrocities in human history or whether it was simply a reflection of the type of event that had occurred at many other times and places. Those who relativize the holocaust by seeing it simply as another case of atrocities in human affairs tend to downplay its lasting significance for German national identity. In contrast, those who perceive the banality as unique in human affairs maintain that Germany must confront in some major way the significance of the event for a national identity. In the absence of an adequate historical resolution, some degree of collective guilt is likely to remain. What continues to remain uncertain is what form of atonement would be appropriate for remembering such a difficult past.

The biblical notion "let he who is perfect, throw the first stone" is implicit in the responses of many Americans who believe that as a nation we have failed to give adequate recognition to the atrocities of our own past. Our own history includes the systematic annihilation of American Indians by settlers bent on confiscating tribal lands, the brutality directed toward captives transported from Africa for the American institution of slavery, and the vigilante activity of the Ku Klux Klan. In recent years, controversy has surfaced over appropriate ways to remember Columbus's discovery of America and the American bombings of Hiroshima and Nagasaki. The sense of collective guilt by the new generation of Americans has become muted through the notions that "we were not alive at the time," "we had nothing to do with such practices," and besides, "we don't do that kind of thing anymore." Yet, the issues continue to surface among subgroups of the population who see themselves as disadvantaged by the ways in which the past is selectively remembered. Confronting a painful past can never be easy, even for those who are young enough to bear no direct responsibility for what happened. The sense of a society as a moral community must necessarily take into account the full scope of its social heritage.

The ending of the cold war has required several countries of the world to rethink their national identities and what they are to become in the years ahead. The disillusionment in the Soviet Union with the communist experiment has led to widespread chaos and uncertainty both about their recent past and what the future holds. Americans think of themselves as having won the cold war, but are also faced with uncertainty about what their future holds. International affairs were more coherent when we had the Soviet Union as an arch enemy. The struggle between the forces of good and evil had a unifying effect on the nation that is now missing. While images of another world war have grown dim, few Americans believe that the world has become a less dangerous place with the breakup of the Soviet Union. As a result, such questions as who we are collectively and what we are to become are now subjected to new forms of reflection. The new generation is necessarily faced with the task of refining and clarifying our recent social heritage.

Disturbing a National Identity

All collective traumas have some bearing on national identity. While in some cases national trauma results in enhancing a sense of unity within a society, there are other cases in which collective traumas have fragmenting effects. Feelings of alienation depend in some measure on the predictions that are made about the outcome of events. For example, during the early years of the American Revolution, the outcome was by no means evident. Had the insurgency been suppressed by the British, the heroic figures that now loom larger than life would have been designated as criminals and punished accordingly. Had the American Civil War resulted in a stalemate or a victory for the Confederacy, we would now have two nations rather than one. The implications are clear that there are few inevitabilities in the outcomes of historical events. Through the epic struggles of the American Revolution and the American Civil War we came to recognize more clearly what it means to be an American.

The social heritage provides us with an everyday blueprint and a sense of social continuity. A serious crisis of meaning surfaces when we can no longer make assumptions about the continuity of social life as it is known and understood. Such was the case with the trauma of the Cuban Missile Crisis. For a few days in October of 1962 there was a disturbing possibility that human life on this planet would be extinguished within a matter of days. There had been no previous episode in the history of the world in which the stakes were so high and the fate of the world in so few hands. The moral fiber of society itself was called into question with the possible use of nuclear weapons for the destruction of civilization. The crisis intruded into everyday consciousness and temporarily brought into focus "unthinkable" prospects for the human condition. The continuity of social life from one generation to the next seemed doubtful. The desire for peace and tranquillity came to be temporarily juxtaposed against the possibility of annihilation.

Of all disruptions of the social system, few events in the history of the nation matched the emotional intensity of collective responses to the assassination of President Kennedy. While we usually think of the political process as falling within the realm of the secular and profane, under conditions of trauma our usual way of thinking is changed. Extraordinary events border on the sacred rather than on the mundane. It is not the event itself that conveys a sense of the sacred, but our responses to events that bestow upon them a sense of awe and the feeling that they are not to be taken lightly. Sacred events are extraordinary; there is something mysterious about them; and they command our attention and respect.

The assassination of President Kennedy became a sacred event to Americans. Analogies were drawn between the death of Kennedy, the assassination of President Lincoln, and the crucifixion of Jesus Christ. Each constituted a human sacrifice in cementing the bonds of society as moral community. Through bloodshed, suffering, and death, the sacred character of social life became rejuvenated. For a few days following Kennedy's assassination, the nation became totally engrossed in the news media coverage of the event and in the collective mourning process. The sadness of specific individuals became linked with the sadness experienced by others. Quiet reflections were directed toward the meaning of society, its sacred values, and what it is to become. At both conscious and latent levels, it tapped into hopes and aspirations for the nation as well as into the underlying fears and anxieties. Kennedy, in effect, became sanctified and loomed larger than life as a sacred symbol of tragedy and heroism in American life. Few events in the history of the nation had such unifying effects through a collective mourning process.

As one of the primary living symbols of the nation, the presidency and its occupant are important ingredients of society as moral community. The president speaks on behalf of the nation, represents the nation on ceremonial occasions, and occupies a primary position of trusteeship. While Americans have a legal right to say negative things about their president, he is the symbolic leader of the nation. It is perhaps because of the central place of the presidency in the sacred pantheon of the nation that a great deal of disbelief and denial accompanied the criminal charges that were brought against President Richard Nixon.

While the Bill of Impeachment in the House of Representative charged President Nixon with "high crimes and misdemeanors," many Americans had difficulty in dealing conceptually with what they were hearing. The importance of the presidency to the affairs of the nation was of such a magnitude that efforts were made to neutralize the effects of criminal conduct. Defects both in individual officeholders and in the social system were evaluated in attempts to restore a sense of moral community. In the orations that were given at Nixon's funeral, an emphasis was placed upon an evaluation of his contributions to the nation. Few references were made to the Watergate affair and "the obstruction of justice." Selective inattention to "the higher immoralities" helped to sustain and reinforce the image of society as moral community.

Some level of deviance and criminality may be necessary within a social system for establishing the boundaries around acceptable conduct. However, if the perceptions of deviancy take the form of widespread beliefs about hidden conspiracies, the society itself is in trouble. This occurred with the widespread fear of hidden communists in our midst during the 1950s. Political demagogues were building their careers around unsupported allegations against American citizens. The allegation that many Americans were withdrawing their allegiance from the United States and promoting the communist cause resulted in mass hysteria that resembled the witch-hunt of an earlier time. Through drawing upon the latent fears of the cold war, high levels of suspicion and distrust were directed toward American citizens. Tranquillity in the social realm was disrupted through the political preoccupation with determining who was or was not a communist or a communist sympathizer. Democratic principles were compromised as hundreds of Americans lost their jobs on the basis of nothing more than the claim that they were communists, communist sympathizers, or a security risk to the United States.

The emergence of social turmoil and collective violence conveys disturbing implications for the moral conscience of society. For example, the civil rights movement called into question the contradictions inherent in American racial policies and practices. The traditional forms of racial segregation and discrimination stood in sharp contrast with the political values of freedom and equality, as well as with the constitutional guarantee of civil liberties for all citizens. Such contradictions had taken the form of a contested struggle. Americans watched television with sadness and dismay as police violence was directed toward peaceful demonstrators. The millions of television viewers constituted a type of judiciary as attention became focused on issues of racism and social justice. Few Americans were able to remain indifferent to the issues that were dramatized. The moral conscience of society had been turned upon itself through the confrontations growing out of the civil rights movement.

The complex interdependency of the many parts of a modern society, greatly increases the probability for its disruption. Technological accidents and the failures of the economic system reflect the process of historical drift toward unwanted and uncontrolled outcomes. If our field of symbolic meanings is suddenly plowed up by tremendous changes in the social order, the firmness of our grasp of reality is weakened and our sense of connection grows fragile. The intrusion of traumatic events into the fabric of social life requires a great deal of remedial work in the maintenance of society as moral community.

As societies have grown in size and increased in complexity they become increasingly vulnerable to disruptions by those who are angry and hostile toward the established social order. Terrorists are well aware of this complex interdependency and are able to disrupt the orderliness of social life with only a limited amount of resources. Exploding bombs in public buildings, releasing poisonous gases in subways, serial murders, political assassinations, and placing explosives aboard aircraft are attention-getting strategies that provide recognition for the disenchanted and highly alienated members of a society. Thus, deviants and social misfits play an important role in the creation of traumatic events in the social realm.

The scope of the conditions promoting serious disruptions of everyday life are thus wide-ranging and unpredictable. The shock effects of the many ways in which a modern society can be disrupted point toward the complex role that custodians of the social order are required to play. It is for this reason that authority figures become the focus of attention in the collective desire for circumventing future occurrences of the types of trauma that have surfaced in the recent past.

Trusteeship

Under conditions of national trauma, the performance of authority figures is subjected to close scrutiny. This is because authority figures are entrusted with the task of maintaining society as a moral community. As custodians of the social order, those in top positions of power and authority are assumed to be competent and are expected to make decisions for the common good. Through being granted the right to make decisions that bind others, authority figures incur obligations for the conduct of societal affairs and trustee responsibilities for the effective management of group resources. The sense of comfort with living in a society is grounded to a large degree in respect for authority and the belief that the leadership decisions and actions are directed toward the best interests of the country.

The trauma of the Japanese attack on Pearl Harbor was intensified by the failure of our military commanders to take the measures that were necessary in view of the threat of war and the mounting political tensions with the Empire of Japan. Had the military commanders in Hawaii exercised sound judgment, they would have recognized the need to disperse our Pacific fleet, rather than concentrate it at Pearl Harbor. Some form of surveillance of the surrounding area should have been undertaken to give some advance warning of any impending enemy attack. In military training exercises in Hawaii, war games routinely had been played around developing a response to a surprise Japanese attack on Pearl Harbor. The irony of such a rehearsal is that it was not regarded as a realistic possibility, and our military forces were caught completely off-guard when the attack did occur. The military commanders in Hawaii had failed to exercise properly the authority that had been delegated to their command.

The incompetence of authority figures may not grow out of their personal qualities and attributes so much as from evaluations of their performance. For example, during the Great Depression the public viewed President Herbert Hoover as cold, uncaring, and cynically indifferent to the problems of those who were suffering. While this imagery may not have been warranted, it did grow out of the worsening of economic conditions during his tenure in office. As president, he had failed to exercise the authority of his office to stem the tide of economic deterioration. Hoover was not evaluated in terms of his moral character or his good intentions so much as in terms of his lack of effectiveness in producing desired results.

The crisis of authority becomes evident with the occurrence of a colossal blunder. As a case in point, we may note Kennedy's authorization of the Bay of Pigs invasion. The plans for the invasion of Cuba by refugees from Castro's regime had been initiated by the CIA during Eisenhower's administration. Kennedy had been assured by his advisers that any attempted invasion would serve to precipitate a mass uprising in Cuba that would result in the overthrow of Castro's regime. All of his advisers endorsed the plan to go ahead with the invasion. Some individuals on Kennedy's staff had serious reservations about the plans, but remained silent. The subsequent assault on the beaches resulted in a disaster. Castro had advance information and was prepared for a slaughter of the invaders. We were not in a position to follow through with an air strike without running the risk of a war with the Soviet Union. The fiasco became a major source of embarrassment to Kennedy and to the United States. A crisis of authority had resulted from a faulty decision-making process.

There is a tendency for authority figures to surround themselves with subordinates and advisers who are like-minded individuals. The affairs of state are assumed to run more smoothly if subordinates endorse and support the lines of action recommended to them. Very often, however, the emphasis on group consensus becomes so great that the critical abilities of advisers and subordinates recede into the background. Through positive reinforcements of each other, an inner circle of political advisers may develop a sense of invulnerability and believe in the infallible correctness of the decisions that they are making. Apparently, it was such a faulty form of decision making that resulted in the quagmire of our involvement in Vietnam and the tragedy of the *Challenger* explosion.

The failure of those in top positions of authority to consult with those experts who were opposed to the Vietnam War resulted in a serious crisis of authority in the social realm. Those who early opposed the war and who maintained that it was a war we could not win were never admitted to the central circle of decision makers. Instead, they were negatively stereotyped as "unpatriotic, disloyal, and soft on communism." The deep divisions within the society over the war reflected a lack of public support for what had been designated as a national priority.

Twenty years after the fall of Saigon, Robert McNamara, Secretary of Defense during the Vietnam War, published a memoir admitting that serious mistakes were made in the conduct of the war. His sense of remorse was a result of the fact that, although he recognized that it was wrong to continue the war, he did nothing about it. At the time, there was strong opposition both in Congress and among the military to any critical assessment of our policies in Vietnam. Only those who were "team players" were allowed to participate in the decision-making process. Thousands of American lives were lost in Vietnam long after McNamara and other senior leaders at the center of power knew that the war was a mistake. The use of deception and misrepresentation in continuing the war made a major contribution to the loss of confidence in political authority in our society. Those entrusted with managing the affairs of state had failed to reflect the integrity that was necessary for effective leadership.

A loss of confidence in political authority also grows out of the excessive use of force in attempts to maintain law and order. The violence directed toward peaceful demonstrators during the Democratic Convention in 1968 was seen as unnecessary by many Americans who were opposed to the Vietnam War. Rather than restoring order, the use of police violence during an urban riot frequently intensifies the disturbance. Attempts to suppress a demonstration protesting the bombing raids in Cambodia during the Vietnam War resulted in the slaying of students at Kent State University by the Ohio National Guard. Such excessive use of the coercive powers of the state become problematic in view of the rights of democratic participation and social protest in an open society.

When those in positions of authority become intolerant of public demonstrations or dissent, society tends to lose its coherence as a moral community. Officials frequently attempt to uphold and reinforce traditions and vested interests long after they have outlived their historical usefulness. For example, a great deal of the trauma surrounding the civil rights movement grew out of the police violence that was directed toward those engaged in peaceful demonstrations. Attempts were made to prop up a system of special privilege for white Americans at the expense of racial minorities.

In the social heritage of the nation, traumas are drawn upon in shaping collective identities, in setting national priorities, and in providing guidelines for what to do or not to do in any given case. We negotiate between the past and the future through our concern about historical repetitions. Serious disruptions of the tranquillity of everyday life tend to be remembered and to become embedded in collective perceptions of society as moral community. Such perceptions provide a close link between self-identity and national identity. Some hold a strong sense of integration and correspondence between self and society, while others develop a sense of estrangement from society and the culture it manifests. The comfort of living in modern society is shaped to a very large degree by perceptions of collective mastery over the challenges that emerge in unexpected ways.

Bibliography

Allan, George. 1986. *The Importances of the Past.* Albany: State University of New York Press.

Bellah, Robert N. 1975. "Civil Religion in America." In *Life Styles Diversity in American Society,* ed. Saul D. Feldman and Gerald W. Thielbar, pp. 16–34. Boston: Little, Brown.

Berger, Peter L. 1967. *The Sacred Canopy.* Garden City, NY: Anchor Books.

Chapman, William. 1991. *Inventing Japan: The Making of a Postwar Civilization.* New York: Prentice-Hall.

Durkheim, Emile. 1961. *The Elementary Forms of the Religious Life.* New York: Collier Books.

Hamilton, V. Lee. 1978. "Who Is Responsible? Toward a Social Psychology of Attribution." *Social Psychology* 41: 316–327.

Hiller, Harry H. 1986. *Canadian Society: A Macro Analysis.* Scarborough, Ontario: Prentice-Hall Canada.

Janis, Irving L. 1989. *Crucial Decisions: Leadership in Policymaking and Crisis Management.* New York: Free Press.

Leone, Bruno. 1986. *Nationalism: Opposing Viewpoints.* St. Paul, MN: Greenhaven Press.

Lipset, Seymour Martin. 1963. *The First New Nation: The United States in Historical and Comparative Perspective.* New York: Basic Books.

Lowenthal, David. 1985. *The Past Is a Foreign Country.* New York: Cambridge University Press.

Maier, Charles S. 1988. *The Unmasterable Past: History, Holocaust, and German National Identity.* Cambridge, MA: Harvard University Press.

Manschreck, Clyde L. 1971. *Erosion of Authority.* Nashville: Abingdon Press.

Moorhead, G., R. Ference, and C. Neck. 1991. "Group Decision Fiascoes Continue: Space Shuttle Challenger and Revised Groupthink Framework." *Human Relations* 44: 539–550.

Naveh, Eyal. 1993. "'He Belongs to the Ages': Lincoln's Image and the American Historical Consciousness." *Journal of American Culture* 16: 49–57.

Niemi, Robert. 1993. "JFK as Jesus: The Politics of Myth in Phil Och's Crucifixion." *Journal of American Culture* 16: 35–40.

Nisbet, Robert A. 1968. *Tradition and Revolt.* New York: Random House.

Reischauer, Edwin O., and Marius B. Jansen. 1995. *The Japanese Today: Change and Continuity.* Cambridge, MA: Belknap Press.

Simon, Yves R. 1980. *A General Theory of Authority.* Notre Dame, IN: University of Notre Dame Press.

Udoidem, S. Iniobong. 1988. *Authority and the Common Good in Social and political Philosophy.* New York: University Press of America.

Vaughan, Diane. 1996. *The Challenger Launch Decision: Risky Technology, Culture, and Deviance at NASA.* Chicago: University of Chicago Press.

Warner, W. Lloyd. 1953. *American Life: Dream and Reality.* Chicago: University of Chicago Press.

Part II

Case Studies of National Trauma

3 • The Great Depression

The Great Depression of the 1930s was the most severe trauma the nation had experienced since the Civil War. The severity of the collapse of the economic system caught most Americans by surprise. The stock market crashed, banks failed, industrial production was severely curtailed, and unemployment rates escalated. Personal fortunes were lost and millions of Americans faced near starvation. The economic system had failed to work, and levels of helplessness and hopelessness reached unprecedented levels within the general population.

The economic trauma did not grow out of a single episode, but out of a series of shock waves that had cumulative effects on the social system. The Great Depression had its beginning with the stock market crash of 1929 and ended with mobilization of the nation for waging World War II. During the interval between these two events, American capitalism was in a state of crisis. The economic euphoria of the 1920s came to be replaced with unprecedented economic hardship. While all major segments of society were affected, the severity of the economic decline was experienced unevenly among subgroups of the population. The millions of Americans who experienced a rough time prior to the Great Depression were devastated by the shock effects of the economic collapse. Damaged lives were becoming increasingly evident. But, even the more privileged members of the American middle class were frequently faced with cuts in pay and were required to manage with diminished resources. Before the Great Depression ran its course, all major sectors of society confronted adversity and the system became permanently changed.

The business cycle was very much a part of the American experience. There were many economic expansions and times of prosperity followed by economic contractions. President Herbert Hoover was optimistic and designated the economic downturn as a "depression." In his view, the term "panic," a term that had been used previously to describe deteriorating economic conditions, was unwarranted in the early 1930s. He persisted in holding the view that the economic downturn was a normal and natural process. The base-building that occurs during a recession was seen as providing the foundation for even greater prosperity in the future. As the depth and severity of the Great Depression became clear, however, few could remember economic conditions that were worse, and there was little evidence for the view that the future would be better any time soon.

The initial jolt to the economic system came with the stock market crash on October 24, 1929. Prices dropped sharply, and thousands of individual investors found their personal finances to be in shambles. The initial trauma of the Great Depression fell disproportionately upon the more privileged members of society who had overextended themselves in the financial markets. The reversal of fortunes among investors symbolically represented the beginning of the hard times that were to follow.

The crash of the stock market in 1929 was not followed by a turnaround in prices as some of the leading experts on the stock market had predicted. Instead, stock prices continued their precipitous decline. The losses that were initially defined as "paper losses" subsequently translated into "real losses" from the panicked selling that followed. The failure of the stock market to recover from its catastrophic collapse contributed to a sharp reversal in public attitudes. Previous attitudes of greed and economic euphoria were transformed into attitudes of fear. As fear descended on the market, brokerage houses were swamped with sell orders as investors attempted to cut their losses. Before the bear market of the early 1930s ran its course, the Dow Jones Industrial Average dropped to a low of 41, down from a high of 381 on September 3, 1929. The 90 percent decline in stock prices translated into severe economic losses for investors. About $30 billion in assets had vanished, a sum approximating the total cost of World War I to the United States. The trauma of the stock market losses became a forerunner of more pervasive economic calamities that were to follow.

The second wave of the economic collapse occurred in the banking industry. Banks failed at an alarming rate during the early 1930s. The banks got into a lot of trouble because they had failed to maintain adequate cash reserves, had made risky investments, and had loaned money to people who could not repay. Individual depositors responded with shock and alarm as banks failed and their money evaporated. The use of banks for depositing personal savings and weekly paychecks had been based on the assumption that funds would be available when there was a need for them. Checking and savings accounts vanished as the banks went under. The scope of the bank failures generated an atmosphere of panic. There was a run on banks as depositors scurried to get their money back. The available resources in the banks were quickly exhausted, and the banks became insolvent. Banks became the object of a great deal of anger and hostility as a result of foreclosures on mortgages, the loss of depositors' savings, and the worsening of economic conditions.

By 1933, industrial production fell to about one-third of its 1929 total, and the U.S. gross national product was trimmed to half of what it had been four years earlier. A dark cloud descended over a nation that had control over vast natural resources, with an agricultural system unsurpassed in its capacity for food production, and with an industrial base for producing vast quantities of consumer goods and services. The production of such consumer items as automobiles, refrigerators, and washing machines necessarily depends on assumptions about a predictable market and consumer buying power. The business sector cannot sustain a high level of production for very long under conditions of falling prices, falling demand, and escalating corporate losses. American consumers no longer had prosperity-level resources for purchasing the products of industry. Production was curtailed. plants were closed, and thousands of employees received their layoff notices.

Reasonable estimates place the overall unemployment rate for the nation at about one-fourth of the civilian labor force by 1933. Thirty-seven percent of nonfarm workers were unemployed. Out of a civilian labor force of 51 million, about 13 million workers found themselves unemployed. In several metropolitan areas, the unemployment rates were more than 50 percent. Employment opportunities were vanishing, and for millions of those who were employed, the rate of pay was severely cut. The average weekly earnings of production workers in manufacturing had dropped from $25 in 1929 to about $17 by 1933. The income levels for about three-fourths of those who were employed fell below the minimum necessary for maintaining a decent standard of living. The families of several million workers had no income of any kind.

The American dream had turned into a nightmare. Life plans were shattered, families were disrupted, and several million Americans became homeless. The collapse of the economic system caused widespread suffering and unhappiness in the personal lives of individuals throughout the country. Men and women who had thought of themselves as self-sufficient found themselves standing in bread lines and making use of soup kitchens to alleviate their hunger pains. Many of those who took advantage of the limited relief available did so with a personal sense of embarrassment and shame.

One of the many dramatic episodes of the Great Depression consisted of the veterans' march on Washington in the late spring of 1932. The veterans camped out with their wives and children in city parks, dumps, empty stores, and warehouses. A sense of desperation was written across the faces of those who participated in daily marches around the White House. The veterans came to demand an advanced payment of the bonus that had been promised to them for military service in World War I. The poverty-stricken veterans hoped to get about $500 each, which would provide temporary relief from their personal suffering and the suffering of their families. While the veterans marched to call attention to their plight, they were met with a governmental response that seemed to be cold and indifferent. President Hoover was embarrassed with what he saw happening in the nation's capital and maintained that the demonstrators were "communists" or "criminals," rather than veterans.

Out of a sense of despair the veterans persisted in their demands and refused to obey orders to move out of Washington. A military unit under the command of General Douglas MacArthur was dispatched to forcefully disperse the demonstrators. Veterans who had served their country in the trenches of World War I were now faced with tanks, gas grenades, machine guns, and rifles with fixed bayonets. More than 100 demonstrators were injured in the forceful dispersal. The coercive powers of the state had been employed to suppress public expression of discontent. The veterans were bitter as they left the Washington area. All evidence pointed to the conclusion that the nation was ungrateful for the personal sacrifices they had made. The nation had failed to respond to their needs in a time of trouble.

Even the forces of nature seemed to be conspiring against human hopes for a secure world and a better life. Contributing to the depth of the Great Depression, a prolonged drought resulted in the most devastating agricultural disaster in American history. The drought lasted throughout the 1930s and was frequently accompanied by unprecedented heat waves. Overplowing and overgrazing of the Great Plains were man's contribution to what became known as "the dust bowl." The affected area extended from the Mississippi River to the Rocky Mountains and from North Dakota to Texas. The top soil became airborne when the high winds came. Clouds of dust covered the landscape, entered houses around windows and doors, and made breathing difficult. The shifting sands altered the landscape and made a vast land area uninhabitable.

Food shortages, and in many cases near starvation, were encountered by farm populations dependent on the annual crop yield. Even under the best of circumstances, making a living through farming in desert-like conditions is difficult. Thousands of families were forced off the land when crops were destroyed by dust storms, loans could not be repaid, and banks foreclosed on farm mortgages. Farm laborers lost their jobs as a consequence of the government policy of removing land from production in order to prop up farm prices. A mixture of hope and despair was associated with the mass migration of hundreds of thousands to other parts of the country. The pathos of the mass migration was captured in John Steinbeck's novel, *The Grapes of Wrath*. The quest for new beginnings and a more favorable life stood in sharp contrast to the reality shock of transient camps and finding nothing more than temporary work at very low wages. Feelings of bitterness and disillusionment grew out of the recognition that hard times had affected all areas of the country.

An increasing proportion of Americans saw themselves as living in an environment that was unresponsive to their personal needs and interests. Those in positions of political authority were seen as failing to provide adequate leadership and as being indifferent to the suffering that was occurring throughout the country. Under existing conditions, society could fulfill neither the economic nor the spiritual needs of the general population. Many intellectuals embraced communism as the only viable system for alleviating the deep troubles the country was facing. People came to believe that capitalism was in a state of crisis. Those pressing for remedial action encountered resistance from those who wished to maintain the status quo. The impact of the Great Depression on American society was of volcanic proportions.

The Crisis of Capitalism

The crisis of capitalism grew out of the failure of the economy to provide for either the needs of individuals or the needs of the social system. All of the markets of the American economy were out of alignment and in serious trouble. The financial markets were in a state of turmoil, the labor markets failed to provide employment, and the commodity markets were faced with surpluses that could not be sold. The contradictions of capitalism were evident in the agricultural sector. Farmers were faced with food that could not be sold, while millions of Americans suffered from hunger. Impersonal forces were operating that were understood neither by business leaders nor government officials.

In contrast to the public view that President Hoover was indifferent to economic hardships, he had taken an active role in appealing to business corporations to take voluntary measures for alleviating the crisis. For example, he called for a voluntary freeze on wage reductions. He argued that business corporations would benefit in the long run if they undertook voluntary measures to stem the tide of economic deterioration.

The Ford Motor Company responded to the president's appeal by announcing that wage levels would not be reduced, but instead would be increased to $7 a day for production workers. The role of the Ford Motor Company in stemming the tide of economic deterioration, however, was short lived. The annual sales of automobiles dropped from more than 5 million in 1929 to slightly more than 1 million in 1932. Economic hardships had resulted in consumers making drastic cuts in their discretionary spending. Ford followed the general trend in industry by seriously curtailing production and laying off thousands of workers to reduce payroll costs. In Detroit, Toledo, Cleveland, and other industrial cities of the Midwest, more than half of the labor force was required to join the ranks of the unemployed.

President Hoover attempted to reassure the nation that all was well. He asserted that in the long run the nation would benefit from the present difficulties. Adversity, in his view, would contribute to strong moral character. Individuals should show more initiative and try harder to solve their own problems. In his view, governmental initiatives in the area of welfare would only lead to chronic dependency. The government, particularly the federal government, should minimize its role in the lives of private citizens. He was, in effect, drawing upon older ideologies that had outlived their historical usefulness. His political agenda included an emphasis on protective tariffs (which intensified the economic crisis on a worldwide basis), an emphasis on tight money policy when there was a need for easier access to credit, and an emphasis on governmental economies when there was a need for economic stimulus. Many Americans saw Hoover's political measures as the source of the problem rather than the solution.

Hoover maintained that unemployment relief should be the primary responsibility of charitable organizations and local governments, not the federal government. He strongly held the conviction that voluntary cooperative action at the local level could not only relieve the distress but also reinforce national values promoting an ethic of social responsibility. The ethic of social responsibility called for the more prosperous members of society to provide help for the less fortunate who were in need. Many local officials initially agreed with President Hoover. Serious efforts were directed toward implementing the tradition of private philanthropy for meeting the needs of the suffering.

The cities of New Orleans, Minneapolis, and many others made a concerted effort to draw upon local resources for dealing with the emergency. All were destined to fail. The local resources that were mobilized turned out to be far too limited for dealing with economic problems that were increasing in severity. The increasing number of unemployed men, homeless families, and hungry school children quickly exhausted all available local resources. Unemployment and homelessness were increasing at the same time that tax revenues were decreasing at both the local and the federal levels. Hoover's orthodox emphasis upon an annually balanced federal budget stood in contrast to the growing need for government assistance in the general population. Voluntary forms of relief could not keep pace with the accelerated economic deterioration. Families in serious trouble were required to do the best they could with the limited resources they had available.

Following in the tradition of private philanthropy, the city of Philadelphia was authorized by the Pennsylvania legislature to borrow $3 million for relief and to establish a private agency for its administration. Providing relief for the unemployed, the homeless, and hungry children quickly exhausted the funds that had been made available. By the middle of 1932, about 57,000 families in Philadelphia were left to fend for themselves. No form of public assistance was available. Similar episodes occurred in metropolitan areas throughout the country. Voluntary forms of relief could not keep pace with the economic collapse. Local governments could not begin to solve the welfare problems and the many needs for relief.

The conclusion became inescapable that only the federal government had the resources that were necessary for dealing with the emergency. Voluntarism on the part of business corporations and charitable organizations had failed to adequately deal with the emergency. As a result, the crisis of capitalism became a crisis of authority in the political realm. Those holding positions of power and trusteeship had failed to act when action was necessary. It was not so much that the president and the Congress were indifferent to the problems that were developing; rather, the crisis stemmed from an intellectual failure to recognize that older ideologies and historical precedents were not adequate for dealing with the seriousness of the economic collapse. Viewing the emergency as only a temporary one that would eventually correct itself was not good enough. Such views subsequently came to be regarded as reflecting attitudes of benign neglect and cynical indifference.

In the final analysis, the crisis of capitalism produced a loss of confidence in the economic system. Business corporations responded by "battening down the hatches," so to speak, through their retrenchment policies. Banks responded by foreclosing on mortgages when homeowners were unable to repay. With plant closings and layoffs, the unemployed were required to fend for themselves. There were no provisions for unemployment compensation or transitional measures for relocating workers. Those looking for work confronted a labor market in which no jobs were available. Individuals faced scarcities and shortages in their personal lives, while corporations and farmers were confronted with surplus production. In effect, neither corporate America nor the American government were able to deal effectively with the problems of economic failure.

The many oral histories of the Great Depression and the pathos in the letters written to Eleanor and Franklin Roosevelt revealed symptoms of trauma resembling those of combat veterans. Sleep disturbances, eating disorders, feelings of detachment and estrangement from others, and a sense of emptiness were evident. The letters to the Roosevelts were disproportionately from women and reflected the many aspects of appeals for help out of feelings of desperation. The letters revealed a sense of no other place to turn and a conviction that the president and his wife were sympathetic to their suffering and would be willing to provide personal help.

Economic Hardship

Throughout most of the human past, deprivation and hardship were the normal state of affairs for most people. Industrialization and urbanization changed that. In the decade following World War I, the purchasing power of the American family was increasing; the overall standard of living was improving; and people were living longer. The types of goods and services available to the masses had previously been limited to only the very rich. While not shared uniformly, the overall prosperity in the United States during the 1920s produced a state of euphoria. The production and distribution of automobiles, telephones, radios, refrigerators, and other consumer durable goods pointed toward a future that would be even better. Materialistic values were given free reign by mass advertisers who encouraged people to want more, to spend more, and to consume more. It was no longer simply a system that was concerned with meeting the survival needs of the population; it now placed an emphasis on generating wants and desires for commodities that did not exist previously.

The American values of individualism and consumerism were counterproductive during the economic setback of the 1930s. A larger number of Americans had come to want and expect a type of lifestyle they could no longer have. The success theme in American culture had always placed an emphasis on the correspondence between merit and reward, between what people deserve and what they actually get. While pockets of poverty persisted throughout the 1920s, there was a general belief in the United States as a land of opportunity: Any man or woman with a lot of initiative and hard work would be able to make it within the system. Subscribing to these values contributed to the anguish of the millions who blamed themselves for their troubles, rather than seeing hardship as a result of a system failure.

The economic hardships of the Great Depression fell disproportionately upon the family unit. The family has always been one of the primary organizational units within a society. When the family is functioning properly, it provides a major source of life satisfaction, a place to retreat from the world, and a place to pursue central life interests within a context of security and intimacy. The effective link of the family to the larger society, however, is dependent upon some minimal level of financial resources. Conditions of crisis surface when parents lack the resources to adequately serve as providers and caretakers for their children and for each other.

At the time of the Great Depression, families were organized along more traditional lines than they are today. It was the husband's primary responsibility to be the breadwinner, while the wife stayed home to do the chores and raise the children. As a result, most households had a single wage earner. When the husband was laid off, no other source of income was available. If the unemployment continued for very long, the savings were soon exhausted, insurance policies were cashed, and furniture and other possessions were sold or pawned to obtain the money needed for survival. Credit was frequently used for buying food or paying the rent, and loans were sought from friends and relatives. Debts piled up, obtaining food became more difficult, and conflicts within the family intensified.

Many of the conflicts within the family grew out of the psychological effects of unemployment on the breadwinner. In a society that places a positive value on work, the self-esteem of men was heavily dependent upon success in performing the provider role. The meaning of work, however, had many facets that went beyond the paycheck for paying the family bills. Having a paid job served to validate social worth and to establish a social identity. The routines associated with keeping work schedules, completing assigned tasks, and meeting family financial needs were important sources of personal stability and order. Then as now, employment served as a psychological stabilizer in the lives of individuals.

A social vacuum often developed with the loss of occupational status. The loss of a job required developing a new self-identity, and this was in part forced on the unemployed by the responses of others. Children frequently looked upon their fathers as failures, and wives frequently complained that their husbands were not trying hard enough to find work. Many of the unemployed tended to withdraw from others. Friends dropped off, they went to church less frequently, and there was less interaction with neighbors. Within the family, husbands became gloomy, detached, and unable to communicate effectively with other family members. A sense of apathy and despair grew out of the unemployed seeing themselves as "damaged" or "defective" because of their inability to find work. They were thrown back on their own coping resources at a time when these resources had become fragile.

The unemployed men were disproportionately unskilled and semi-skilled workers who had limited experiences with job hunting. The skills required in mining, steel mills, and automobile plants were not skills that could be transferred to other lines of work. The inability to find work was accompanied by the feeling that one's skills and abilities had little value in the labor force. Standing in long lines with others seeking work, and pounding the pavement day in and day out, frequently resulted in feelings of futility. Previously, a job had been thought of as primarily something offered by an employer. Such was not now the case. Working at odd jobs at a very low rate of pay was the very best that many could do. It was not a matter of not putting enough effort into looking for work. The jobs simply were not available.

The unemployed had time on their hands, but it was not time that was suitable for the pursuit of hobbies, sports, or other creative and meaningful uses of leisure. It was coerced leisure accompanied by the lack of a sense of connectedness. Having husbands around the house all day added to the daily hassles experienced by wives. Couple interactions frequently became hostile as arguments surfaced over money matters, child-rearing practices, and relationships with relatives. While some couples were able to maintain the coherence of family life under conditions of economic adversity, most were not. Family relations were seriously affected by husbands who had developed attitudes of fatalism and helplessness, by children who had lost their respect for parental authority, and by wives who attempted to manage a household with diminishing resources.

Some husbands and fathers abandoned their families and joined the army of those drifting around the country in search of work. Without any means of financial support, wives gathered up their children and moved in with parents or other relatives. Being unable to support oneself or to care for one's children was associated with attitudes of despair. Households became overcrowded and levels of stress increased when limited resources had to be shared with needy relatives. Something was wrong with the system when some households became seriously overcrowded at the same time that there were empty apartments and houses because of the inability of potential tenants to pay the rent.

Without places to live and with no jobs available, several hundred thousand Americans were required to take to the road. Several of these were families who packed up their belongings in an old automobile and headed out for greener pastures. The poverty-stricken nomads were seeking escape from intolerable conditions in their present environment. Usually, migration is associated with optimism about greater opportunities elsewhere and hopes for a better life. There were little grounds for optimism among those uprooted from their homes by dust storms or among those in urban areas who had confronted homelessness and near starvation. The nomads of the Great Depression were forced to move, and the quest for a better life was limited primarily to the need for subsistence.

About 200,000 of the wanderers were adolescents and young adults who joined the homeless traveling around the country in search of work and subsistence. Under normal conditions, young adults would enter the labor force after the completion of schooling. Then as now, there was a low tolerance for the vacuum that is created when young adults are neither in school nor in the labor force. Both male and female adolescents, whose families could not support unproductive members, joined the homeless nomads searching for work and subsistence. The availability of food was associated with gluttonous eating only to be followed by near starvation when food was not available. The transient population had lost the safety and security of their previous lives and confronted serious threats of victimization. Under conditions of hunger, fights broke out over access to garbage pails that were placed in alleys in back of restaurants. For many, life had become harsh and brutal.

The primary mode of travel among the poverty-stricken was through hopping freight trains and riding in empty boxcars. Hopping a freight train is a dangerous, risk-taking activity. Several hundred were killed or seriously injured in the process. Initially, the railroads attempted to stop the practice by arresting the transients for trespassing. When the number of transients reached several hundred thousand, the railroads became somewhat sympathetic to their plight, and out of a sense of futility stopped the practice of arresting and prosecuting them. The railroads, however, continued to be concerned with trespassing and hired their own detectives to remove transients from the trains and railroad property.

Attitudes were ambivalent in the communities that became hosts to the transients. The ambivalence centered around some degree of generosity in making food available while having an interest in getting them out of town as soon as possible. Many relief stations provided only two meals a day, and these frequently consisted of no more than weak soup and a limited amount of bread. In some communities the soup kitchens were made available for no more than three days for any given person and then he or she was expected to move on. The strangers in town were frequently seen as being undesirable and of questionable character.

A new vocabulary surfaced for describing the homeless and the unattached who were drifting. The term "tramp" was used for describing individuals who were seen as unwilling to work and simply looking for a handout, while the term "hobo" was used for describing men who were willing to work when work was available. The hobos were frequently accepted as men who were down on their luck, and there was sometimes a willingness to share the limited work available. The tramps, by way of contrast, confirmed the stereotypes of the underprivileged. They were seen as "lazy," "shiftless," and as "con artists." Thus, in any given case, the widely used phrase "brother can you spare a dime" was met with judgments about the validity of the need for help relative to the probability of being taken in by an operator. The begging frequently consisted of reference to "having a bad run of luck" and "having children who were hungry." Only a few defined the problem as one of system failure, rather than in terms of the perceived qualities and attributes of the unfortunate.

The transients became aggregates or collections of individuals who settled in empty lots, city dumps, or some other vacated land space within communities. The "hobo jungles" were comprised of people who had been brought together by fate and had no ongoing relationships with each other. The dwellers of these "jungles" were an assortment of people who would prefer to be someplace else. All major cities had such areas in which the homeless congregated. These areas became known as "Hoovervilles" and were characterized by make-shift shacks that had been constructed from whatever materials were available to provide some protection from the wind, the cold, and the rain. The newspapers that were used as sources of warmth became known as "Hoover blankets." Many of the homeless survived only through begging or scrounging through garbage cans or garbage dumps in search of food.

When the severity of the Great Depression reached its peak in the early 1930s, there was no other major subgroup of the population as severely affected as the African Americans. In all areas of the country, the level of economic deprivation was consistently greater for blacks than for whites. Unemployment had reached 50 percent among blacks by 1932, and among those who were employed, there was a sharp drop in wages. Routinely, blacks faced a labor market in which whites had received preferential treatment in hiring and job security. African Americans were among the last hired and among the first to be dismissed when layoffs became necessary. At the outset of the Great Depression, the majority of blacks in the United States lived in rural areas. Several hundred thousand of them were sharecroppers, who in 1930 had an average annual income of only $295 per year. With the sharp drop in farm prices during the 1930s, the economic hardships increased dramatically for black families that were dependent upon farm labor as the source of income.

Blacks in urban areas had routinely fared better than their rural counterparts in terms of income. With the onset of the Great Depression, however, there was a reversal in the sense of well-being. The unemployment rates for blacks in urban areas were 30 to 60 percent higher than for whites. As jobs became scarce, blacks and ethnic minorities were least likely to find employment; and when payrolls were reduced they were among the first to join the ranks of the unemployed. Having no stable source of income, the health of many black families became seriously impaired as a result of the reduced expenditures for food. Disproportionately, black families were reduced to the subsistence level. The jarring effects of the Great Depression were severe for most of the population, but among those routinely underprivileged, the effects were catastrophic.

The American middle class was also confronted with economic deprivation during the Great Depression. While the levels of suffering did not match that of the lower socioeconomic levels, many did face wage cuts and sporadic work opportunities. Several adaptive responses emerged as coping mechanisms. Priorities were reordered as the importance of money came to be downplayed and the intrinsic rewards of social relationships came to be emphasized. Particularly along these lines were the themes of positive thinking and the importance of getting along with people. The best-selling book of the decade was Dale Carnegie's *How to Win Friends and Influence People*. Movies became increasingly popular; people turned to them for vicarious thrills. Identification with the celebrities of popular entertainment served as compensation for what was missing in their personal lives. The many forms of diversion reflected ways of coping with problems that could not be confronted and solved directly.

Remedial Action

Serious problems of social inequality surfaced with the unfolding of the Great Depression, and discontent was expressed in organized protest. In Chicago, riots broke out in protest against landlords who had evicted tenants because of their inability to pay the rent. Labor turmoil and strikes became widespread in response to deplorable working conditions and cuts in pay. Stores were looted in Oklahoma City and Minneapolis by hungry people who were seeking food. Farmers in Iowa organized to protest falling farm prices by pouring out milk and withholding their products from the market. Pigs by the thousands were floated down the Missouri River to dramatize the plight of farmers in producing a product that could be sold only at a loss. Unemployed men and women marched on City Hall in Los Angeles, Cleveland, Philadelphia, and other cities to call attention to their plight and suffering. In Madison, Wisconsin, unemployed workers took over the state capital and for several days enacted mock legislation that was seen as being necessary. Suffering at the grassroots level led to a clamor for remedial action at the political level. Never before had so many Americans suffered from hunger or lived under such wretched conditions.

The hard times seemed to confirm what the socialists had been saying for a long time about the contradictions of capitalism. The earlier writings of Karl Marx and Friedrich Engels had predicted that a revolution would grow out of a cataclysmic depression and an intensification of misery for the masses. Although the American communists saw conditions as ripe for revolution, the unfolding of historical events suggested that revolution was not the only response to economic misery. Rather than a clamor for revolution, the focus of most Americans was on personal troubles and daily hassles. Although one-third of the population was "ill-fed, ill-clad, and ill-housed," there was no widespread call for revolution.

Most Americans did not want a revolutionary overthrow of the system, but only access to those resources that were needed to relieve their suffering through reform. The attention of most people was directed toward the immediate concerns of everyday life. Wearing handed-down clothing, buying day-old bread, eating less meat, growing gardens, and canning were typical of the economies initiated in the management of daily affairs.

The American Communist Party made a concerted effort to recruit members of the working class and racial minorities into its movement. These efforts turned out to be a dismal failure. Blacks were unsympathetic to the communist cause, in large measure because they saw the movement as an attempt to exploit them for ends that were not their own. The classical theories of Marx and Lenin had failed to address the issue of race in their condemnations of the capitalist system. The members of the working class were less concerned with political ideologies than with getting a fair share of the rewards that modern industry had to offer. The aspirations of industrial workers were believed to be better served through labor negotiations than through a revolutionary overthrow of the system.

The turmoil of the 1930s was of a sufficient magnitude that all things seemed possible. The growing levels of discontent when combined with the political activities of extremist groups produced a potentially volatile situation. In the presidential election of 1932, Roosevelt responded to the voices of discontent. His campaign was constructed around the promise that the federal government would take an active role in addressing the problems of the Great Depression. A concerted effort would be made to restore confidence in the country through direct action at the center of power.

In his inaugural address, Roosevelt observed, "The only thing we need to fear is fear itself." He noted the vast resources of the country, maintained that a great deal of repair work was needed in the social realm, and called for collective and cooperative efforts in addressing the serious problems of the nation. Roosevelt's subsequent "fireside chats" made full use of the radio as a medium of communication and conveyed to the nation a personal sense of warmth, closeness, and caring. As is frequently the case in times of crisis, a charismatic leader had emerged to symbolize the hopes and aspirations of his constituents. Many Americans soon came to regard Roosevelt as standing alongside Washington and Lincoln in providing the greatest leadership the nation ever had.

During the first few months of Roosevelt's administration, extensive executive and legislative initiatives were undertaken. These included creating policies for regulating banks and insuring deposits in order to restore confidence. The rights of labor unions to organize and to engage in collective bargaining were recognized. Federally funded emergency projects were initiated to provide employment. The explosion of collective reforms manifested the replacement of "systems defects" for what had previously been defined as "defects of individuals." Roosevelt drew upon the notion of a crisis as both "danger" and "opportunity." The crisis provided an opportunity to initiate changes that had long been needed. The political process, however, became increasingly rancorous as the initiatives for change collided with strong vested interests.

Among the initiatives undertaken through New Deal legislation, few matched the symbolic significance of the Social Security Act. Some saw the social security measures that called for unemployment compensation and old-age pensions as the beginnings of "a welfare state" and argued that too much power was being concentrated in the federal government. Support and opposition came to be crystallized along social class lines. Deficit spending to support New Deal legislation was seen by some as undermining the foundations of the American economy. In effect, "capitalists" did not want social security. However, in retrospect, several historians have noted that it was Roosevelt and the New Deal legislation that saved the capitalist system. According to some historical analyses, "It was social security or the barricades." Without major reforms, the integrity of the private property system was in jeopardy. Stemming the tide of economic collapse served to circumvent the discontent and turmoil that was developing at the grass-roots level.

The remedial measures initiated under the New Deal legislation did not solve the basic problems of the Great Depression. At the time neither Roosevelt nor his advisers could see the full scope of the efforts that would be required for economic recovery. Some of the conservatives were outraged in 1938 when the president succeeded in getting $3.7 billion from Congress for public spending. We now recognize that even this amount was far too little to get the job done. The civilian unemployment rate was still 15 percent as late as 1940. It was not the New Deal that brought an end to the Great Depression, but the Japanese attack on Pearl Harbor. Gearing up for wartime production provided the type of stimulus that was needed for economic recovery. Full employment was not achieved until about 15 million Americans were in uniform and $50 billion were spent annually for the war effort. Unemployment vanished as men and women previously on the margin of the labor force found themselves at the center of the war effort. Economic hardship and despair came to be replaced by renewed optimism and a new set of opportunities.

The Legacy of the Great Depression

While no one yet understands the precise reasons for the severity of the economic collapse, we can now see some of the measures the government can take to avoid the type of catastrophe that occurred in the 1930s. There are now procedures in place for drawing upon professional expertise in regulating the American economy. The creation of the Council of Economic Advisers was a direct outgrowth of the Great Depression. Macroeconomic theories became more fully developed, and we now have more dependable knowledge for reducing the severity of economic recessions. The Federal Reserve Board now plays a central role in fine-tuning the American economy. Interest rates may be reduced, or the money supply increased, to offset the severity of a recessionary swing. It is now recognized that an increase in government spending, or a reduction in taxes, can have a stimulating effect on the American economy. Thus, we now have a much clearer understanding of the macro-forces that are operating and how to offset some of the serious problems that developed during the Great Depression.

The central role of the federal government in the economic affairs of the nation became well established. Through speaking in the name of society, the scope and functions of the federal government came to be legitimated and elaborated. What previously had been defined primarily as personal troubles were increasingly seen as public issues. Taking steps to promote stability within the economic realm became one of the major responsibilities of government. No modern government can afford to ignore sharp increases in the rates of unemployment or sharp drops in the standard of living in the general population. An overriding political challenge has become that of meshing the needs of individuals with the needs of the social system.

Such measures as unemployment compensation and social security are now perceived as necessary and as forms of entitlement. The taken-for-granted provisions of social security have greatly altered the ways in which individuals build their life-worlds. For example, the young married couples of today seldom plan to have children in order to have someone to look after them in their old age. This was a major reason for having children prior to the Great Depression. Adult children do not regard it as a personal responsibility to provide for the economic needs of their aging parents. Private pension plans and social security benefits have made a substantial contribution to personal independence and to the quality of life among the aged. Access to desired resources provides a greater sense of personal dignity in the later years than was the case when aged parents were more heavily dependent upon their children.

Collective memories of the Great Depression became muted during the economic prosperity of the postwar years. Experiences with the economic hardships of the 1930s became frozen in the past, and the nation came to be caught up in consumer-oriented lifestyles. From the many oral histories of the Great Depression, it becomes clear that collective memories take a selective form. In reflections on the 1930s, there is a certain amount of denial of the economic hardships among those who made it through with limited psychological scars. Most individuals thought they had fared pretty well in comparison to others they knew who had suffered more. While painful memories tend to be downplayed over time, they are sufficiently embedded in collective consciousness that they may be drawn upon when the need arises. The Great Depression serves as a major reference point for making evaluations when there is a sharp drop in stock market prices, an increase in bank failures, an increase in unemployment rates, or a deep recessionary swing in the business cycle.

The trauma of the Great Depression conveyed the message that individual initiatives and motivations were not enough, in and of themselves, for a fulfillment of the American dream. The structure of opportunities is a property of a social system. Whether solving basic social problems or promoting acquisitive individualism is to become the national priority is currently subject to political debate. Attitudes of cynical indifference toward social problems are likely to result in unintended consequences. High rates of crime, an increase in personal pathologies, and the recurrence of civic disorders are likely outcomes of the failure of a social system to provide for the basic needs of its members. The legacy of the Great Depression serves as a reminder of what happened in the past and of the type of collapse and calamity that could happen again.

In summary, the impact of the Great Depression on American society was extensive. An entire generation continued to bear what Caroline Bird called "the invisible scar." The lives of individuals became closely linked with historical circumstances. Through confronting hard times and moving beyond them, an older generation of Americans came to hold a special appreciation for the material abundance of the postwar years. While few looked upon increased income as increased increments of human happiness, there was an overall appreciation for the advances that had been made in the economic realm. For the generation seriously scared by the Great Depression, economic prosperity was not taken as self-evident. Knowing what both hard times and prosperity were like contributed to a keen awareness of the limitations and prospects of the human condition.

Bibliography

Allen, Frederick Lewis. 1940. *Since Yesterday: The 1930s in America.* New York: Harper and Row.

Amenta, Edwin, and Sunita Parikh. 1991. "Capitalists Did Not Want the Social Security Act: A Critique of the 'Capitalist Dominance' Thesis." *American Sociological Review* 56: 124–132.

Bakke, E. Wright. 1940. *Citizens Without Work.* New Haven, CT: Yale University Press.

Bendiner, Robert. 1967. *Just Around the Corner: A Highly Selective History of the Thirties.* New York: E.P. Dutton.

Bergman, Andrew. 1971. *We're in the Money: Depression America and Its Films.* New York: Harper Torchbooks.

Bernstein, Irving. 1985. *A Caring Society: The New Deal, the Worker, and the Great Depression.* Boston: Houghton Mifflin.

Billington, Monroe. 1982. "The New Deal Was a Joke: Political Humor During the Great Depression." *Journal of American Culture* 5: 15–21.

Bird, Caroline. 1966. *The Invisible Scar.* New York: D. McKay.

Brunner, Karl, ed. 1981. *The Great Depression Revisited.* Boston: Martinus Nijhoff.

Buss, Terry F., and Stevens Redburn. 1983. *Mass Unemployment: Plant Closings and Community Mental Health.* Beverly Hills, CA: Sage.

Elder, Glen H., Jr. 1974. *Children of the Great Depression.* Chicago: University of Chicago Press.

Feather, Norman T. 1990. *The Psychological Impact of Unemployment.* New York: Springer-Verlag.

Galbraith, John Kenneth. 1988. *The Great Crash of 1929.* Boston: Houghton Mifflin.

Garraty, John A. 1987. *The Great Depression.* New York: Doubleday Anchor.

Gibson, Donald E. 1992. "Post-Industrialism: Prosperity or Decline?" *Sociological Focus* 26: 147–163.

Goldston, Robert. 1968. *The Great Depression: The United States in the Thirties.* Greenwich, CT: Fawcett Premier.

Graubart, Judah L., and Alice V. Graubart. 1978. *Decade of Destiny.* Chicago: Contemporary Books.

Hobson, Archie, ed. 1985. *Remembering America: A Sampler of the WPA American Guide Series.* New York: Columbia University Press.

Jenkins, J. Craig, and Barbara G. Brents. 1989. "Social Protest, Hegemonic Competition, and Social Reform." *American Sociological Review* 54: 891–909.

Klingaman, William K. 1989. *The Year of the Great Crash.* New York: Harper and Row.

Komarovsky, Mirra. 1940. *The Unemployed Man and His Family.* New York: Dryden Press.

McElvaine, Robert S. 1984. *The Great Depression.* New York: Times Books.

Mitchell, Broadus. 1947. *Depression Decade.* Vol. 9 of *The Economic History of the United States.* New York: Rinehart.

Nash, Gerald D. 1979. *The Great Depression and World War II.* New York: St. Martin's Press.

Newman, Katherine S. 1988. *Falling from Grace: The Experience of Downward Mobility in the American Middle Class.* New York: Free Press.

Piven, Frances Fox, and Richard A. Cloward. 1979. *Poor People's Movements: Why They Succeed, How They Fail.* New York: Vintage Books.

Recken, Stephen L. 1993. "Fitting-In: The Redefinition of Success in the 1930s." *Journal of Popular Culture* 27 (winter): 205–222.

Rollins, Alfred B., Jr., ed. *Depression, Recovery, and War: 1929–1945.* New York: McGraw-Hill.

Shannon, David A., ed. 1960. *The Great Depression.* Englewood Cliffs, NJ: Prentice-Hall.

Sternsher, Bernard, ed. 1969. *The Negro in Depression and War.* Chicago: Quadrangle Books.

———. 1970. *Hitting Home: The Great Depression in Town and Country.* Chicago: Quadrangle Books.

Terkel, Studs. 1970. *Hard Times: An Oral History of the Great Depression.* New York: Pocket Books.

Ware, Susan. 1982. *Holding Their Own: American Women in the 1930s.* Boston: Twayne.

Watkins, T.H. 1993. *The Great Depression: America in the 1930s.* Boston: Little, Brown.

Wolters, Raymond. 1970. *Negroes in the Great Depression.* Westport, CT: Greenwood Press.

4 • The Japanese Attack on Pearl Harbor

Americans encountered one of the more traumatic and consequential events in the history of the nation on December 7, 1941. The millions of Americans who were listening to their radios were shocked by the news that interrupted their regular programs. Suddenly and without warning, military forces from Japan had launched an aerial attack on the American naval base at Pearl Harbor. The integrity of the United States as a nation had been violated; the orderliness and security of everyday life had been disrupted. The damage was extensive and fatalities were high, including civilian as well as military personnel. It was clear that a serious national emergency existed.

It was an early Sunday morning in Hawaii when the attack occurred and the initial responses were those of shock, disbelief, and denial. Radio announcers found it necessary to emphasize again and again the importance of the newsworthy event and to repeat "this is an attack." Many observers initially thought that what they were seeing was simply another drill by the relatively large military force that was concentrated on the islands.

Japanese aircraft carriers supported by heavy cruisers had moved secretly and inconspicuously across about 2,000 miles of ocean to assemble in a wedge-like formation for the assault on Hawaii. The attack was an outgrowth of the planning that had been in process for several years. As dawn was breaking at Oahu, wave after wave of Japanese assault planes pounded the naval base at Pearl Harbor. The meticulous preparations for the attack could not have been more successful. The easy targets and the complete surprise of the Americans resulted in a military victory for the Japanese that exceeded their expectations.

The peace and tranquillity that Americans enjoy on Sunday mornings had contributed to their vulnerability. The relaxed atmosphere that prevailed in Hawaii seemed far removed from any immediate threat of war. When the scope of the damage was assessed, it was clear that a large part of the American Pacific Fleet had been destroyed or incapacitated. Nineteen ships were sunk or seriously damaged, including six battleships. Additionally, 188 of the planes on the ground at Hickham Field were destroyed. More than 2,000 American sailors, soldiers, and civilians were killed, and more than an additional thousand were wounded. Aerial and naval assaults had been launched simultaneously against American bases in the Philippines, Guam, and Midway.

The news of the Japanese attack intruded into the daily lives of Americans and had a dramatic impact. Very few Americans who were alive at that time have difficulty in remembering the activities in which they were engaged when they heard about the attack on Pearl Harbor. The event became a marker in the personal lives of men and women. A reference point had been created for separating the past from the present and from the events that were to follow. The world had undergone drastic change and could never be the same again. Social worlds and personal lives had been exposed to a shock of volcano-like proportions. Subsequent memories of life events were to be organized around what happened prior to Pearl Harbor and what happened afterward. Personal biographies were becoming linked with the unfolding of historical events.

The level of shock among Americans was comparable to what it would have been had the invasion been from Mars, and nearly as unbelievable. The trauma to the nation was intensified because the attack was launched by the Japanese. The attention of Americans had been riveted to the German blitzkrieg in Europe—within a relatively short period of time the German army invaded and conquered not only Austria, Czechoslovakia, Hungary, and Poland, but also the Netherlands, Belgium, and France. All had fallen to the onslaught of the German army and England appeared to be next. Americans had thus followed with interest and anxiety the developments in Europe, while giving less attention to the expansionist policies of Japan in China and Southeast Asia.

The emotional shock of the attack was followed by intense feelings of sadness. The immediate feelings of sadness grew out of the loss of lives at Pearl Harbor and the conditions under which the deaths had occurred. The news media played upon the tragedy by elaborating accounts of experiences in Hawaii, with particular emphasis on the acts of heroism on the part of both the men who had died and those who had lived. Attention was also given to the impact of the casualties upon surviving family members, their communities of origin, and their close friends. The sadness growing out of the loss of lives from the Japanese attack was further intensified by an awareness that World War II would be a long and drawn-out war. Hundreds of thousands of American lives would be lost before it was over.

The sense of shock and feelings of sadness within the American population were also accompanied by intense levels of fear. The world had lost its predictability, and there was uncertainty over the possibilities of additional calamities to follow. Some expected the attack on Pearl Harbor to be followed by an invasion of the American West Coast. Many expected bombing raids on American cities and towns. The fear bordered on mass hysteria as thousands of people from Southern California to Alaska scanned the skies for approaching Japanese aircraft. There were numerous reports of Japanese submarines sighted by people living on the West Coast; many of these submarines were, perhaps, whales. Assumptions about the probability of an invasion or the eventual outcome of the war could not be made with any reasonable degree of certainty. The nation had been militarily and psychologically unprepared for the emergency that was now being confronted.

The anger of Americans was intensified by the perception that the attack was unprovoked and had been launched without warning. There was no formal declaration of war. The Japanese ambassador had received instructions to announce to the State Department that they were breaking diplomatic relations with the United States. However, the Japanese ambassador was unable to get an appointment at the State Department on a Sunday morning. He did not succeed in delivering the message until about an hour after the attack had occurred. His message was received with a cool and hostile response. The entire nation was outraged. An assault on the integrity of the United States as a nation had occurred. Images of the Japanese as devious, cowardly, evil, and unpredictable were elaborated.

To everyone it was apparent that the United States could neither remain isolated from world affairs nor sustain the role of a neutral observer. Isolationism was dead, never to return. The wars in Europe and Asia had become worldwide in scope, and we were involved. Beyond this, it was a time in which it was difficult for the individual to know what he or she should believe. Anything and everything seemed possible. For many Americans, the idea of war conjured up images of chaos and carnage. The attack on Pearl Harbor was seen as a forerunner of the shocks and suffering that were soon to be encountered.

Millions of lives had already been lost in Europe and Asia, and millions more would be lost before the war was over. Many Americans would now be required to join the ranks of the military dead. The trauma was especially great for the families of those going off to war. Husbands would be separated from their families, and the continuity of family life would be broken for an extended period of time. Levels of emotional intensity ran high in families who clearly recognized the dangers and the absurdities of war. Parents would see their sons depart for a war from which they might never return.

Listening to the news with some degree of desperation and helplessness was evident throughout the country. The crisis was intensified by the speed with which the Japanese army invaded and occupied such widely dispersed geographical areas a Manila, Guam, Hong Kong, Shanghai, and Singapore. All of this was accomplished by the end of February 1942. The early tide of the war favored the Japanese, and levels of panic and hysteria mounted. Would there be an invasion and conquest of the continental United States? If so, millions of lives would be lost, and Americans would be required to live in an occupied country.

The generalized anxieties about the war and its eventual outcome soon crystallized into sets of specific concerns, including questions about our lack of preparedness at Pearl Harbor, what to do about the Japanese Americans living on the West Coast, and how to mobilize the resources of the nation for bringing the war to a decisive, expedient, and dramatic end. In addressing these concerns, the United States as a nation would be permanently changed. In response to the lack of preparedness for World War II, the United States would assemble the most awesome military arsenal the world had ever known. In response to the mass hysteria over Japanese Americans living on the West Coast, the civil rights of American citizens would be violated. In developing the atom bomb for ending the war, the world could never again be the same. From the events set in motion by the jolt of Pearl Harbor, the United States was thrust into a position of world leadership, and American lifestyles were permanently altered.

Lack of Preparedness

The trauma of the Japanese attack on Pearl Harbor was intensified by the fact that the United States had been caught unprepared. As a nation we had failed to develop an adequate awareness of the importance of the wars in Europe and Asia for our own national security. The impact of the lack of military preparations had now contributed to a collective sense of vulnerability.

Before the attack on Pearl Harbor, the conflict between Japan and the United States over supremacy in the Pacific had escalated following the Japanese invasion of China and Japan's announcement of plans for increasing its influence in Asia. Peacefully inclined officials in Japan were replaced by those with a military bent, and diplomatic relations deteriorated rapidly as Japan prepared for war. The military presence and political commitments of the United States in the Pacific were seen by the Japanese as major obstacles to the attainment of their national objectives. The United States embargoed the shipment of scrap metal and oil to Japan to slow down their military momentum. The threat of Japan to the security of the United States had been underestimated.

Many of the overriding anxieties of the day were still directed toward the problems of the Great Depression and the extremely high levels of unemployment and economic hardship that the nation recently had encountered. The major problems were defined by some as economic problems, and a great deal of attention was directed toward the contradictions inherent in the market system and the necessary role that the government must play. While there was a great deal of uneasiness about what was happening in Europe, this uneasiness was not linked to planning for the heroic undertaking that was to follow. Apparently humans have a great deal of difficulty in identifying the most appropriate things to worry about. Ambivalence about world events and the lack of public support for the buildup of the machinery of war resulted in inactivity when circumstances called for decisive action.

The lack of preparedness at Pearl Harbor was a single episode in the lack of preparedness for a war that many saw as inevitable but hoped would never occur. Memories of the trench warfare and heavy casualties of World War I were still vivid in the memories of many Americans. Thousands of veterans returned to their communities only to continue suffering from the carnage and futility of trench warfare and from the devastating effects of exposure to chemical warfare. The mental anguish and physical pain engendered by the war had not ended for many American veterans with the formal end to the war itself. Many Americans had seen our involvement in World War I as a senseless undertaking, and many veterans believed the nation was ungrateful for the sacrifices they had made. Some resolved that never again should the United States become involved in "someone else's war." In the presidential campaign of 1940, Franklin D. Roosevelt promised that if he were elected "American boys would not have to fight on foreign soil."

The unbelievable lack of preparedness at Pearl Harbor was partially an outgrowth of the deep-seated isolationism in American thought. Very early, President George Washington in his Farewell Address had advised the nation against becoming involved in foreign wars. Our geographic isolation from Europe had provided us with the opportunity to go it alone and to develop our own national identity with its own distinctive qualities. The general mood of the country had been one of a desire for stability and a wish not to become involved in the rancorous conflicts and wars of Europe. Many Americans shared the view expressed by George Washington. Foreign problems were defined as foreign problems, not as American problems. This view was deeply embedded in American consciousness and reinforced by the widespread disillusionment over the outcomes of World War I.

The lack of military preparedness at the time of Pearl Harbor was thus an outcome of the mood of the country. Neither the American people nor their representatives in Congress had been in favor of the financial costs that would be involved in a military buildup. Given its geographical separation from Europe and Asia, the wars in those parts of the world did not constitute an immediate threat to the national security of the United States. The attack on Pearl Harbor changed all of that. The lack of preparedness was seen by many as the collective responsibility of the entire nation. There were still serious questions to be raised about why our military commanders in Hawaii had been caught so completely off guard by the Japanese attack.

Military officials had known that a crippling attack on our naval forces in the Pacific had been a standard part of Japanese strategic planning for more than a decade. "How would you carry out a surprise attack on Pearl Harbor" had been a standard examination question for the cadets graduating from Japan's naval academy. Signal Corps intelligence had established that top naval officers in Japan were engaged in planning for a major attack on Pearl Harbor and deliberating on the most feasible way of doing it. As the diplomatic relations between the United States and Japan reached the breaking point, every major American commander should have known of the impending danger. Why then was the base at Pearl Harbor characterized by such a relaxed atmosphere? Why were between one-third and one-half of all naval officers on shore leave? Why was there no surveillance of Hawaii's perimeter? Why was such a large part of our Pacific fleet concentrated in a single location? Several investigative commissions and more than forty volumes of documents have failed to come up with rational answers to these questions.

On January 26, 1942, a commission investigating the disaster at Pearl Harbor found both Admiral Husband E. Kimmel, the commander of the U.S. Pacific Fleet, and General Walter C. Short, the commander of the army unit in Hawaii, guilty of a dereliction of duty. Each was guilty of not having done what a prudent military commander should have done under the circumstances. While each commander had advanced military information on an impending Japanese attack, neither believed the attack would occur at Pearl Harbor. After the war several retrospective evaluations pointed to the conclusion that Kimmel and Short had been used as "scapegoats." They may have failed to do what they should have done, but there were many issues of responsibility that remained unresolved. Foremost among them were issues related to why officials in Washington who knew of an impending attack had not relayed this information to the commanders in Hawaii.

Officials in both the State Department and the War Department had been well aware of the possibility of a military assault following the deterioration of diplomatic relations with Japan. Intercepted messages sent to envoys from Tokyo indicated the intent to break off diplomatic relationships, and this was generally understood to mean war. Nevertheless, despite the advanced knowledge of an impending attack, top military and diplomatic officials expressed shock and surprise along with the rest of the nation when the attack did occur. Wishful thinking had generated both an unwarranted optimism and an unbelievable state of unpreparedness.

A major conspiracy theory that surfaced after the war implicated both Franklin D. Roosevelt and Winston Churchill. According to the theory, both knew of Japan's plans, but wanted Japan to strike first in order to arouse public indignation and support for the war. If it was indeed true that Roosevelt knew of Japan's plans and waited for events to unfold as expected, the scheme could not have been any more successful. Americans were outraged by the attack, and opposition to American involvement in World War II vanished immediately. Allegedly, a relaxed but jubilant Churchill called Roosevelt shortly after the attack and then went to bed and slept soundly. America's future was now linked with that of Britain in the pursuit of the war effort. The question of responsibility for unpreparedness quickly receded into the background as anger and hostility mounted toward Japan.

Internment of Japanese Americans

Conditions of trauma tap into the reservoir of emotions that lie beneath the surface in everyday life. Such was clearly the case in public responses to the Japanese attack on Pearl Harbor. Hostility toward Orientals living in the United States and in Hawaii provided the raw material for a great deal of speculation about how and why the event occurred and what was likely to happen next. Hundreds of rumors initially surfaced about the part local Japanese had played in the success of the attack. The attack was obviously well planned and based on accurate information about the position of American military units in Hawaii. How could the Japanese have known so much if local residents had not been involved in treachery and sabotage? Rumors also spread among the Japanese themselves that the American army planned to kill all residents of Japanese ancestry. While these rumors quickly subsided in Hawaii, from the lack of confirming evidence, additional rumors persisted on the mainland and contributed to the incarceration of a large number of American citizens. Constitutional guarantees of due process were suspended and basic civil rights were seriously violated.

For several weeks following the attack on Pearl Harbor, the intense outrage and hostility toward Japan became directed toward the Japanese Americans living on the West Coast. They were here, living as aliens in our midst, and symbolic of what had surfaced as manifestations of evil. General John L. DeWhitt, the commanding general of the Western Defense, was vehement in his view of Japanese Americans as enemies in our midst. He saw them as comprising a vast espionage network that would aid the enemy in any planned invasion of California. The newspapers on the West Coast also drew upon and sensationalized public sentiment against those of Japanese ancestry. Even the distinguished journalist Walter Lippmann defined the Japanese Americans as a menace and urged "mass evacuation and mass internment." The nation wanted revenge.

The deep-seated racial prejudice toward Orientals prior to the war now became ethically embellished and perceived as justified. The combination of extreme racism with anger and fear produced a highly volatile situation. Out of a sense of outrage and anger, banks in California froze the funds of Japanese American depositors and refused to cash their checks. Japanese American professionals and businessmen lost their clients: Doctors lost their patients, businessmen lost their customers, and lawyers lost their right to practice law. Grocery stores refused to sell them food, and business establishments refused to provide basic services. In effect, Americans of Japanese decent were abused and stigmatized with the accusations of disloyalty.

By executive order from President Roosevelt, "military camps" were authorized for the removal of Japanese Americans from the West Coast. The executive order was consistent with the prevailing sentiment of political and military leaders throughout the country. Even the Supreme Court ruled that the rights guaranteed to American citizens by the U.S. Constitution could be suspended under conditions of war or threats to national security. Given the devious attack on Pearl Harbor, an invasion of the West Coast was perceived as a realistic possibility. All precautions should be taken to ensure that any such invasion would not be facilitated by the spies and saboteurs who were living here. Doubts about the loyalty of Japanese Americans and the hysteria of the times resulted in the most serious violation of civil rights in the history of the country.

There were about 110,000 Japanese Americans living on the West Coast at that time, and most of them had been born in the United States. They thought of themselves primarily as Americans, but like other ethnic groups, they had retained their social heritage and aspects of lifestyles associated with their country of origin. Many had become successful as businessmen and farmers and had believed in the American dream. Although many were moving toward the American mainstream and shared the sense of indignation over the attack on Pearl Harbor, sinister characteristics were imputed to all of them. Their Japanese ancestry was taken as evidence of obvious and collective guilt.

General DeWhitt issued a military proclamation setting a curfew for

Japanese Americans and restricting their travel to within a five-mile radius of their homes. Shortly afterward, all Japanese Americans living in California, Oregon, and Washington were ordered to report to assembly points for evacuation. The order included all Americans with any trace of Japanese ancestry, including Japanese women who had married American men and orphan children who had been adopted by American parents. The "trail of tears" had been the only precedent for such an extensive program of mass evacuation: During Andrew Jackson's administration, orders were given to relocate all American Indians living east of the Mississippi River. The forced relocation of Japanese Americans was the first time the U.S. government had "imprisoned" such a large group of people in barbed-wire enclosures on the basis of nothing more than their ethnicity. There were no formal charges against them, there was no trial by jury, and there was no direct evidence of subversive activity.

The Japanese Americans were notified to report to assembly points on a given day for relocation. They had between twenty-four hours and two weeks to report to the assembly point. They were permitted to keep only the personal property they could carry with them. Homes and businesses were sold for whatever price anyone was willing to pay. In some cases, neighbors took advantage of the situation, acted like scavengers, and offered outrageously low prices for homes, cars, household furniture, and other private property. The Japanese Americans salvaged what they could, but enormous economic and personal losses were suffered. A great deal of personal and family archival materials were trashed or burned. The loss of jobs and personal property resulted in a great deal of confusion for the people involved. Social worlds were crumbling, their prior sense of well-being was seriously disturbed, and the future became uncertain.

After being held in temporary camps, in some cases up to six months, the Japanese Americans were loaded in boxcars that would provide transportation to places unknown to them. American citizens were herded by armed guards with fixed bayonets. The relocation movement was, in effect, a form of incarceration. The internment camps were located in desolate areas far removed from the West Coast. The camps, hastily constructed by the Army Corps of Engineers, were like concentration camps. The temporary housing consisted of barracks that were overcrowded, and few of the amenities associated with normal living were available. Entire families were frequently housed in a single room. There was little protection from winter storms and the scorching summer heat. The camps were surrounded by dual barbed-wire fences, and the guard towers were manned with machine guns. American citizens found themselves in the absurd position of being held as prisoners of war within their own country.

As the tide of the war changed, and it was apparent that Americans would eventually win, there was an official recognition that a mistake had been made. The Supreme Court reversed itself in declaring the evacuation and internment of Japanese Americans to be an illegal act. The Japanese Americans were now free to go. But where could they go? They had been deprived of their jobs, their homes, and their previous property. The negative sentiment directed toward them had not diminished. Those released from the internment camps had very little to return to. They now confronted the problem of picking up the pieces and rebuilding a life for themselves in a hostile world.

War Mobilization

The Japanese attack on Pearl Harbor transformed American society into a moral community. News accounts of personal tragedies at Pearl Harbor, accounts of heroism, and accounts of personal sacrifices tapped a responsive chord. The intensity of the national trauma had extinguished any hopes for a better world anytime soon. The attack on Pearl Harbor put an end to this possibility. We were at war and the level of emotionality ran high. The sadness inspired by the casualties at Pearl Harbor was accompanied by high levels of anger and hostility toward Japan. We had been "dastardly attacked" and were now engaged in an epic struggle, not of our own choosing, between the forces of good and evil. The world increased in complexity, but the inevitable plan of action came to be characterized by an unambiguous simplicity. We were the good guys and they were the bad guys, and it was a war that we must win.

In the days and weeks following the attack on Pearl Harbor, patriotic music was given a prominent place in radio programming. The multiple themes of the music were directed toward building up hatred for the enemy and bolstering courage, bravery, national commitment, and self-sacrifice. Popular war heroes were celebrated and commemorated in ballads, linking them with heroic figures from the past. Kate Smith's emotional rendition of "God Bless America" is still remembered by most older Americans, and in the early part of the war, her recording was played repeatedly. Maintaining morale on the home front was recognized as a necessary ingredient for sustaining and intensifying commitment to the war effort. Many people left their radios on throughout the day to listen to the music and to stay informed about any major developing events.

The necessity of producing planes, tanks, ships, submarines, and other instruments of war provided an empirical test of the productive potential of our industrial enterprise. The conversion of the American economy to a war economy, immeasurably assisted by the existence of excess capacity and high unemployment, was achieved rapidly. All forms of industrial production were placed under the authority of the War Production Board. Assembly lines for making automobiles were converted into the production of planes, tanks, and military vehicles. The last civilian car for the duration of the war came off the assembly line early in 1942. Production centers throughout the country were transformed into the production of military technology. By the end of the war, the United States had produced nearly 300,000 aircraft, over 70,000 ships, and nearly 90,000 tanks. The capacity of the American industrial enterprise turned out to be the decisive factor in the eventual outcome of the war. A giant had been created, and it was the American industrial enterprise that was to dominate the world economy for years to come.

Manpower shortages were created in the civilian sector as millions of young, able-bodied men volunteered for or were conscripted into military service. Women found employment in jobs that were formerly limited to men. They vacated the household and became riveters, welders, and forklift operators, demonstrating that women have the capability of performing successfully in what previously had been defined as only masculine occupations. Discrimination in employment on the basis of gender temporarily receded into the background.

The long-term employment problems and economic hardships of the Great Depression were replaced by job opportunities and new forms of abundance. Displaced farm workers migrated to urban centers and found employment in factories at wage levels far above that to which they had been accustomed. Southern black sharecropping plummeted toward its ultimate doom. The labor shortage created new opportunities for many of those who had been seriously disadvantaged during the era of surplus labor and unemployment during the Great Depression. The labor shortages were especially beneficial to underprivileged groups, such as the physically handicapped, young adults, older workers, and blacks. Workers who had been on the margin of the labor force now found themselves located at the center of the war effort. The new opportunities that were made available at the individual level were accompanied by a clear recognition of danger at the national level and by an awareness that sacrifices would have to be made.

The movies, the stage plays, the comics, and other forms of popular entertainment also went to war. Hollywood became geared up to turn out a large number of patriotic movies to inform, to entertain, and to inspire. The movies provided dramatic stories that permitted individuals to personalize historical events and to vicariously participate in them. The movies also focused on major happenings on the home front and frequently used humor to provide comic relief from the tragedies of war. The comics also played their part as such superheroes as Batman, Superman, Captain America, and the Green Hornet lent their support to the war effort through fictionalized accounts of encounters and triumphs over the evil men of Germany and Japan.

In collective memories, World War II came to be described by some as "the last great war." Such a designation was not accompanied by images of the enormous casualties that were sustained. The costs to the families, lovers, and friends of the thousands of Americans who were killed or seriously injured in the war were glossed over. The collective emotions of sadness and anger had produced a nationally unprecedented sense of cohesion. Group differences that had divided the nation disappeared or were suspended as nearly all segments of the population became engrossed in the war effort. The war was looked upon as a great war in the sense of its unifying effects for the country. The reference was to an implied set of criteria for group effectiveness. In contrast to the stalemate in Korea and the unpopular war in Vietnam, the national commitment to winning World War II was clear, definite, and widely accepted. The danger of an external threat had generated a blending of personal goals and national objectives into an inseparable pattern. The war brought out what some saw as the best of human characteristics: a sense of purpose, a commitment to ideals that stood above personal avarice and greed, a sense of belonging, and a sense of national commitment.

Perceptions of the Japanese Warrior

During the war, movies, cartoons, and other forms of war propaganda were designed to incite hatred, anger, and hostility toward Japan. The brutality of the Japanese soldier was prominently emphasized in both news reports and fictionalized accounts. Americans were deeply moved by news accounts of the forced "death march" at Bataan and by other reports of the brutal treatment that prisoners of war received at the hands of the Japanese. Accounts from the Philippines suggested widespread looting and rape of civilians by the Japanese army of occupation. The rules of war and the code of honor that had been associated with wars in Europe seemed to be lacking in the Japanese army. The surprise attack at Pearl Harbor and the subsequent accounts of Japanese atrocities suggested that they were a brutal, fanatical, and formidable foe.

In the early part of the war, General Jonathan Wainright had surrendered the American bastion at Corregidor after food, military equipment, and other supplies were running out. While resistance to the end may have been heroic, it was also looked upon as senseless. Why sacrifice American lives for a battle that could not be won? Continued resistance, at best, could only postpone for a little longer the inevitable fall of the Philippines to the military forces of Japan. From the American standpoint, very little would have been accomplished through continued resistance. Further, international agreements among the nations of the world had called for the humane treatment of prisoners of war.

The Japanese military ideology held otherwise. The Japanese soldiers looked upon prisoners of war as "cowards," "garbage people," and "defective human beings." Any soldier that allowed himself to be captured deserved harsh treatment. The surrender at Corregidor was seen by the Japanese as symbolic of the lack of will among Americans to resist an enemy of superior moral fiber. Their military code placed an obligation on the Japanese soldier to die in battle or to commit suicide rather than to be taken as a prisoner of war.

Images of the fanatical commitment of Japanese soldiers were reinforced in the later part of the war with the surprise and horror associated with the organization of a Kamikaze Corps. This corps was comprised of Japanese pilots who had volunteered for suicide missions that called for diving their planes into American ships and losing their lives in the process. The principle of deliberate self-sacrifice was not new to the Japanese, nor to the ideals of warriors the world over. Extraordinary bravery and self-sacrifice have always provided the raw material for military decorations and awards. Early in the war, a few American pilots had voluntarily dived their planes into Japanese ships, thus sacrificing their lives. But, what was new in the later part of the war was the systematic organization of a suicide corps among Japanese pilots.

In organizing the suicide missions, emphasis was placed upon legendary beliefs in a sacred shield that had protected the islands of Japan. In August 1281, a Chinese armada of 3,500 ships with about 100,000 men aboard was moving toward an invasion of Japan. Because of internal wars and conflicts, Japan was in no position to turn back the assault. The Japanese were expecting defeat, captivity, or death, when divine intervention occurred. The invasion was halted by the emergence of a sacred wind. A violent typhoon sank most of the ships, destroyed the attack, and preserved the integrity of the islands of Japan. The terrified invaders returned to China never again to attempt such an invasion. The national mythology of Japan held that their islands continued to be protected by a sacred shield.

Drawing upon historical precedent, the term "kamikaze" (sacred wind) was employed to provide inspiration for the Japanese pilots. Implementing the suicide missions resulted in the creation of human gods. Once Japanese pilots volunteered for a suicide mission, they were automatically placed in the realm of the sacred, both in terms of self-identities and in the responses by others. There was an aura of extraordinary and awesome proportions that came to surround them. They were elevated above the mundane aspects of everyday life and set apart from ordinary human beings. They came to be admired by the Japanese as "thunder gods" who had no earthly desires.

To the American military, the Kamikaze pilots were not viewed as demons endowed with extraordinary personal qualities but rather as a practical problem that had to be dealt with. American planes had become more efficient and had greater maneuverability than the Japanese Zero. Intense anti-aircraft barrages from American ships limited the effectiveness of the suicide missions. Further, the pilots employed by Japan were not adequately trained because of the shortage of fuel for planes. Had the suicide missions been organized sooner, the defeat of Japan would probably have been more difficult; however, they represented, at best, acts of desperation.

While the damage from the Kamikaze attacks was extensive, the more important message that Americans received pertained to what was likely to happen with the eventual invasion of the islands of Japan. Some estimates held that nearly a million American lives would be lost in the final assault. Memories were vivid of the heavy casualties sustained by American forces in the conquest of Pacific islands held by the Japanese. Any military assault on the Japanese homeland was expected to be met with tenacious and violent resistance from the entire population, including old men, women, and children. Many Americans believed that the soldiers who had survived the war in Europe would be transferred to the Pacific for the final assault on Japan. The number of gold stars in the windows of American homes would greatly increase.

Ending the War

Well before the defeat of Nazi Germany, the eventual outcome of the war with Japan was no longer in doubt. The United States would win. But it was unclear how long would it take and how many American lives would be lost. Propaganda in Japan was preparing the population to resist for as long as 100 years if necessary. Japan had recognized our technological and materialistic superiority, but saw their own moral fiber and the spirit of the Japanese people as the decisive factor in the long run.

To Americans, the concern was with getting the war over with as soon and as expediently as possible. It was expected that the Japanese would continue to fight even when it was obvious they could not win. Such had been the case in the war against Nazi Germany. The defeat of the German army in the Battle of the Bulge made it evident that Germany would lose the war. Yet, the resistance continued even after the Allied forces had crossed the Rhine River and pursued their advance toward Berlin. The Germans continued fighting until the Americans and the British met the Russians at the Elbe River. Given the tenacity of Japan in pursuing the war, there was little reason to believe that their resistance would be any less than that of the Germans in resisting a foreign invasion of their homeland.

Plans were already under way for an invasion of Kyushu, the southern-most of the main islands of Japan, when the Americans succeeded in exploding the world's first atomic bomb at a site near Alamagordo, New Mexico. The United States had been working on the development of an atomic bomb throughout the war. President Roosevelt had been influenced by a letter from Albert Einstein suggesting the feasibility of such a weapon from theoretical work in the field of nuclear physics. Further, there was the possibility that German scientists were working on a similar project. If a nuclear device could be used as a military weapon, it was better for us to do it, thus getting a jump on our adversaries. The development of the bomb was seen as a possibility from the scientific knowledge that had been developed over the first several decades of the twentieth century. The background theoretical work had been completed, and it was simply a matter of time before that knowledge would be put to use. Following Roosevelt's request, Congress appropriated funds for developing the atomic bomb without actually knowing what they were supporting.

The untimely death of President Roosevelt in April 1945 was traumatic to the nation. Roosevelt's charismatic style had provided the nation with a sense of security and confidence in his leadership. There were doubts about whether Harry Truman as the new president had the political experience and the sophistication that was necessary for dealing effectively with the job at hand. The war was winding down in Europe, but the problem of defeating Japan remained a major challenge. Few presidents had entered the office with so many complex issues to resolve within such a short period of time. For example, the secrecy surrounding the development of the bomb had been of such a magnitude that even the vice president of the United States had not been informed about the progress of the Manhattan Project. Truman found himself required to make one of the more controversial decisions any president of the United States ever had to make.

What should or could we do with the atomic bomb now that we had it? Truman's resolution of this issue mirrored the sentiment of the nation in his commitment to end the war as soon, as decisively, and as expediently as possible. In ending the war, nothing less than unconditional surrender would be acceptable. Following up on the suggestion that Japan may be willing to surrender, an ultimatum was issued at the Potsdam Conference. However, at that time there were three important items of information that could not be revealed to Japan for strategic reasons: (1) The United States had developed an atomic bomb; (2) Russia had agreed to enter the war against Japan ninety days after the surrender of Germany; and (3) the United States had already decided to permit the Japanese to keep their emperor. These three items of information may very well have influenced a decision to surrender rather than to continue the war.

The abruptness with which World War II ended is similar to the abruptness with which it started. Both the beginning and the end dramatized the capacities of modern societies for institutionalized violence. Daily activities around the world were disrupted by the news bulletin on August 6, 1945, that the city of Hiroshima had been destroyed by an atomic bomb, a new weapon of historically unprecedented proportions. The city of Hiroshima was demolished and the fatalities far exceeded the number that had been expected. Three days later, a second bomb was dropped on the city of Nagasaki. Approximately 200,000 lives were lost from the aerial assaults using nuclear weapons. The bombing of Hiroshima and Nagasaki had provided Americans with an opportunity both to avenge the attack on Pearl Harbor and to end the war.

Qualitative changes in the human condition occurred with the development of the atomic bomb and a demonstration of its destructive potential through its use on human populations. Slow death from radiation sickness among thousands of civilians at Hiroshima and Nagasaki produced some degree of uneasiness about the possibility that we had solved one problem but had created additional problems of an even greater magnitude. The survivors at Hiroshima and Nagasaki were faced with serious psychological trauma from seeing their social world instantly vaporized by a weapon about which they had no knowledge. In the months and years afterward, survivors watched with anguish as their friends and family members perished from radiation sickness. For some there was also the horror of giving birth to deformed monstrosities or the shame of being marked by stigmatized scars from the nuclear explosion.

The end of the war was met with jubilant responses in the United States. The victory celebrations were extensive and enthusiastic. Many single women looked favorably upon the prospect of forming intimate relationships with males of their own age level. They had grown tired of having their social interactions limited primarily to other women, the elderly, and children. The veterans were welcomed home as heroes, and ticker-tape parades were held in their honor. The gruesomeness of the war was muted through erecting monuments to commemorate their heroic deeds. The nation was grateful and a great deal of attention was given to the successful reentry of veterans into civilian life.

After most wars, veterans were forgotten once they were no longer needed. But the end of World War II was different from other wars. The veterans provided a great deal of social support for each other and received a great deal of support from others within their communities. The nation was grateful, and the benefits accorded to the veterans were extensive. Employers were required to give back to the returning veterans the jobs they had before going off to war. Women who had worked during the war were expected to give up their jobs, go home, get married, and have babies. Educational benefits were made available through the G.I. Bill of Rights. The government paid the tuition costs of attending a college or a university, paid for the books and supplies, and provided the veterans with a generous living allowance. The impact was sufficiently great that it led to a rapid expansion of colleges and universities throughout the country. Under the Veterans Administration, housing was made available to the returning veterans through guaranteed government loans and at a relatively low rate of interest. Thus, in contrast to other wars, the nation was willing to show its gratitude to the returning veterans.

The social psychology of "the homecoming" had some interesting features to it for the veterans returning from the South Pacific. For example, the marine unit that was involved at the battle of Iwo Jima had been stationed in the Pacific for more than three years. During this time, the unit saw only about six weeks of combat. The battle for Iwo Jima was intense and the casualties were high, but we were victorious. It was to become one of the more highly commemorated victories of the war. In contrast to the veterans in the assault across Germany, however, many of the veterans in the Pacific had a great deal of time on their hands, during which they fantasized about what life was like in their home towns and how glorious things would be when they returned. The longer they were away, "the greener the grass grew" in their home towns. They glorified family life, getting married if they were single, owning their own home on their own lot, and having a lot of children.

They had assumed that nothing would change while they were gone. This turned out not to be the case. They had changed, their home towns had changed, and the people they knew had changed. They returned to a world that was less familiar than they had imagined. The problems were especially intense for the men who were married prior to going into the service. Some wives felt that the long years of separation had not been a part of their marriage contract. Fathers who had left when their children were very young or had not yet been born returned to children who did not know them. Their families had become independent and had managed to get along without them while they were gone. The veterans themselves had changed in personalities and preferences as a result of the war experience. The initial separation in going to war had been painful, and the readjustments after the war were often difficult. It is perhaps for these reasons that the divorce rate was disproportionately high for the veterans returning from the war. The costs of the war went far beyond the immediate cost of participating in the war itself. The personal lives of individuals had been turned upside down by one of the major national traumas of the twentieth century.

Bibliography

Adams, Michael C. 1985. *The Best War Ever: Americans in World War II*. Baltimore: Johns Hopkins University Press.

Benedict, Ruth. 1989. *The Chrysanthemum and the Sword: Patterns of Japanese Culture*. Boston: Houghton Mifflin.

Bundy, McGeorge. 1988. *Danger and Survival: Choices about the Bomb in the First Fifty Years*. New York: Vintage Books.

Daniels, Roger. 1975. *The Decision to Relocate the Japanese-Americans*. Philadelphia: J.B. Lippincott.

Grodzins, Morton. 1949. *Americans Betrayed: Politics and the Japanese Evacuation*. Chicago: University of Chicago Press.

Hoehling, A.A. 1963. *The Week Before Pearl Harbor*. New York: W.W. Norton.

Hoopes, Roy. 1977. *Americans Remember the Home Front*. New York: Hawthorn Books.

Kennett, Lee. 1985. *For the Duration: The United States Goes to War*. New York: Charles Scribner.

Kimmel, Husband E. 1955. *Admiral Kimmel's Story*. Chicago: Henry Regnery.

Lord, Walter. 1957. *Day of Infamy*. New York: Holt, Rinehart, and Winston.

McWilliams, Carey. 1944. *Prejudice, Japanese-Americans: Symbols of Racial Intolerance*. New York: Little, Brown.

Millis, Walter. 1947. *This is Pearl!* New York: William Morrow.

Millot, Bernard. 1970. *Divine Thunder*. New York: Pinnacle Books.

Morganstern, George. 1947. *Pearl Harbor*. New York: Devin-Adair.

Mosse, George L. 1990. *Fallen Soldiers: Reshaping the Memory of the World Wars*. New York: Oxford University Press.

Naito, Hatsuho. 1989. *Thunder Gods: The Kamikaze Pilots Tell Their Story*. New York: Dell.

Nam, Charles B. 1964. "Impact of the 'G.I. Bill' on the Educational Level of the Male Population." *Social Forces* 43: 26–32.

Neuman, William L. 1963. *America Encounters Japan: From Perry to MacArthur*. New York: Harper Colophon.

Prange, Gordon W. 1982. *At Dawn We Slept: The Untold Story of Pearl Harbor*. New York: Penguin Books.

Rhodes, Richard. 1986. *The Making of the Atomic Bomb*. New York: Simon and Schuster.

Rushbridger, James, and Eric Nave. 1992. *Betrayal at Pearl Harbor: How Churchill Lured Roosevelt into World War II*. New York: Touchstone Books.

Selden, Kyoto, and Mark Selden, eds. 1989. *The Atomic Bomb: Voices from Hiroshima and Nagasaki*. Armonk, NY: M.E. Sharpe.

Shibutani, Tamotsu. 1966. *Improvised News: A Sociological Study of Rumor.* Indianapolis: Bobbs-Merrill.

Smith, Bradford. 1948. *Americans from Japan.* Philadelphia: J.B. Lippincott.

Smith, C. Calvin. 1986. *War and Wartime Changes.* Fayetteville: University of Arkansas Press.

Tateishi, John. 1984. *And Justice for All: An Oral History of the Japanese-American Detention Camps.* New York: Random House.

Terkel, Studs. 1984. *"The Good War": An Oral History of Word War Two.* New York: Ballantine Books.

Theobald, Robert A. 1954. *The Final Secret of Pearl Harbor: The Washington Contribution to the Japanese Attack.* New York: Devin-Adair.

Thomas, Gordon, and Max Morgan Witts. 1978. *Enola Gay.* New York: Pocket Books.

Toland, John. 1982. *Infamy: Pearl Harbor and Its Aftermath.* New York: Doubleday.

Vatter, Harold G. 1985. *The U.S. Economy in World War II.* New York: Columbia University Press.

Waller, George M. 1976. *Pearl Harbor: Roosevelt and the Coming of the War.* Lexington, MA: D.C. Heath.

Ward, Stephen R., ed. 1975. *The War Generation: Veterans of the First World War.* Port Washington, NY: Kennikat Press.

Wilson, John P. 1989. *Trauma, Transformation, and Healing.* New York: Brunner/Mazel.

Wohlstetter, Roberta. 1962. *Pearl Harbor: Warning and Decision.* Palo Alto, CA: Stanford University Press.

5 • The Communist Menace

Following the defeat of Germany and Japan, international tensions were of a sufficient magnitude that many Americans did not believe that World War II had really ended. A war with the Soviet Union was believed to be inevitable. For example, General George Patton at the end of the war with Germany observed that we might as well proceed to take on the Russians. In his view, we would have to do this sooner or later, so why not just get it over with. Patton's view on the inevitability of war with the Soviet Union was shared by many Americans. A military defeat of the Soviet Union was seen as necessary for producing a peaceful world.

Most Americans had been emotionally drained by the trauma of World War II and were oriented toward returning to the normality of business as usual. Those occupying positions of political leadership could not, however. Much of the world was in shambles. The ruins and rubble of war were evident in bombed-out cities, depleted economic resources, and in serious shortages of food, medical supplies, and other necessities for sustaining large populations. It was a monumental task to build a new world order. The conditions under which men and women live had permanently changed, and the world could never again be the same. Hopes for a better world collided with painful memories of the recent past and fears and uncertainties about the future.

World War II had an indelible impact on American perceptions of the postwar world. The United States had been thrust into a position of world leadership, and it was apparent that we could no longer be guided by the isolationist sentiment that prevailed prior to the war. The world had become more interdependent. The happenings in remote places were now seen by Americans as having a direct bearing on our own national security. The calamities of World War II provided the background for conceptualizing and defining the new world order. The generation that directly encountered

World War II was the generation that would shape national policies and priorities for many years to come. Historical precedent was drawn upon in setting national priorities and in allocating national resources.

Memories of World War II

Memories of the surprise attack on Pearl Harbor and our lack of preparedness for the war became deeply embedded in American consciousness. "Remember Pearl Harbor" was a major slogan for mobilizing national resources during World War II. The slogan, however, took on a modified form as it subsequently became embedded in collective memories. Remembering the surprise attack on Pearl Harbor and our lack of military preparedness for World War II served to shape national priorities for the next fifty years. Americans came out of World War II preoccupied with national security and a resolve to never again be caught unprepared militarily.

The dangerous possibilities of the postwar world were seen as resembling the world of the 1930s. Historical analogies with the events and conditions leading up to World War II were drawn upon for clarifying what must be done in the new world order. Particularly important in these analogies were perceptions of the similarities between the Soviet Union and Nazi Germany. The specific enemy had changed, but the political conditions of the world were seen as bearing a striking resemblance. We were determined to avoid the historical mistakes that were believed to have caused World War II.

The totalitarianism of the Soviet Union was seen as resembling the totalitarianism of Nazi Germany, the ruthlessness of Joseph Stalin was seen as resembling the ruthlessness of Adolph Hitler, the purges in the Soviet Union were seen as resembling the holocaust of Nazi Germany, and the domination of the countries of Eastern Europe was seen as resembling the Nazi conquest of surrounding countries. In effect, the dangers of extremism on the left were seen as resembling the dangers of extremism on the right. Each constituted a threat to the integrity of the democracies of the world. Accordingly, the late 1930s and early 1940s were remembered as times in which we had failed to anticipate and prepare for the role we would be required to play in world affairs. We had failed to make advance preparations for the heroic undertakings of World War II. We were determined that it would not happen again.

The perceived evil of Joseph Stalin and other communist leaders was of sufficient magnitude to preclude any form of compromise or quest for diplomatic solutions to the problems of the cold war. The Munich episode was deeply embedded in collective memories. At the Munich Conference in 1938, Neville Chamberlain, the prime minister of England, had followed a policy of appeasement in an attempt to placate Nazi Germany and hopefully to offset another major war in Europe. The appeasement strategy failed to work, and Chamberlain became disgraced as a result.

In dealing with the Soviets, American presidents from Harry Truman through Ronald Reagan responded to the Munich analogy by conveying an image of "being tough on communism" and rejecting any notion of "appeasement" or "compromise." Being "soft on communism" was an image to be avoided at all cost. Only the image of forceful resistance was seen as being politically tenable. To stop the spread of communism, nothing short of superior military force and the threat of retaliatory annihilation were seen as viable options.

The absence of reasonable options for diplomacy and negotiation left us with only the use of force or the threatened use of force for dealing with international conflicts and tensions. Only the development of military technology superior to that of the Soviet Union would save us in a hostile world. The stockpiling of nuclear weapons was seen as imperative for maintaining our military superiority. Yet we recognized that our monopoly control over nuclear weapons would not last for very long. By having knowledge that such weapons were possible, other countries would be able to mobilize their resources for producing atomic bombs.

Our monopoly control over the atomic bomb lasted for only four years. In September 1949, samples of unusually high levels of radiation taken by a long-range reconnaissance plane provided overwhelming evidence that the Soviets had exploded a nuclear device similar in magnitude to the one that had been exploded at Alamagordo, New Mexico. The Soviets had developed the bomb much sooner than anyone had expected. As a result, any remaining doubts about the technological capabilities of the Soviet Union vanished instantly. The world had become more dangerous, and it no longer seemed self-evident that we would be able to win a future war with the Soviet Union. Suspicions emerged that the Soviets could not have developed the bomb so quickly without receiving secret information from scientists working on the Manhattan Project.

Intolerance for a long and complex struggle was manifested in the claim that we should initiate a preemptive strike against the Soviet Union. The speed with which the Soviets had developed the atomic bomb suggested that our military superiority may be of short duration. Remembering the success of the Japanese attack on Pearl Harbor, the advantage of early initiatives in the conduct of war appeared to be evident. Rather than just reacting to what the Russians were doing on the world scene, a carefully planned nuclear strike could have a crippling effect on the Soviet Union that would solve the communist problem once and for all.

Containment of Communism

All advances that were made under the banner of communism any place in the world were assumed to reflect the unfolding of a master plan that had originated in the Soviet Union. Extraordinary forms of cunning, deceit, and political sophistication were being attributed to the inner circle of the Communist Party in Moscow. Such attributions provided a ready-made framework for simplifying the many faces of evil in world politics. The fall of the nationalist government in China to the communist forces was seen as promoted by the Soviet Union, as was the expanding memberships in the communist parties of Italy and France, and the seizure of power by the Communist Party in Czechoslovakia. The cold war was becoming an extraordinary confrontation with a unified form of evil. Stopping the spread of communism was taking the form of a moral crusade.

A series of international events within a relatively short period of time added to the perceived realism of the threat of communism: Evidence was obtained that the Soviet Union was now engaged in a crash program to develop its military capabilities. The overthrow of the nationalist government in China substantially increased the land area of the world now under communist control. Further, the French were having difficulty in their efforts to suppress communist insurgency in Vietnam. Applying a "worst case" scenario, Americans saw the common thread of all these events as pointing toward a master plan that had originated in Moscow.

In June 1950, the communist forces of North Korea launched a broad-scale attack against the Republic of South Korea. The North Korean army was well trained and had been armed with weapons from the Soviet Union. The objective was clearly that of seeking a unification of Korea as a communist state. Because Americans saw the invasion as a part of a master plan to spread communism, they responded with anger and indignation. The efforts of the United States resulted in a condemnation of the invasion by the United Nations and an endorsement of military intervention to preserve the integrity of the Republic of Korea. American troops assigned to the occupation of Japan were reassigned to Korea. They lacked training and preparation for their combat assignment and sustained heavy losses in setting up a defense perimeter just north of the city of Pusan at the southern tip of the Korean peninsula.

Following a successful landing of American troops at Inchon and the subsequent buildup of military forces under the command of the United Nations, the North Korean army was driven back across the thirty-eighth parallel, the dividing line between North and South Korea. The tide of the war had shifted, and the American army continued its advance through

North Korea. The policy of containing the spread of communism had been altered by the field commanders in Korea. Our objective was changed to one of unifying Korea under a noncommunist government. The resistance of the North Korean army was minimal as American forces aimed for control of Korea all the way to the Yalu River. What was expected to be an easy victory was soon to become a military disaster. More than 100,000 Chinese troops crossed the Manchurian border into Korea, transforming the war into a large-scale military encounter.

The conduct of the war resulted in a major controversy between the field commanders in Korea and the official policies of our government in Washington. General Douglas MacArthur wanted to conduct bombing raids in Manchuria to cut off the enemy supply lines into Korea. President Truman was concerned with a containment of the war and with avoiding American involvement in a land-based war in China. By limiting the war, a stalemate developed, and an easy victory for either the Chinese army or the American army was no longer a realistic possibility. The heavy losses in the fighting for the hills along the battle lines of Korea came to resemble the absurdity of the trench warfare of World War I. Neither side could make a major advance against the other without sustaining unacceptable losses.

The continuation of a war that we could not reasonably expect to win resulted in low levels of morale for American army personnel. The night patrols, the assaults on enemy-held hills, and the heavy artillery bombardments resulted in heavy casualties for both sides. Throughout the war, a concern for the possible use of nuclear weapons was paramount. Several military commanders had recommended the use of nuclear weapons to break the stalemate. Earlier in the war, General MacArthur's staff had worked to identify suitable targets in North Korea and in China for the use of nuclear weapons. Even Truman had refused to rule out the possibility of using nuclear weapons in Korea. Our allies in Europe were especially concerned that the conduct of the war in Korea could lead the Soviet Union into an active military involvement and thus precipitate World War III. Neither the Soviet Union nor the United States would endure a crushing military defeat in a conventional war; they would be forced to use nuclear weapons.

One of the more dramatic episodes of the war was when President Truman fired General MacArthur. A crisis of authority resulted from General MacArthur's refusal to adhere to policies originating from Washington on the conduct of the war. MacArthur believed that as field commander he should be permitted to do whatever was necessary to win a clear victory in the war. He publicly pronounced that bombing raids should be conducted on the other side of the Korean border and that we should make use of Chinese nationalists both as combat soldiers in Korea and for a subsequent military overthrow of the communist government in China. Such views were incompatible with the policy of limiting the war to Korea and minimizing the risk of an all out war with the People's Republic of China or with the Soviet Union. Sober minds at the center of power in Washington did not regard the Korean War as providing the proper time or place for the final showdown with the communist nations of the world.

Following a negotiated settlement of the war, Americans were shocked by the news that there were American POWs who chose to go to China, rather than be repatriated to the United States. The war had been prolonged because of the difficulties in resolving the POW issue. More than 100,000 Chinese soldiers had surrendered during the war as a means of getting out of communist China. The Republic of China wanted them all back, while the United Nations negotiators insisted that repatriation should be a voluntary choice on the part of the individual soldier.

The news that several American soldiers selected the option of living in China alarmed the nation. Why did this happen? How did this happen? In public discourse the term "brainwashing" was frequently used. The alarm, in part, grew out of the belief that the Chinese had developed new techniques of "thought control." "Brainwashing" suggested that American values could be swept aside and replaced by a communist ideology. The hysteria of the times pointed toward the insidious character of communist attempts to manipulate and control thought processes. The conduct of American soldiers who were prisoners of war was subject to debate for many years to come.

The tensions generated by the Korean War provided the immediate background for broadening collective definitions of the communist menace. Our capacity to contain the international spread of communism was seen as limited by the insidious influences of the communists hidden in our own society. Communism came to be perceived as both an external threat and an internal menace. Just at the POWs had been brainwashed as captives in Korea, American citizens in their everyday lives were considered susceptible to communist ideologies. The fear of communism that was deeply embedded in American history transformed into mass hysteria. While there was little we could do to prevent Soviet initiatives on the world scene, there was something we could do about the hidden enemies in our midst.

Hidden Enemies in Our Midst

Fear of hidden communists had its roots in responses to the nineteenth-century efforts of American workers to unionize. Some of the early labor unions drew upon a revolutionary rhetoric, calling for the development of union solidarity, a revolutionary overthrow of the capitalist system, and a control of the factory system by industrial workers. Most members of labor unions found the revolutionary rhetoric to be unacceptable. Their primary interest was in getting a fair share of the rewards that modern industry had to offer. The labor unions that gained the largest following were those seeking such practical benefits as a shorter work week, better working conditions, and higher wages. All labor unions, however, were seen by many business leaders and government officials as being engaged in an attack on the social system. Unions were widely publicized as being under the control of "communists," "bolsheviks," "anarchists," "reds," or other foreign elements that were engaged in activities designed to overthrow the free enterprise system.

The communist revolution in Russia reinforced these underlying fears. While the communists were not the primary agency in the overthrow of the czarist government, they were successful in gaining control of the government once a revolution had occurred. Through developing a small cadre of dedicated revolutionists, they were in a position to take advantage of the confusion of the situation and thus gain control. In the United States, the response was one of dismay over what had happened in Russia. Communism was no longer an abstract set of ideological principles; it had become a central ingredient in practical politics. Many believed that something similar to what had happened in Russia could also happen here. Through infiltrating labor unions, it was believed that skilled revolutionists could create a unified labor movement and, through a general strike, gain control of the social system. Private property would then be replaced by collective ownership and control.

Responding to the Red Scare of the 1920s, Attorney General A. Mitchell Palmer ordered simultaneous raids on scores of cities across the nation. More than 6,000 suspected communists were arrested, frequently manhandled, and thrown in jail. Those arrested were denied legal counsel and held for days or weeks without any explicit charges against them. Newspapers gave extensive coverage to reports from Mr. Palmer's office on the gigantic plot against the safety of the country. While no evidence was found of plans for an insurrection, the hysteria of the times mounted. Under the wartime Sedition Act, several hundred alien residents were deported. Most were guilty of nothing more than holding radical views on political issues.

Memories of the economic hardships of the Great Depression added to the uneasiness of many Americans about the communist threat. Political and economic discontent were seen as providing the raw materials for an ascendancy of communism both within the United States and the rest of the world. Millions of otherwise reasonable citizens believed that a communist revolution in the United States could occur at any time. Several prominent Americans expressed admiration for the strong and effective leadership of Adolph Hitler in dealing with the communist menace. Germany had initiated a policy of "exterminating" communists before their attention had been directed toward "the Jewish question." Killing the communists was one way of dealing with them.

While anticommunist sentiment in the United States became muffled during World War II, with the Soviet Union as our ally in the war against Nazi Germany, perceptions of the communist menace resurfaced as soon as the war was over. In response to the communist menace, the House Un-American Activities Committee was set up in 1945 as a permanent congressional committee to investigate subversion in American life. Special attention was given to the alleged influence of communists in labor unions, the entertainment industry, churches, and universities. Several prominent Americans were called before the committee and questioned extensively about their political attitudes or any connection they may have had with a radical cause. The hearings frequently resembled an inquisition, and guilt was frequently assumed at the outset. Witnesses found themselves harassed by the committee without the protection of due process that would have been available in a court of law. Unwarranted allegations replaced solid evidence, and several people were sent to prison on charges of perjury or for refusing to answer the outrageous questions in the committee's interrogation. The rights of individuals to have political convictions without being required to reveal them to their government was violated.

Individuals who were investigated by the committee became stigmatized, lost their jobs, and had their names placed on a blacklist. Those who lost their jobs encountered closed doors when they sought employment elsewhere. Several hundred names were included on the blacklist on the basis of nothing more than the charge of having a friend or an acquaintance that was a "leftist" on the political spectrum. Communist leanings had been imputed to those who had publicly expressed pro-working-class sentiments during the 1930s, had participated in peace demonstrations, or had supported whatever was defined as a radical cause.

Prominent men and women in the television and movie industries were denied future employment. Employers ran the risk of "guilt by association" if they hired any of the alleged subversives on the blacklist. Further, those on the blacklist were placed under surveillance by the Federal Bureau of Investigation. Their activities were monitored, notes were taken on who they interacted with, and their garbage was examined for any mail thrown out. Divorces, suicides, illnesses, and heart attacks were prominent among those who had been stigmatized by the charges leveled against them. A sense of despair resulted from harassment, having their jobs lost, and having their reputations ruined.

The nation was appalled in 1948 at the testimony of Whittaker Chambers and Elizabeth Bentley before the House Un-American Activities Committee. Both Chambers and Bentley had defected from the American Communist Party and, in their testimony before the committee, alleged that communists were employed within the American government and that these communists were engaged in espionage for the Soviet Union. The notion that there was "a spy ring" that included top government officials generated alarm and anger among those who saw the world as engaged in a dramatic struggle between the forces of good and evil. The perceived failures of American foreign policy took on new forms of meaning and justification.

The McCarran Internal Security Act of 1950 called for the mandatory registration of "communist-front" organizations and for the construction of concentration camps. The camps were authorized for the purpose of interning all suspected subversives if the president or the Congress were to declare a national emergency. The legislation also specified that those suspected of disloyalty could be held in detention without trial by jury or a formal hearing. Six camps were established in 1952 and maintained until the early 1960s. The Bureau of Prisons renovated old POW camps and the detention camps that had been used for the internment of Japanese Americans during World War II.

Congressional and state legislative committees regularly published lists of suspected communist-front organizations. These included groups that advocated world disarmament, peace, more effective labor unions, or greater racial and economic equality. The turbulence of the times seemed to call for "100 percent Americanism," and this meant avoiding any form of criticism of the status quo. The climate of opinion did not favor the emergence of groups with a focus on the troubles or the problems of the social system. The claim that social life is something less than it can or ought to be was seen as unpatriotic and potentially subversive.

The notion that some American citizens had formed a personal allegiance with the Soviet Union to promote international communism developed into mass hysteria. The international situation seemed so complex that many individuals became unclear about what they should believe. The jolt of their experiences with World War II had generated a predisposition to believe that anything, or everything, was a realistic possibility. Political demagogues and opportunists seized upon the opportunity to promote their own careers through making outrageous claims about the treachery and subversion in American life. Simplistic explanations were offered to provide coherence to world affairs.

Confusion and uncertainty over the scope of clandestine operations on behalf of world communism became prominent in American concerns. Some believed that the concessions President Franklin D. Roosevelt had made to Joseph Stalin at the Yalta Conference had been prompted by communist sympathizers in the State Department. Others maintained that the hidden communists in the State Department had either permitted or promoted the fall of China to communism. The dividing line between secrecy and conspiracy grew thin in perceptions of the planning phase of government operations. It was widely believed that a large number of Americans were engaged in subversive activities to promote the cause of communism. Perceptions of the Soviet threat were now broadened to include the traitors in our midst who were committed to undermining the American way of life.

The complacency of Americans about their security in peacetime was shattered. The tensions of the cold war mounted with the fear that secret information about nuclear weapons, NATO defenses, and the codes used in our military operations were being passed on to the Soviets. The expanded scope of our own intelligence operations in other countries added credibility to the belief that clandestine operations had become widespread on a worldwide basis. The claim that American traitors were transmitting valuable, high-level, secret information to the KGB was generally accepted as valid, or at least as plausible. The climate of the times was favorable to the notion that treason was a growing industry, and there was no shortage of traitors who were willing to benefit from it.

As the level of hysteria mounted, both those involved in shaping public policy and those government employees who had access to classified information were potentially subjected to the charge of disloyalty. The rhetoric of the day included allegations against individuals as being "soft on communism," being "sympathetic to the communist cause," or affiliating with "known communists." The failure to take a strong anticommunist stand was seen as evidence of having communist leanings. The fear of communism in public attitudes provided new opportunities for ambitious politicians. The career of Richard Nixon, and several others, was advanced by promoting a personal image of being tough on communism while casting doubts about the loyalty and patriotism of the political opposition.

McCarthyism

The term "McCarthyism" entered the American vocabulary to describe the fanatical beliefs about the pervasiveness of disloyalty among Americans. Senator Joseph McCarthy delivered a speech in Wheeling, West Virginia, in February 1950 in which he claimed that communists had infiltrated each of our major institutions and were working to undermine the American way of life. McCarthy asserted that a communist blueprint was being carried out for infiltrating and infecting our schools, churches, labor unions, the news media, the arts, mass entertainment, voluntary associations, and virtually all agencies of government. McCarthy claimed that he had a list of known communists in the State Department, and that these hidden communists were responsible for failures in American foreign policy. The fears, anxieties, and frustrations of the cold war were being given free reign in the political arena.

Whether or not McCarthy actually believed what he was saying is a debatable issue. It is clear that he never actually had a list of "known communists" as he had claimed. The list was a form of histrionics and pure fabrication. The verdict of history is that he was a little man with big political ambitions. He drew upon collective fears and anxieties for building a political constituency as no other man had done in the history of the nation. His appeal, in part, grew out of his image as a lone individual who was taking on the big institutions, such as the State Department and the army, and was having a major impact on them. Admiration for him may very well have provided compensation for the political alienation of Americans who felt helpless and overwhelmed by the complexity of the issues the nation confronted.

Few Americans had doubts about the seriousness of the communist menace. Memories were still vivid of how we had neglected to take seriously the threats of Nazi Germany and the Empire of Japan. The type of conspiracy theory that had previously been applied to Japanese Americans during World War II was now being applied to ordinary citizens. The targets of suspicion and distrust included the foreign born, civil rights advocates, peace groups, and participants in many other types of social movements. All were subjected to critical scrutiny. By a strange system of logic, all those who held views that were to the left of the political center were being lumped into the communist category. The war-like atmosphere of the day called for the creation of "a moral community," and nothing less than full compliance with the national goal of stopping communism was regarded as socially acceptable. The residual patriotism held over from World War II was being directed toward the perceived threat of communism.

The public pronouncements of J. Edgar Hoover, as director of the FBI, added credibility to McCarthy's claims. According to Hoover, the close monitoring of communist activities since the 1920s had indicated increased sophistication in the use of mass agitation, subversion, and infiltration techniques. Both Hoover and McCarthy claimed that hidden communists were to be found lecturing in our universities, preaching from America's pulpits, among those writing scripts and acting in television and movie productions, and among candidates for political office. The difficulty in identifying a communist was reflected in Hoover's comment: "Most communists are ordinary-looking people, like your seat mate on the bus or a clerk in one of your neighborhood stores."

McCarthyism as a political ideology resembled the witchcraft theories of an earlier time. In witchcraft theory, it was assumed that there was a cohesive, well-organized, and zealously committed group of individuals who had entered into a conspiracy with the Devil. A demonic order was seen as co-existing alongside the legitimate and normative order of everyday life. Beliefs about the sources of evil had changed, but the system of logic was remarkably similar. Speaking in defense of a person accused of being a communist was considered evidence of disloyalty to the United States. Thus, those who recognized McCarthy as a demagogue were hesitant to speak out against him or to defend those who were outrageously charged with having communist leanings.

Before McCarthyism ran its course, charges were made against each of our major institutions. McCarthy and his supporters claimed that an epic struggle was under way for control over the minds and souls of the masses. Public schools and universities were seen as in a position to politically indoctrinate students with the communist way of thinking. McCarthy's claims were sufficiently credible that universities throughout the country required professors to sign loyalty oaths as a condition of employment. FBI agents routinely checked libraries to identify those professors and graduate students who had checked out books written by Karl Marx or by other known communists. Professors who had joined left-wing organizations during their youth, or who had friends that were known communists, were suspected of disloyalty and dismissed from their jobs. Textbooks and library books by American authors, both past and present, were scanned for themes that were seen as sympathetic to the communist cause.

Conformity became the rule of the day. College professors altered their lecture notes to remove any suggestion of controversial ideas. State legislatures enacted laws prohibiting controversial speakers from being allowed on college campuses. Banning controversial speakers from campus was based on the view that students were highly receptive and gullible when exposed to subversive ideas. Only a purification of the system could assure that "American values" would be transmitted and the "American way of life" would be preserved. The ideals of academic freedom and open inquiry in a democratic society were put on hold.

Many people in the entertainment industry and in the news media found their careers in ruins on the basis of nothing more than the charge that they had communist leanings, that they had associated with someone in the past who was a known communist, or that they could actually be a communist or a communist dupe without even knowing it. While McCarthy's outrageous claims did not result in a single conviction of subversion or espionage, he did win a sizable constituency of admirers by drawing upon latent sentiments and collective fears. Perhaps no other political figure in American life had been more successful as a demagogue in drawing upon the darker side of the national consciousness. Before McCarthy was censured by the U.S. Senate for his unethical conduct, hundreds of individuals lost their jobs and found their careers in ruins.

Only those public officials who supported McCarthy or were militant in their public pronouncements about communism, were regarded as patriotic and loyal Americans. For example, the John Birch Society questioned the loyalty of President Dwight Eisenhower. It was noted that the Soviet's highest military honor had been bestowed upon him, that he had failed to support Senator McCarthy's campaign against hidden communists, and that he had opposed increasing federal expenditures for defense. Past public service was not regarded as sufficient evidence of present intentions and commitments. Even General George C. Marshall, the chief architect of our military victories in World War II, was accused of being "a dedicated, conscious agent of the communist conspiracy." As secretary of state, Marshall was seen as a central figure in "the communist-directed Truman administration."

Following the censure of McCarthy, the FBI continued to maintain extensive secret files on private citizens. The justification for the files was that it was necessary to identify and monitor the activities of those individuals who constituted a security risk to the defense and integrity of the United States. However, the files created through the covert activities of the FBI went far beyond any concern for national security issues. They contained highly private information that could be drawn upon for discrediting or embarrassing individuals when it was politically expedient to do so. Hundreds of individuals were denied government employment on the basis of unconfirmed information that had been assembled in the files.

Some alleged that the decisions of the Supreme Court were guided by communist influences. Such was particularly the case when the decisions of the court upheld the Bill of Rights. The Supreme Court's decision on school desegregation received special attention. In linking the decision with communism, it was alleged that the court had been guided by "the works of Karl Marx," and that the case had been instigated by communist agitators, rather than "by the Negroes themselves." Some extremists alleged that all civil rights activity represented the unfolding of a communist plot.

McCarthyism had a sufficient impact on American consciousness that it did not dissipate with his demise. Following his death, McCarthy became a martyr for radical-right groups that sought to continue his legacy. The primary danger to the United States, they argued, was not the Russians nor the Chinese communists, but the evil men and women in our own country who were working to promote the ascendance of communism. The agenda of the radical right called for the removal of the United States from the United Nations and the buildup of strong military forces to defend our borders. Domestic policies called for exposing or eliminating the hidden enemies in our midst, rescinding the "communist" legislation of the New Deal, and purifying the American way of life. The purification was to consist of a blending of religious and political fundamentalism with an emphasis upon rugged individualism and the free enterprise system. While such extremism failed to achieve center stage, it did add to the uneasiness of the times and selectively reflected the tensions of the cold war and the fear of communism.

The preoccupation with the communist menace during the 1950s deeply scarred the moral and ethical foundations of American society. The traditional commitments of Americans to maintaining an open and democratic society were compromised. The basic rights of individuals to criticize their government collided with charges of disloyalty, and the demand for conformity had corrosive effects on the integrity and vitality of the system. The self-righteousness of those promoting the anticommunist campaigns had more damaging effects on the American system than any espionage or subversion that may have occurred. The McCarthy episode serves as a grim reminder of the political opportunities that are available to a demagogue within a democratic society.

The threat of communism had become intolerable to Americans. By the early 1950s the tide of international events was perceived by many Americans as favoring the Soviets. While the United States had developed into an industrial giant, intense feelings of national insecurity persisted. The collective emotions of anger, fear, and uncertainty that had generated a sense of moral community in resisting the threat of Germany and Japan had been extended to the cold war with the Soviet Union. We continued to be involved in an epic struggle between the forces of good and evil. The quest for moral purification within the country was accompanied by preoccupation with protecting our borders and effectively resisting the spread of communism to any other place in the world.

The primary trauma of the communist menace, however, grew out of what Americans did to themselves. The "nightmare in Red" reflected the suspicions and distrust that were directed toward American citizens who had been defined as traitors and subversives. Government actions, at both the national and state levels, were described by Truman as "getting the government into the business of thought control." The harassment of individuals on the basis of unwarranted allegations violated the basic rules of our justice system. Hundreds of individuals found themselves stigmatized in their communities, avoided by former friends, and unable to continue their careers. While the hysteria over the hidden enemies in our midst had subsided by the early 1960s, the nation was on the verge of encountering the terrifying implications of the Cuban Missile Crisis.

Bibliography

Adler, Les K. 1991. *The Red Image: American Attitudes Toward Communism in the Cold War Era*. New York: Garland.

Allen, Frederick Lewis. 1952. *Only Yesterday: An Informal History of the Nineteen-Twenties*. New York: Bantam Books.

Barnett, Frank R., William C. Mott, and John C. Neff, eds. 1965. *Peace and War in the Modern Age: Premises, Myths, and Realities*. Garden City, NY: Doubleday Anchor.

Bauer, Raymond A., and Edgar A. Schein, eds. 1957. Brainwashing. *Journal of Social Issues* 13, no. 3: 1–61.

Belfrage, Cedric. 1973. *The American Inquisition, 1945–1960*. Indianapolis: Bobbs-Merrill.

Bentley, Eric, ed. 1971. *Thirty Years of Treason: Excerpts from Hearings before the House Committee on Un-American Activities, 1936–1968*. New York: Viking Press.

Broadwater, Jeff. 1992. *Eisenhower and the Anti-Communist Crusade*. Chapel Hill: University of North Carolina Press.

Callahan, David. 1990. *Dangerous Capabilities: Paul Nitze and the Cold War*. New York: Harper Collins.

Caute, David. 1978. *The Great Fear: The Anti-Communist Purge Under Truman and Eisenhower*. New York: Simon and Schuster.

Ewald, William Bragg. 1986. *McCarthyism and Consensus*. Lanham, MD: University Press of America.

Fehrenbach, T.R. 1963. *This Kind of War: A Study in Unpreparedness*. New York: Macmillan.

Fried, Richard M. 1990. *Nightmare in Red: The McCarthy Era in Perspective*. New York: Oxford University Press.

Gaddis, John Lewis. 1972. *The United States and the Origins of the Cold War*. New York: Columbia University Press.

Halberstam, David. 1993. *The Fifties*. New York: Villard Books.

Hastings, Max. 1987. *The Korean War*. New York: Simon and Schuster.

Heale, M.J. 1990. *American Anticommunism: Combating the Enemy Within*. Baltimore: Johns Hopkins University Press.

Hoover, J. Edgar. 1958. *Masters of Deceit: The Story of Communism in America and How to Fight It*. New York: Henry Holt.

Inglis, Fred. 1991. *The Cruel Peace: Everyday Life and the Cold War*. New York: Basic Books.

Karp, Walter. 1974. *Indispensable Enemies: The Politics of Misrule in America*. Baltimore: Penguin Books.

London, Kurt. 1968. *The Permanent Crisis: Communism in World Politics*. Waltham, MA: Blaisdell.

Maslow, Will. 1957. "The Witness before the Congressional Committee." *Journal of Social Issues* 13, no. 2: 12–16.

Parenti, Michael. 1993. *Inventing Reality: The Politics of the News Media*. New York: St. Martin's Press.

Pincher, Chapman. 1987. *Traitors*. New York: Penguin Books.

Prange, Gordon W. 1986. *Pearl Harbor: The Verdict of History*. New York: McGraw-Hill.

"Remembering the Blacklist: A Word that Marks an Era." 1994. *New York Times*. July 31, p. 16.

Rovere, Richard H. 1970. *Senator Joe McCarthy*. New York: World.

Schrecker, Ellen. 1994. *The Age of McCarthyism: A Brief History*. Boston: St. Martin's Press.

Shils, Edward A. 1956. *The Torment of Secrecy*. Glencoe, IL: Free Press.

Stouffer, Samuel A. 1955. *Communism, Conformity, and Civil Liberties*. Garden City, NY: Doubleday.

Whitfield, Stephen J. 1991. *The Culture of the Cold War*. Baltimore: Johns Hopkins University Press.

6 • The Cuban Missile Crisis

The atomic bomb was America's major trump card in the early years of the cold war. Following the surrender of Japan, the armed forces of the United States were rapidly demobilized, while the armed forces of the Soviet Union were not. The large number of divisions in the Soviet army would give them a major advantage in any conventional, land-based war. The use of nuclear weapons was a key ingredient in plans for America's defense of Western Europe and its own territories. Americans were disturbed by the refusal of the Russians to be impressed by the fact that we had the atomic bomb.

Following World War II, there initially was hope for creating some mechanism for international control over nuclear weapons. The need was evident, since it would only be a matter of time before nuclear capability among the nations of the world had proliferated. The debates among Americans over the international control of nuclear weapons, however, were fraught with a basic contradiction. We had a monopoly control over nuclear weapons and were not willing to give up that control voluntarily. Given the atmosphere of suspicion and distrust between the Soviet Union and the United States, there seemed to be no reasonable mechanism for banning the use of nuclear weapons as instruments of war.

The bombs used on Hiroshima and Nagasaki were primitive in comparison to the destructive potential of the bombs being developed by the early 1960s. The cold war game became one of intensifying the level of terror for any adversary considering a first strike. The aim was to intensify the enemy's sense of vulnerability through developing weapons with increased explosive capability and elaborating more efficient systems for the delivery of nuclear weapons to predetermined targets.

Preparing for the contingency of a first strike against the United States, and the need for immediate retaliation, the Strategic Air Command had

B-29 bombers in the air continuously with sealed orders on targets within the Soviet Union. At a moment's notice the bombers could be on their way. Mirroring widespread sentiment within the nation that World War III was inevitable, General Curtis LeMay, the commanding officer of the Strategic Air Command, once argued that we should simply launch a nuclear attack on the Soviet Union. We were ahead of the Soviets and could win, which may not be the case in the future.

In addition to the continuously airborne bombers, we also developed secret missile sites at remote areas within the United States. The missile sites were comprised of silos from which rockets armed with nuclear warheads could be fired at the Soviet Union. It was assumed that an initial strike from the Soviet Union would be directed toward densely populated and industrialized areas. Through locating missile sites in such remote areas as Montana and Western Nebraska, we would be able to retaliate. Given the vast geographical area of the United States, any initial strike could not wreak immediate and total havoc on all parts of the country.

Additionally, we developed nuclear submarines armed with weapons aimed at the Soviet Union. The game became that of "mutually assured destruction." One side could not attack or annihilate the other without also being destroyed in the process. A quick and decisive response to any nuclear attack by either side was required. In science fiction, speculation was directed toward the possibility of developing a "doomsday machine." Such a device was conceptualized as one that would be triggered automatically by any bomb that was dropped by an enemy nation. This would set in motion a nuclear chain reaction that would destroy the entire world. The rhetoric of the cold war took the form of an Orwellian "double speak" in the argument that the way to achieve peace and security in the world was to prepare for war.

Soviet Missiles in This Hemisphere

Of all the crises of the cold war, none matched the severity and intensity of the Cuban Missile Crisis. On the evening of October 22, 1962, President John F. Kennedy went on television to make an important announcement to the nation and to the world. The United States had discovered that Soviet missile bases were being constructed in Cuba, only ninety miles off the coast of Florida. With missiles in Cuba armed with nuclear warheads, all regions of the United States would be in easy range. All American cities would be vulnerable to nuclear attack. Kennedy noted that the installation of missiles in Cuba was regarded as an act of aggression that could not be tolerated. Kennedy declared that we would do whatever was necessary to get the missiles out of Cuba.

Kennedy forcefully announced his plan of action. A strict quarantine would be placed around Cuba. The blockade would maximize the use of American forces to stop further Soviet work on the missile sites. Further, the Strategic Air Command was placed on the highest alert ever. Kennedy announced that we would increase our surveillance of Cuba and increase our readiness for a further response if it were necessary. Any nuclear missile launched from Cuba to any part of the Western Hemisphere would be regarded as an act of war against the United States. Kennedy announced that this would require a full retaliatory response against the Soviet Union.

For most Americans this was the most terrifying experience of their lives. The possibility of a nuclear war in the next few days had become a realistic possibility. The worst of nightmares about nuclear war seemed on the verge of being enacted. Even before the Cuban Missile Crisis, a large number of Americans believed a nuclear war was inevitable. Their perception of when a nuclear war was likely to occur, however, was far enough into the future that they would not have to confront the issue today, although it was not far enough in the future to free themselves of an underlying anxiety about its occurrence. Many Americans believed that neither they, nor their children, nor their grandchildren, would live to the year 2000. Now that we were on the brink of nuclear war, the planning of personal lives became greatly shortened.

The potential outcomes of the crisis could not be reasonably assessed by drawing upon historical precedent. There had been no previous episode in the history of the world in which the stakes were so high and the fate of the world in so few hands. If the worst possible scenario had been enacted, all traditions, lifestyles, and social relationships would have been irretrievably altered. One's physical safety and personal security could no longer be taken for granted. The decisions made at the centers of power in the United States and the Soviet Union were seen as having potentially drastic consequences for the personal lives of individual men and women throughout the world.

Continuation with everyday life seemed meaningless. For example, students who were working toward a college degree, or were involved in long-range planning for a career in law or medicine, became concerned about what they were doing. Why defer immediate gratification for long-range planning if it is all to end in the futility of nuclear destruction? Why go to class or work on a research paper if there is to be a total destruction of the world as it is known and understood in the next few days? Some were reminded of the secretaries in Berlin at the end of World War II who were filling out requisitions for next year's office supplies while the Russian soldiers were marching through the streets. Because they were not personally able to do anything about the big issues facing the world, most people continued with business as usual. It became difficult to know what one ought to believe or ought to do under such extraordinary circumstances.

The Soviet Union was even more terrified by Kennedy's announcement. Officials in the Kremlin knew several things that Kennedy and his Security Council did not know. For example, we did not know that some of the missiles in Cuba had already been armed with nuclear warheads. Had we launched bombing raids on the missile sites, as some of Kennedy's military advisers had recommended, it would have meant World War III. We also did not know that the Soviet military unit in Cuba was also armed with tactical nuclear weapons. Had we invaded the island to remove the missiles, as some of Kennedy's advisers recommended, the results would have been disastrous.

The Soviets also knew that they had lost partial control over their military unit in Cuba. For example, in the midst of the crisis, one of the American U-2 planes flying over Cuba was shot down. It was regarded as an invasion of Cuba's air space by the Russian advisers. Such a line of action was neither authorized nor approved by officials in Moscow. The tensions in the world were too great to risk a minor event precipitating a nuclear holocaust.

The message sent to the Soviets by the Americans was that the cost of resistance to demands for a removal of the missiles would be too great. Full nuclear retaliation would be used as a last resort if all other attempts at persuasion failed or if a nuclear weapon was fired from Cuba. From Kennedy's standpoint, a strong and decisive response to the Soviet threat was seen as necessary. The use of threats and counter-threats in a context involving nuclear weapons, however, constituted an extraordinary degree of risk taking. Both the Soviets and the Americans risked being boxed into a corner from which there would be no avenue of retreat. If the conflict escalated to the point of no return, there was no decision to be made. No option short of full nuclear retaliation would remain.

Contingency plans were directed toward the use of successive military strategies if the Soviets failed to give in to our demands. Our first strategy was the blockade to stop Russian ships from delivering missiles to Cuba. The blockade included hundreds of ships and nearly 1,000 aircraft. It was one of the more formidable armadas ever assembled in the history of the world. If this did not work, there was the possibility of air strikes against the missile sites. Further, more than 100,000 troops had been assembled in the Southern United States for a possible invasion of Cuba.

On October 24, the world was glued to their television sets and radios as Soviet ships moved toward the American blockade that had been placed around Cuba. We had embarked on a course of action in which the outcome could not reasonably be predicted in advance. Would the Soviet ships attempt to run the blockade? Clearly, the confrontation contained all of the ingredients for a dangerous escalation toward war. We were prepared to do whatever was necessary to stop the Soviet ships. We had no way of knowing what the Soviet response would be.

People around the world drew a sigh of relief when the Soviet ships suddenly stopped dead in the water and turned back. The more intense phase of the Cuban Missile Crisis had passed. However, work on the missile sites continued, and additional negotiations with the Soviets were necessary.

In pursuing the cold war, it was assumed that decision makers in both the Soviet Union and the United States were guided by rational calculations of national self-interest. Accordingly, it was assumed that neither side could launch a nuclear war without risking its own annihilation in the process. The Cuban Missile Crisis called into question such assumptions about the rationality of decision makers. The risk of nuclear war increased dramatically when the Soviet Union placed the missiles in Cuba and during the events that followed. Conditions of reciprocal suspicion and distrust, bordering on paranoia, are not favorable to calm and rational decision making. At what point would the issues of face-saving and national pride, in an atmosphere of fear and anger, result in the use of nuclear weapons as an act of desperation?

Rational decision making can occur only if the decision makers have access to all relevant information. The conflict between the United States and the Soviet Union resulted in a breakdown of communication between them. Negotiating a settlement to the crisis was difficult because there were no direct lines of communication between Washington and the Kremlin. We had to communicate either through the Russian ambassador or through KGB agents in the United States who were known to the CIA. This was a relatively slow and cumbersome process. How can crisis management follow rational procedures if the antagonists cannot communicate directly with each other in a highly volatile situation. An inappropriate reading of the cues and intentions of the other could have disastrous consequences. One of the immediate actions, once the crisis subsided, was to install a hot line between the White House and the Kremlin, so that the president of the United States could communicate directly with the premier of the Soviet Union if this became necessary in the future.

On October 26, a break came in the crisis. Khruschev privately sent a message to Kennedy announcing a set of terms for a resolution of the crisis: The Soviet Union would withdraw its missiles from Cuba (1) if the United States would formally pledge not to invade Cuba and (2) if the United States would remove from Turkey its Jupiter missiles that were aimed at the

Soviet Union. The Soviets had installed the missiles in Cuba in response to the American strategy of locating missiles adjacent to their borders.

Kennedy accepted Khruschev's terms with some qualifications. He would publicly make a pledge that the United States would not invade Cuba, but he did not want to announce to the world that he had agreed to remove our missiles from Turkey. For political reasons, Kennedy did not wish to convey the image that he was willing to appease or compromise with the Russians. At the same time, however, Kennedy privately assured Khruschev that we would remove the missiles from Turkey. Khruschev found this agreement to be acceptable, thus ending the most dangerous crisis in the history of the world.

The trauma of the Cuban Missile Crisis was primarily an outgrowth of the power struggle between the leadership of the Soviet Union and the leadership of the United States. The drama of the confrontation between Kennedy and Khruschev was being enacted while the rest of the world watched in terror. Most Americans perceived Kennedy as a man who had demonstrated forceful leadership and saw Khruschev as a man who had backed down. The missiles were removed from Cuba, and the entire world drew a sigh of relief. Confusion remained, however, over the rapidity with which we had been brought to the brink of nuclear war. We had made it through the Cuban Missile Crisis, but the cold war was far from over.

Fear of Nuclear War

The acute trauma phase of the Cuban Missile Crisis quickly subsided in the consciousness of Americans. To dwell on "what might have been" would have had a pathological quality about it and would be counter-productive to the everyday task of getting on with the business of living. Yet, the fear of nuclear war persisted within the general population, and policymakers reviewed over and over again the lessons to be learned from the crisis for future forms of international confrontation.

The fear of nuclear war in the general population took the form of several questions that could not be answered with confidence: Is World War III inevitable? What is the probability that a nuclear war will occur in the next few years? How will a nuclear war start? Will there be an advanced warning or will it begin suddenly and unexpectedly? Will it be possible for humans to survive a nuclear war? These questions attempted to link personal biography with historical circumstances. While the inherent uncertainty of the historical context precluded clear and definitive answers, these questions were of sufficient importance that some form of response was necessary.

The mushroom cloud over Hiroshima had become a major symbol of the challenges and dangers of the world in which we live. The symbolism of the bomb went far beyond the recognition of it as a weapon. It had become a device for destroying the world. Nothing humans had ever made before had such tremendous power and destructive capability. Both in Japan and the United States there were some who believed that the scientists and technicians who had worked on the bomb as well as the military, who had a new instrument of war at their disposal, had welcomed the opportunity to try it out on Japanese cities. Thus, the complexity of the motives for using the bomb resulted in the conclusion that the future of our nation and the survival of our species could not be taken as self-evident.

The genocidal component of the nuclear arms race was reflected in the view that an overkill capacity had been developed during the course of the cold war. A sense of uneasiness resulted from comparisons of the atomic bombs dropped on Japan with the more sophisticated weapons that were subsequently developed. The bombs at Hiroshima and Nagasaki were primitive compared to the bombs that had been developed by the time of the Cuban Missile Crisis. A single hydrogen bomb now had an explosive capacity that greatly exceeded that of all the weapons denoted during World War II. The explosion of any one of these bombs on a large metropolitan area would result in a disaster unprecedented in human history. The full scope of the catastrophe could not be adequately comprehended.

Given the number of nuclear bombs that had been developed, all major cities in both the United States and the Soviet Union could be smashed flat within a matter of minutes. In public discourse on the effects of a nuclear war, it was noted that from the fireballs and the firestorms of nuclear explosions, the temperature of the earth would reach levels matching the surface of the sun. It was believed that the land surface of the earth would be seared and the oxygen in the atmosphere would be depleted. The heat generated would be sufficiently intense to melt the polar ice caps, which would result in the flooding of a great deal of the land surface of the planet. Immense amounts of gamma radiation would be released over a large geographic area. Death would result not only from the concussion of the explosion, but also from asphyxiation. Survivors of the initial blast would likely die from acute radiation sickness within a short period of time.

The view was widely held that humans were not yet prepared for having such weapons at their disposal. A nuclear war of the scale that the United States and the Soviet Union were capable of waging could end civilization in minutes, and the greater part of the world's population could be dead within days or weeks. Some believed that a great deal of the earth's animal and plant life would be destroyed as well. Thus, it was not a matter of either side bombing the other "back to the stone age"; it was a matter of the survival of the human species itself.

Some observed that the need for speed in the retaliation process increased the risk of a nuclear war being started by accident. In a tactical plan for nuclear war, it is important to launch one's rockets before they are destroyed on the ground. The result was a war environment unprecedented in human history. In previous wars, the mobilization of the entire population was necessary for successfully undertaking a major war. In contrast, a nuclear war could run its full course before most of the population were even aware that it had started. Once the weapons were in place, the keys could be turned and the buttons pushed by only a few individuals. Mobilization of public opinion for waging a war had become neither necessary nor relevant.

We usually think of fear as a physiological and a cognitive response to some impending danger. At the individual level, conditions of fear generate such physiological reactions as an increase in the production of adrenaline and an increase in the sugar count in the blood stream. These are adaptive responses for "fight or flight"—a mobilization of internal resources for aggressive behavior or to maximize one's capacity for flight. When fear is pervasive and extends over a long period of time, however, it tends to be maladaptive. Chronic stress that cannot be confronted directly tends to show up in such depressive symptoms as feelings of tiredness and sleep disorders. The fear of nuclear war was a chronic form of stress that required some form of adaptive response. For most people, the fear of nuclear war became muted through some form of denial and repression. Uncertainty about when the war would come, if ever, resulted in the removal of concerns about everyday life.

Within the general population, however, there was more than a passing concern with the threat of nuclear war. Immediately following World War II, the tensions were downplayed because the United States was the only country that had the bomb. During times of crisis, however, the latent fears were temporarily brought to the surface. This occurred with the news that the Russians had now developed the bomb, when the Russians launched the first man-made satellite, with the tensions mounting during the Berlin Airlift, and particularly with the news of the Cuban Missile Crisis. Americans had demonstrated their willingness to use nuclear weapons on civilian populations. There was little reason to believe the Russians would be any more restrained.

Fear of nuclear war was brought under control through rationalizations and wishful thinking. New emphasis was placed on thinking positively and downplaying negative thoughts. The beliefs in the American system were evident; including the optimistic views that the United States will develop a defense against nuclear bombs, that the creative genius of Americans will permit us to solve whatever problems confront us, and that public authorities will make decisions that are in the best interests of the country. If our destiny lies in the hands of powerful others, the best we can hope for is that they are benevolent and will make decisions that are compatible with our own best interests.

Worry about the immediate threat of nuclear war was also downplayed through attitudes of fatalism: "Since there is nothing we can do about the world situation, why worry about it." Humans have always been faced with the problems of adapting to the "unshakable facts" of their existence. Attention should be directed toward doing something about those problems that are within our personal control, such as the challenges of everyday living, not the complicated issues of international affairs. Such attitudes minimized the stress resulting from the threat of nuclear war.

"Selective inattention" was one way to cope with the threat of nuclear war: There are good times and bad times, and the bad times can be endured if we "think positively" and avoid "negative thoughts." Conditions of stress and tension within the social realm can be endured if we look for "the silver lining." The economic prosperity generated by the wartime economy had translated into increased purchasing power and a higher standard of living for most Americans. A prominent view was that "we should count our blessings." Troublesome circumstances can be trivialized by maximizing a focus on that which is worthwhile and gratifying. Such a style of coping tends to equate problem-solving with the avoidance of worry and tension. The underlying aims were to avoid confrontation, to relax, to downplay the importance of a difficult situation, and to permit problems to disappear with the passing of time.

Thinking and talking about the painful possibilities of "what could happen" tend to have "magical" or "taboo" qualities about them: Talking about an event can "magically" cause that event to occur, while there can be a social stigma or a disdain toward those who bring up such unpleasant "taboo" topics for conversation. At some level of consciousness, many recognized that never before in history had so few been able to destroy so many in so short a time; that nuclear weapons are almost entirely offensive, not defensive; and that the continued stockpiling of nuclear weapons increases rather than decreases a sense of national security. Yet, in interpersonal conversations most people preferred to avoid openly reflecting on such disturbing topics. Dwelling on painful or disturbing possibilities can only have uneasy or morbid consequences. Thus, it is better not to think about or talk about such matters.

While adults were developing coping mechanisms for downplaying their level of stress, the tensions stemming from the threat of nuclear war surfaced for children and adolescents. The Civil Defense program in the public schools that called for "duck and cover" exercises had unexpected psychological consequences for children. Many children concluded that because of their preparation they might survive a nuclear war but their parents would not. Fears were directed toward "being stuck" and not having anyone to take care of them. While a few adolescents were fascinated with the idea of nuclear weapons, most were strongly antinuclear and expressed anger at the older generation for playing with their future and perhaps depriving them of the opportunity to grow up and live out their adult lives. Typical responses of adolescents reflected a mixture of anger with feelings of hopelessness and helplessness. The majority of adolescents were doubtful that either they or their country could survive a nuclear war. Very few adolescents expressed any interest in personally making plans for surviving a nuclear war.

The encounter of adolescents with the Cuban Missile Crisis was subsequently followed by a set of attitudes that were disturbing to many adults. By the middle 1960s, many young adults were openly expressing their anger toward the older generations and placing their faith exclusively in their own generation. This was reflected in the viewpoint that "no one over thirty years old is to be trusted." Resentments about the world that had been created for them by the older generation were translated into attitudes of distrust toward authority and established institutions. Rather than working within "the system," an emphasis was placed upon seeking self-fulfillment through impulsive actions. The focus was on "here and now," rather than on a future that required making long-range plans and deferring immediate gratifications. The pervasiveness of such attitudes was reflected in the number of those who dropped out of school, became sexually permissive, and experimented with mind-altering drugs. In the face of an uncertain future, the hedonistic view of "living for today and letting tomorrow take care of itself" became evident.

Surviving Nuclear War

During the Cuban Missile Crisis, there was a run on supermarkets. Preparing for a nuclear catastrophe was one way people could translate their underlying fear and anxiety into a specific line of action. Through storing up provisions for survival, they were preparing for the worst possible scenario. Some included the purchase of guns in their preparations. It was believed that it would be necessary to have some way to defend oneself and one's family if there was a breakdown in law and order following a nuclear war. Since there was no realistic way of knowing what the world would be like, survival may very well require being prepared for drastic measures.

The American emphasis on personal mastery and control was reflected in the construction of fallout shelters. Rather than fatalistic resignation in the face of nuclear war, it was believed that individuals could take matters into their own hands. Accordingly, during the late 1950s and early 1960s a small number of Americans constructed bunkers in their backyards. The bunkers were cellar-like constructions covered with several feet of dirt and stocked with food and water in sufficient supply to survive for several days following a nuclear war. When asked what they would do if neighbors attempted to force their way into their fallout shelters, the response was frequently, "We'd just have to shoot them." Personal survival was defined as the major objective in these cases, and self-interests were assigned higher priority than communal interests.

The construction of fallout shelters was also accompanied by a great deal of black humor. Salesmen from construction companies offering fallout shelters frequently claimed that "Our work is guaranteed" and "If the shelter fails to work, we promise to refund your money." Such uses of humor were responses to the tensions of the cold war. It was a way of providing relief from the stress that many people were experiencing. The human absurdity of mutual destruction was easier to deal with through humor than through taking the issues at face value.

Many major cities throughout the country began planning civil defense strategies. Columbus, Ohio, for example, predicted that the bomb would fall at the intersection of Broad and High Streets (the city center). Assuming that there would be about a thirty-minute advance notice of an impending nuclear attack, what should be the civil defense response? Should plans be made for evacuating the city or should plans be made for going underground?

If the city is to be evacuated, what are the contingency plans that must be made? Are the food supplies in the surrounding countryside adequate to feed the evacuated urban dwellers? If the city is to be evacuated, what should be done with the poisonous snakes in the zoo? Should they be shot? And what about the prisoners in the Ohio State Penitentiary that was located in the city? Should the guards just walk away, and if so, what should be done with the inmates? In planning for an evacuation of the city, it was decided that the streets should all be transformed into one-way streets leading out from the center of the city. A practice evacuation was held, and the result was a massive traffic jam. The planning for civil defense in American cities was seen by many as an exercise in futility.

A variety of viewpoints came to be expressed over the issue of whether there would be survivors following an all-out nuclear war. Some turned to the sacred scriptures for insights into the aftermath of nuclear war and maintained that not all would perish. Here it was noted the world was once destroyed by a great flood, and there were survivors. Noah and his family had been chosen by God to perpetuate the species. This view held that a merciful God would provide humanity with an opportunity for a fresh start. Some asserted that humanity can and will survive the grimmest of holocausts. Enough people would survive a nuclear war to gradually repopulate the earth. The survivors will have an opportunity to build a new social order that will be a substantial improvement over the old one.

Others took a more secular approach and came to less optimistic conclusions. Several scientists elaborated on the concept of "a nuclear winter" and maintained that there would be no survivors. The debris released into the atmosphere from the explosions of a nuclear war would alter the earth's climate by blocking out rays from the sun. The rapid drop in temperature would soon result in a heavy snowfall covering the millions of burned bodies in major metropolitan areas. Drastic environmental changes would occur as temperatures dropped to severely low levels. The plant and animal life upon which humans depend for food would be extinguished. The disappearance of the dinosaurs from a drastic change in climatic conditions was drawn upon as a precedent.

Appraisals of the aftermath of nuclear war suggested that the planet would become engulfed in "a long darkness" devoid of life forms. If this ever occurred, the result would be a human absurdity. The designs and imperatives of the technology elaborated to increase the sense of national security would result in the ultimate in human insecurity and vulnerability. Since it would be our own end, the nuclear holocaust came to be perceived as a form of self-destruction. The bumper sticker "Better Red than Dead" reflected the desperation growing out of the awareness of the potential for human annihilation. The destruction of civilization or living under communism was a choice that few Americans were willing to make.

"The long darkness," or "the nuclear winter," argument may be understood as a plausibility argument growing out of conditions of uncertainty. Such concerns stem from an inability on the part of anyone to come up with a realistic set of expectations about what would happen during and after a nuclear war. There are no precedents in the human experience for encounters with such severe environmental changes nor for such dramatic imperatives for human adaptability within such a short period of time. Yet, it is clear that the world could never again be the same. The old world order would be of limited usefulness for any new social world the survivors would be required to create.

We could draw upon neither direct experiences nor rational analysis for a reasonable set of predictions about what the world would be like after a nuclear war. For these reasons, Americans turned to such forms of popular culture as the movies, novels, and music both for entertainment and reflections on their underlying anxieties. Prominent in images of nuclear war were such notions as "doomsday," "Armageddon," "the apocalypse," "total destruction," and "a lifeless planet." Such images conveyed the implication that there would be no survivors of an all-out nuclear war. The planet would join the other planets of the universe on which life had never developed or had been extinguished.

The themes in science fiction about survivors of a nuclear war mirrored the sentiments of the nation. Total annihilation had its limits in the development of a plot. It could only represent the ending, rather than the beginning of a story. Scripts with the theme that a few people would survive a nuclear war permitted giving free reign to the imagination in portraying what life would be like under these circumstances. The environment typically confronted was one of wasted cities, burned bodies, and the destruction of civilization. The survivors of nuclear war were also portrayed as suffering from physiological mutilations and deformities.

The fantasies of popular culture suggested that if only a few survived a nuclear war, the survivors would have a rough time of it. The money in their checking accounts would be useless; food in grocery stores would be contaminated; and there would be no electricity for the use of appliances. The taken-for-granted supports in everyday life would no longer be available. In the absence of law and order, the ugliest side of human nature would be manifested. Because of the loss of the power of the state, human relationships would become brutal, dangerous, and coercive. Self-interests would prevail, and the availability of communal support and mutual caring would have vanished. In effect, with the trappings of civilization stripped away, the social environment would become harsh and unresponsive to personal needs and interests. In the absence of any reasonable knowledge of what social life would be like following a nuclear holocaust, imagination was given free reign in developing notions about the forms of human nature that would be tapped and about the types of men and women who would prevail.

The lessons from Hiroshima had suggested that much more was involved in a nuclear war than the deaths initially resulting from the explosion itself. The acute radiation aftereffects at Hiroshima and Nagasaki were grotesque. Symptoms of "the invisible contamination" included severe diarrhea, ulceration of the mouth, bleeding gums, skin cancer, high fever, loss of hair, low white blood cell count, and damage to the central nervous system. There was also evidence that exposure to high levels of radiation would have gruesome effects on future generations: Children or grandchildren would be born with genetic abnormalities, and deleterious mutations would occur.

In view of such dire consequences, many Americans came to the conclusion that it would be preferable to die rather than to survive a nuclear war. Living out a life of slow death with pain and suffering was not seen as a viable option. Given the perceived environmental effects, sudden death from a nuclear war was seen as preferable to prolonged suffering. The consequences of survival were seen as even more catastrophic than death itself. There are circumstances in which death is preferable to living with intense and prolonged agony.

The death trauma in human affairs is generally combined with some conception of immortality. The sting of death is attenuated through beliefs that the spirits of the dead will be joined with loved ones in the afterlife, that a just God reigns in Heaven and will reward the righteous, that reincarnation will permit returning and starting over again, that the spirits of the dead reside within the community of the living, that one has not really died as long as he or she is remembered, and that continuance is provided through passing on one's genes and family name to the next generation. Such conceptions of immortality lose their applicability if the entire human species is eradicated by nuclear war. Death takes a nihilistic form. Only the rivers and the mountains will remain as the principle of "dust to dust" is applied to the entire human species.

Those who believed that the best way to survive a nuclear war was to prevent one took an active political stand against additional preparations. If there were no reasonable circumstances under which a nuclear war could be fought, then why were we preparing for it? If the United States already had an "overkill" capacity for annihilating all men, women, and children on this planet, why were we putting resources into developing more sophisticated weapons? A large number of books, editorials, sermons, and radical publications expressed anger over the suicidal implications of the escalation toward nuclear war.

Peace advocates overwhelmed by the cold war rhetoric, however, were voices in the wilderness. Residual patriotism from World War II, experiences with the defeat of Germany and Japan, and attitudes of moral superiority became ingredients in the prevailing political ideology. A military buildup to resist the communist challenge received overwhelming support in American public opinion. Within this context, advocates of peaceful coexistence were seen as traitors and subversives. Nothing less than expanding our military power abroad and minimizing dissent at home were seen as viable.

Those at the center of power and influence in our political and military institutions took what they regarded as a realistic and hard-headed approach to matters related to the cold war. Peace advocates were regarded as "soft-headed, misguided idealists" who lacked a realistic understanding of practical politics. The science fiction writers who portrayed nuclear war as a form of doomsday were condemned as overly emotional and hysterical in their approach to issues of national security. The international situation was seen as requiring a macho approach, rather than any form of appeasement or compromise. The issue of what constitutes a realistic threat and what constitutes a neurotic form of anxiety became a part of the uncertainty in responses to the potentials for nuclear war.

Whether the fear of communism was realistic or unrealistic, it is clear that we were operating between the boundaries of order and chaos, between good and evil, between survival and mass destruction. The quest for military superiority precluded a reduction of the arms race even after the capacity for overkill had been developed on both sides of the Iron Curtain. We may never be able to adequately explain or understand the escalation of the arms race between the United States and the Soviet Union. Whatever else future historians may decide, it is clear that misperceptions, misunderstandings, and mass hysteria were among the ingredients involved. But at the level of human action, what is important is not the truth of the matter, by objective criteria, but what people believe to be true. Humans act on the basis of their beliefs, whether they are valid ones or not.

Bibliography

Allison, Graham T., Albert Carnesale, and Joseph S. Nye Jr. 1985. *Hawks, Doves, and Owls.* New York: W.W. Norton.

Barnett, Frank R., William C. Mott, and John C. Neff, eds. 1965. *Peace and War in the Modern Age: Premises, Myths, and Realities.* Garden City, NY: Doubleday Anchor.

Bialer, Seweryn, and Michael Mandelbaum. 1988. *The Global Rivals.* New York: Alfred A. Knopf.

Blight, James G. 1992. *The Shattered Crystal Ball: Fear and Learning in the Cuban Missile Crisis.* Lanham, MD: Littlefield Adams Quality Paperbacks.

Blight, James G., and David A. Welch. 1990. *On the Brink: Americans and the Soviets Reexamine the Cuban Missile Crisis.* New York: Noonday Press.

Bundy, McGeorge. 1990. *Danger and Survival: Choices about the Bomb in the First Fifty Years.* New York: Vintage Books.

Clarfield, Gerard H., and William M. Wiecek. 1984. *Nuclear America.* New York: Harper and Row.

Dyson, Freeman. 1985. *Weapons and Hope.* New York: Harper and Row.

Ehrlich, Paul R., Carl Sagan, Donald Kennedy, and Walter Orr Roberts. 1984. *The Cold and the Dark: The World After Nuclear War.* New York: W.W. Norton.

Garthoff, Raymond L. 1987. *Reflections on the Cuban Missile Crisis.* Washington, DC: Brookings Institutions.

Grinspoon, Lester, ed. 1986. *The Long Darkness: Psychological and Moral Perspectives on Nuclear Winter.* New Haven, CT: Yale University Press.

Harris, John B., and Eric Markusen. 1986. *Nuclear Weapons and the Threat of Nuclear War.* New York: Harcourt Brace Jovanovich.

Kull, Steven. 1988. *Minds at War: Nuclear Reality and the Inner Conflicts of Defense Policymakers.* New York: Basic Books.

Lifton, Robert Jay. 1967. *Death in Life: Survivors of Hiroshima.* New York: Random House.

Lifton, Robert Jay, and Eric Markusen. 1988. *The Genocidal Mentality: Nazi Holocaust and Nuclear Threat.* New York: Basic Books.

Mack, John E., and Roberta Snow. 1986. "Psychological Effects on Children and Adolescents." In *Psychology and Prevention of Nuclear War,* ed. Ralph K. White, pp. 16–33. New York: New York University Press.

McCrea, Frances B., and Gerald E. Markle. 1989. *Minutes to Midnight: Nuclear Weapons Protest in America.* Newbury Park, CA: Sage.

McNamara, Robert S. 1987. *Blundering into Disaster: Surviving the First Century of the Nuclear Age.* New York: Pantheon Books.

Milburn, Thomas. 1977. "The Nature of the Threat." *Journal of Social Issues* 33, no. 1: 126–139.

Mills, C. Wright. 1960. *The Causes of World War III.* New York: Ballantine Books.

Osgood, Charles E. 1966. "The Psychologist in International Affairs." In *Taboo Topics,* ed. Norman L. Farberow, pp. 106–126. New York: Atherton Press.

Paulson, Dennis, ed. 1986. *Voices of Survival in the Nuclear Age.* Santa Barbara, CA: Capra Press.

Popkess, Barry. 1980. *The Nuclear Survival Handbook: Living Through and After a Nuclear Attack.* New York: Collier Books.

Porter, Jeffrey L. 1993. "Narrating the End: Fables of Survival in the Nuclear Age." *Journal of American Culture* 16: 41–47.

Sherwin, Martin J. 1975. *A World Destroyed: The Atomic Bomb and the Grand Alliance.* New York: Alfred A. Knopf.

Smith, Jeff. 1989. *Unthinking the Unthinkable: Nuclear Weapons and Western Culture.* Bloomington: Indiana University Press.

Szumski, Bonnie, ed. 1985. *Nuclear War: Opposing Viewpoints.* St. Paul, MN: Greenhaven Press.

Teller, Edward. 1987. *Better a Shield than a Sword: Perspectives on Defense and Technology.* New York: Free Press.

White, Ralph K., ed. 1986. *Psychology and the Prevention of Nuclear War.* New York: New York University Press.

York, Herbert F. 1987. *Making Weapons, Talking Peace: A Physicist's Odyssey from Hiroshima to Geneva.* New York: Basic Books.

7 • The Assassination of President Kennedy

On November 22, 1963, the daily activities of Americans ground to a halt upon the release of the news bulletin that President John F. Kennedy had been shot in Dallas, Texas. The news was met with shock, disbelief, and incredulity. The early reports were incomplete on the seriousness of the injuries and many Americans were hoping the president would live. While only a small percentage of Americans heard the first radio and television reports on the shooting, a remarkable diffusion of information took place among friends, acquaintances, and even strangers. Most Americans had heard about the tragedy within half an hour after the shooting occurred.

In the early reports, very little information was available on anything more than the details of the motorcade through Dallas and that the president had been shot and had been taken to Parkland Memorial Hospital. The central preoccupation of the nation was with the details of what had happened and whether or not the president would live. University classes were interrupted and canceled, factory workers left their jobs and went home, stores closed their doors, and the everyday activities of the nation ground to a halt. Continuation of business as usual seemed to make little sense in view of the extraordinary events that were happening. Regular television programming was suspended and news coverage continuously reported on the events surrounding the assassination.

The president's motorcade was met with friendly and enthusiastic spectators who had crowded the parade route. Kennedy was in Texas primarily to help unify the Democratic Party and to win support for the next presidential election. In response to the pleasant weather and the friendly crowds, the top to the limousine had been removed and the bullet-proof windows were rolled down. The motorcade had just made a left turn down an incline toward an underpass when the shooting began. Governor John Connally, who was riding in the limousine with the Kennedys, had just commented, "You can't say Dallas isn't friendly to you today." The number of shots and where they came from became topics for debate and discussion for many years afterward. The shooting sequence lasted only about six seconds. Both President Kennedy and Governor Connally had been hit with sniper bullets. The news media repeatedly showed film clips of the motorcade and the assassination in attempts to clarify what had happened from the sketchy evidence available. Film from network coverage of the event, film from home movies, and the photographs taken by spectators were examined extensively as both news analysts and the general public attempted to establish the facts of the case. At the time and in subsequent analyses, there was a great deal of confusion about the details of what had happened.

Many Americans remember the faltering voice of Walter Cronkite, who came close to being emotionally overwhelmed in reporting the president's death. Cronkite's emotional response was similar to the level of emotionality that was being expressed by individuals throughout the nation. The orderliness and predictability of social life had broken down, a tragedy of epic proportions had occurred, and there was a great deal of uncertainty about what would happen next. Throughout the nation, individuals expressed their feelings of shock, disbelief, and horror. Some were stunned to the point of silence, while others were crying without embarrassment and openly expressing their sense of grief.

People turned to family members and close friends for emotional support. Rather than responding to the tragic event as isolated, atomized individuals, the responses were shared and shaped within the framework of small and intimate groups. Phone lines became jammed with the extremely large number of calls that were being made to close relatives and friends. People were reaching out for sources of support, stability, and security. An acute crisis had emerged in the personal lives of individuals. The sense of grief felt by many was as severe as the grief they felt if a close friend or a family member had died.

There was a widespread quest for news, yet it was too early for the news services to provide sufficient information about what was happening. As a result of the uncertainty surrounding the events, people all over the country began creating plausible explanations. Many initially believed that the assassination had been promoted by a right-wing conspiracy. Radical-right groups had been active in the Dallas area and were known to be opposed to the liberal policies Kennedy had promoted. In the absence of official information, others were equally convinced that the assassination had been engineered as a left-wing or communist plot. Castro had been indignant over the Bay of Pigs invasion and believed that Kennedy was planning an invasion of Cuba. Yet others maintained that it was likely the president was shot by a mentally deranged individual. The conflict between conspiratorial and psychological explanations were topics of conversation in small groups all over the country. Attempts were being made to bring some degree of coherence to a senseless, meaningless event.

The initial shock was followed by a sense of national vulnerability. Some felt that the assassination was a forerunner of similar disturbing events that were to follow. The memories were still vivid of the Cuban Missile Crisis and the threat of nuclear war. The orderliness of social life had broken down, and there was a great deal of uncertainty about what was going to happen next. The concern was with whether the assassination was a self-contained event or whether it was an indicator of additional tragedies that were to follow.

Shortly after the assassination, it was established that the shots had come from the sixth floor of the Texas School Book Depository and that the suspect was Lee Harvey Oswald. News accounts were then directed toward his background. Oswald was identified as a misfit and as a troublemaker who had twice been court-martialed as a marine. It was noted that he had formerly renounced his citizenship and traveled to Russia, only to later return to the United States with a wife and a baby daughter. His violent action was understood as growing out of a generalized sense of rage and disaffection. Yet, there remained some uncertainty about his ties to the Soviet Union and his prior public expression of pro-Castro sentiments.

The drama continued to unfold with the conditions surrounding the arrest of Oswald. A police officer, J.D. Tippitt, was killed in an attempt to make an arrest of Oswald in the vicinity of a Dallas movie house. The tragedy for the Tippitt family was shared by the television viewing audience. The dangers inherent in police work became evident, and the images of Oswald took on additional sinister characteristics. Oswald's tenacious assault on symbols of authority reflected the risks to society of highly alienated individuals who direct their pent-up hostility into violent actions. Oswald was suspected of having previously attempted to assassinate a major public figure.

Shortly after the announcement of the death of Kennedy, Lyndon Johnson was sworn in as the thirty-sixth president of the United States while aboard *Air Force One* en route to Washington. It was important for both the nation and the world to be assured of the continuity of the office of the presidency. Also aboard the plane were Mrs. Jacqueline Kennedy, the casket bearing her slain husband, and her brother-in-law, Senator Robert Kennedy. The pilot had received orders to fly a zigzag path back to Washington to thwart any potential plans for intercepting and shooting down the plane.

There was still a sufficient degree of uncertainty about any involvement of the Soviet Union or Cuba to warrant reasonable precautions.

The casket bearing the president was subsequently taken from Bethesda Naval Hospital to the White House to allow close family members and the White House staff to pay their respects. The next day the casket was placed in the rotunda of the capital on the same catafalque that had previously held Abraham Lincoln. Emotional eulogies were delivered by Senator Mike Mansfield, Speaker of the House of Representatives John McCormick, and Chief Justice of the Supreme Court Earl Warren. The eulogies focused on Kennedy's idealism, his personal sacrifice, and the loss to the nation. Throughout the afternoon and night, long lines of mourners silently walked past the closed casket. At times, the line was more than two miles long, and some mourners waited six to eight hours before reaching the capital steps. An estimated 250,000 people showed their respect by silently walking past Kennedy's coffin and the motionless honor guard on duty.

The nation watched on television the expressions of sadness and grief as major political leaders in the United States and from abroad arrived and departed from the White House. It was difficult for Americans not to recall the youth and vigor of Kennedy as they reflected on the heart attack that Lyndon Johnson had had in 1955 and the ages of the men who were next in line for succession to the presidency. John McCormick was seventy-one years of age and next in line to become president if anything happened to Johnson. The next in line was Senator Carl Hayden, who was eighty-six years old.

The sadness on the part of Americans was accompanied by expressions of grief on a worldwide basis. In Tokyo, Buddhist priests offered prayers before a portrait of Kennedy; Nairobi issued a proclamation of pain; news bulletins were displayed on the streets of Seoul; flags were flown at half-staff in London; and mourners marched in commemorative torch parades in Berlin and in Bern, Switzerland. President Kennedy had captured the hopes and aspirations not only of Americans but also of the peoples of the world. Berliners recalled the help provided by Americans during the Berlin Airlift and remembered Kennedy's speech on a visit to Berlin in which he proclaimed "Ich bin ein Berliner." People around the world felt they had lost a personal friend and experienced some degree of insecurity with the loss of a world leader.

On Sunday morning, November 24, the church bells tolled across the country as millions of Americans went to pray. After the emotional drain of the weekend, the day promised to be one of quiet reflections on the tragic events; however, it turned out not the be the case. In Dallas, the television cameras were covering the transfer of Oswald from the city prison to the county jail. The nation was shocked and horrified to witness on live television the shooting of Oswald by Jack Ruby who had suddenly appeared on the scene. The trauma of the viewing audience became intensified. The earlier explanation of Oswald as the lone gunman was suddenly called into question. Why did Ruby shoot Oswald, rather than permit him to go to trial and receive due process in a court of law? The lack of clarity surrounding Ruby's motives was to plague the nation for years to come. Was Ruby acting on behalf of someone other than himself? How did Ruby get through the security guard around Oswald? Was there negligence on the part of the Dallas police in allowing this to happen? The perceived vulnerability of the nation to further unexpected and tragic events continued to build. The stability of the social order seemed to be breaking down.

The handling of the Oswald case by the Dallas police resulted in feelings of uneasiness about the disregard for due process on the part of law enforcement officials. The available evidence against Oswald appeared to be overwhelming, and the assumption of his guilt had been taken as self-evident. Oswald had been exposed to long hours of questioning without the benefit of legal counsel. Throughout, Oswald proclaimed his innocence and had asserted that he was being "set up as a patsy." A hectic atmosphere prevailed at the police headquarters in Dallas, and the television cameras were intrusive. Many Americans had the feeling that the news media were not providing the full story. Doubts were raised about the authenticity of the messages that were being sent. It was unclear whether Ruby's killing of Oswald grew out of his admiration for Kennedy or whether it was a means of circumventing evidence that may have come out in courtroom proceedings.

The following day, the nation was engrossed in television coverage of the funeral ceremony at St. Matthew's Cathedral and the subsequent funeral procession to Arlington Cemetery. The dignity of the ceremony and the symbolism of the funeral march were accompanied by intense feelings of sadness. The funeral march was embellished by an honor guard, muffled drums, a horse-drawn caisson bearing the casket, and a riderless horse with empty boots reversed in the stirrups.

The grief of Americans was shared by people around the world. The heads of state came to Washington to pay their respects and to share in the tragedy. The funeral procession, which was three miles long, included such world figures as General de Gaulle, Emperor Haile Selassie, and the presidents of the Philippines and South Korea. Emissaries represented nearly all the major noncommunist countries of the world. In some respects, the tragedy of Kennedy's death resulted in one of the most impressive summit meetings in history.

His burial in Arlington Cemetery, rather than in the family plot in Massachusetts, indicated that he now belonged to the nation and to the world. Since the days of the Civil War, Arlington Cemetery has been a sacred place for Americans. More than 100,000 of those who made personal sacrifices for their country were buried there. Included are ordinary people as well as the famous.

The ceremony at the graveside included a twenty-one-gun salute and a flyover of fifty jets to represent each of the states. Following the playing of taps and the folding of the American flag, an emotionally drained nation started thinking about returning to business as usual. In the years that followed, millions of Americans made pilgrimages to Kennedy's graveside. Along with the Tomb of the Unknown Soldier and the Lincoln Memorial, Kennedy's grave was to become one of the more sacred places in the consciousness of the nation.

Death Symbolism

Attributes of human mortality were grappled with in individual responses to Kennedy's assassination and his burial at Arlington Cemetery. Foremost among them was the recognition that the high and the mighty are mere mortals like the rest of us. Death is both a universal and a democratic aspect of the human condition. Many Americans remembered the sadness that had accompanied the untimely death of President Franklin Roosevelt during the latter part of World War II. All men and women die sooner or later. Following Kennedy's death, the sense of grief and mourning was shared by the rich and powerful as well as the poor and disadvantaged.

The fundamental absurdity of the human condition is that each of us has an awareness of our own mortality, but we live our lives without knowing when our own death will occur. In our daily lives, we go about business as usual as though we were immortal. At the same time lurking in the back of our consciousness is the recognized fact that sooner or later each of us will die. It is against this background that death serves as a reference point for assessing the meaning of life. President Kennedy had come to symbolize the hopes and aspirations of the nation in the creation of a national agenda that he would no longer be able to implement.

We also collectively have an awareness that there is a proper time to die—such as after a long and productive life, when one reaches old age, or as relief from chronic pain and suffering. The sting of death has a more intense sense of tragedy when it is out of place. The death of the president was seen as a senseless event that should never have occurred by the standards of what is normal, natural, and just within the social realm.

Kennedy's untimely death precluded the fulfillment of the historical destiny of a youthful president. To have his life ended abruptly and without warning was an encounter with absurdity that has no place in a just world.

The youthfulness of Kennedy added to the intensity of the trauma. He was only forty-three years of age when he was elected president, the youngest man ever elected to that office. The aura he brought to the presidency was one of youthfulness, vigor, energy, and idealism. He was the first president born in the twentieth century and was admired by the youth of the nation and regarded as a spokesman for the new generation. Politics had been elevated to a noble enterprise, and Kennedy's style was oriented toward enhancing optimism, idealism, and commitment. To have it all ended at the relatively young age of forty-six precluded him from fulfilling his political promise. Both his family and the nation were deprived of what he had to offer.

In the months and years following the president's assassination, Americans identified closely with the tragedies of the Kennedy family. The president's older brother had been killed during World War II as the pilot of an explosive-laden bomber. His sister, Kathleen, had been widowed during the war and subsequently died in a plane crash. The loss of a valued family member, whether from an accidental death or a casualty of war, is universally a tragic event for the survivors. The tragedies of the death of his children were especially intense for Joseph Kennedy because of the career aspirations he had held for them. The subsequent assassination of Senator Robert Kennedy occurred in California in the midst of a presidential campaign that looked promising. The nation sympathized with the Kennedy family, recognizing that their glories and triumphs had also been accompanied by the unfolding of extraordinarily tragic events.

Following his death, the images and memories of Kennedy became selective and more vivid as they took on sacred qualities. As is generally the case when people die, there it became taboo to say negative things about Kennedy. Criticism of the man and his tenure of office was no longer socially acceptable. There were no references to the narrow margin by which he had been elected president, nor to the fiasco of the Bay of Pigs invasion, nor to the concerns of many Americans with our growing involvement in Vietnam. The rights of Americans to say negative things about their elected officials were temporarily put on hold. In the process of becoming sanctified, Kennedy had been removed from the mundane world of practical politics. Social forces were operating to promote idealization.

Kennedy's idealism was remembered from his speech at Rice University in which he announced the national objective of landing a man on the moon before the decade was over. Others remembered his role in negotiating with the Soviet Union a ban on nuclear testing in the atmosphere. He was seen as providing strong and effective leadership in seeking a resolution of the Cuban Missile Crisis. Still others recalled his style of oratory in which he inspired a sense of social consciousness and clearly indicated a personal commitment to making the world a better place. The themes of his speeches drew heavily on "civil religion" by effectively blending references to God and other sacred symbols with patriotic values in attempts to create a sense of moral community.

The sanctification of Kennedy as an ideal man and the ideal president was frequently associated with collective memories of Lincoln. Each had been assassinated under conditions of crisis and social tension. In Lincoln's case, the Civil War had recently ended, and his assassination was linked with the thousands of soldiers who had sacrificed their lives on the field of battle. His assassination had provided a climax to the end of a bitter war in which mass armies had met on the field of battle and the casualties ran into the millions. The trauma of Lincoln's assassination added to the trauma of the war itself. The enormous task of rebuilding a divided nation remained unfinished. By elevating Lincoln to the status of a martyr, his assassination provided the world with a sanctified model of what a great leader ought to do in the quest for social justice and human rights.

Kennedy was assassinated at a time in which the intensity of the cold war was at its peak. Both the United States and the Soviet Union were building up their military arsenals for the annihilation of each other. Anxieties about a forthcoming nuclear holocaust loomed large. Communist insurgents were on the verge of taking over South Vietnam, and we were in the process of becoming involved. Internally, the United States was deeply divided over issues related to civil rights. Students participating in the voter registration of African Americans had been murdered, governors had defied federal laws on school desegregation, and images were still vivid of law enforcement officials using tear gas and turning police dogs loose on civil rights demonstrators. Levels of fear and tension were high about both what was happening in our own country and what was happening in the world at large.

Political Charisma

Kennedy's administration represented the first of the television presidencies. In the television debate with Richard Nixon, Kennedy came out the clear winner in terms of physical attractiveness. Imagery was beginning to replace substance; symbolic meaning was beginning to replace commitment to specific political issues. Impression management was becoming more evident in the selection of the symbolic leader of the nation. Kennedy was particularly adept in using the new media of communication. His sense of comfort with the press conference, his wit, and his physical attractiveness contributed greatly to the presidential imagery he evoked. Increasingly, the new form of communication was to draw upon the imagery surrounding both the personal life and the family life of the president.

The idealization of Kennedy's immediate family was well under way prior to the assassination. Jackie Kennedy was not only young and physically attractive, but also well educated, refined, and articulate. She brought a level of charm, glamour, and sophistication to her role in the White House that had been missing among the wives of previous presidents. The presence of two young and attractive children added to the image of the ideal man and the ideal family. Many Americans still remember the innocence of the salute of the honor guard by John John during Kennedy's funeral.

The experience of Americans with the assassination crisis precluded thinking about either Kennedy or the presidency exclusively in rational, political, or bureaucratic terms. Instead, the positive images many Americans had held of Kennedy prior to the assassination were elaborated and embellished. Americans came to experience his existence as a unique gift. Emphasis was placed on his intelligence, his good looks, his youth, his wealth, his family background, and his dedication to the American people. In effect, extraordinary qualities were imputed to him, and he was regarded as having sources of wisdom that are not attainable by ordinary mortals.

The personal charisma of Kennedy was well established among his followers prior to his election. The fondness for Kennedy was reflected in his physical closeness with people during his campaign. The large number of people reaching out to touch Kennedy seemed to have a magical quality about it. His enthusiasm and dedication appeared to be contagious, and many felt a sense of security in the prospects for his election as president. The agenda he proposed for the nation tapped into personal hopes and aspirations.

While Americans are frequently ambivalent about their political leaders, there is also an aura of charisma that tends to surround the office of the presidency. The White House is a sacred shrine to Americans, and its occupant symbolically represents the nation. The hopes and aspirations of the nation become vested in the office of the presidency. At the apex of authority, the president is seen as shaping the political agenda of the nation. He has it within his power to recommend and designate priorities in the allocation of national resources. He has the responsibility to serve as the custodian of collective interests in the decision-making process. During times of crisis, the charisma of the man and the charisma of the office provide the raw materials for the creation of a special gift.

Through charismatic identification, Kennedy was looked upon both as "one of us" and as "the best of us." He had a special appeal to the socially disadvantaged and the underprivileged. In contrast to Dwight Eisenhower, who had been seen as a part of "the establishment," Kennedy was seen as a leader from the periphery—a man of wealth and influence who had identified with the underprivileged and defined their problems as his problems. During his presidential campaign in West Virginia, he had visited the coalfields and poverty-stricken areas to listen to the people and to propose solutions to their problems. His leadership style was forceful, and he welcomed the challenge of finding solutions to difficult problems. The people of West Virginia responded to his charm, wit, and insight by giving him a decisive victory in the presidential primary. A state, whose population was 95 percent non-Catholic, clearly demonstrated that a Catholic could be elected as president of the United States.

The assassination was collectively regarded as both a secular event and a sacred event. Some held that, while we cannot know God's will, the nation will become a better place. It was maintained that Kennedy died for what he believed in and as a result we must listen to what he had to say. His death was regarded as his last and his most important act. Some predicted a political and religious awakening in this country as a result of his death. Some college students made a vow to become better informed about political events and to become more highly committed to public service and political action.

The presidential assassination also precipitated a series of judgments about the extraordinary forms of evil that are present within our culture and how our society fails to measure up to its own standards of morality. Some reflected on the pervasiveness of violence in our society and noted that the president had been killed by a gun that Oswald had bought via mail-order. Attention was directed toward "the culture of violence," including the observations that there is a laxity of control over access to guns and ammunition, that violence is one of the more popular themes in mass entertainment, and that the United States has the highest homicide rate of any country in the industrialized world. It was further observed that American history is in large measure a history of violence. Our history has included the forceful transportation of people from Africa to support the institution of slavery. The settlement of our nation has included the systematic annihilation of American Indians and the confiscation of their tribal lands. We have been a warlike people and prone to use force to have our own way. These background sentiments were reflected in the comment of a college student on the day following Kennedy's funeral: "Any love of country I may have had is replaced by a desire to leave this madhouse and become a hermit. Today I am not proud to be an American."

Others noted how American citizens had been denied their basic rights; for example, individuals had been pulled off lunch counters and kicked in the face only because of their race. The injustices that were implicit in the epic struggles of the civil rights movement were brought to the forefront of reflections on society. Memories were still vivid of segregated rest rooms, lunch counters, swimming pools, schools, and buses. Many Americans were being denied their basic constitutional rights because of the color of their skin. Opportunities for African Americans to participate in the political and economic life of the nation were seriously limited. How could we promote the ideals of democracy and freedom on a worldwide basis if we do not practice these ideals at home?

While people were responding to the uniqueness of the event, their responses were conditioned by the routine organization of their personal lives and what they saw as the qualities of people in general. Those who looked upon the assassination as an ephemeral event that would recede into the background as people returned to business as usual made comments such as the following: "It will have little lasting effect on the nation"; "We are a resilient people that have the capacity to solve whatever problems confront us"; "The sense of grief and mourning is a passing phenomenon within the broader framework of social continuity"; "Our political system is superorganic in the sense that it is stable one that is not dependent upon individual men and women"; and "Specific individuals come and go, but the system remains." Some sense of comfort was derived from the notion that, in the final analysis, it is the presidency rather than the specific president that really matters.

Who Killed JFK?

In the days and weeks following the funeral, attention shifted away from Kennedy's idealism and his political agenda to the circumstances of his assassination. Did Oswald act alone or were there also shots fired from the grassy knoll overlooking the motorcade? Was Oswald just the trigger man for some organized conspiracy? Was Lyndon Johnson implicated in some way? Was there political intrigue on the part of some organized group that condones the use of violence to achieve their ends? These are questions Americans raised upon hearing the initial news from Dallas. They were the same questions that were being raised over and over again for many years afterward.

The immediate task of Lyndon Johnson's administration was to move beyond the tragedy of the assassination and to get on with the business of government. Johnson's success in doing this, however, was limited. The assassination did occur in his home state of Texas, and it was known that his relationship with the Kennedys was something less than friendly. Some suspected that Kennedy intended to drop Johnson as his running mate in the next election. While there was never any evidence that Johnson had anything to do with the assassination, there remained the suspicion that if he were not involved he may have been engaged in a cover-up of what he did know. The issues of why and how Kennedy was assassinated remained unresolved.

By presidential order, the Warren Commission was created to investigate the circumstances and causes of Kennedy's death. It did not appear that separate investigations by the FBI, the State of Texas, congressional committees, or other agencies would be able to adequately resolve the many issues of responsibility that were likely to be involved. Suspicions still prevailed that Oswald may have been a sacrificial victim for either a domestic or a foreign conspiracy. The intent was to establish "a blue ribbon" panel of distinguished Americans who would conduct the investigation in a prompt, systematic, authoritative, and dignified manner. Johnson had assumed that the investigative report of such a distinguished panel would bring closure to the case and resolve any remaining doubts. Given the emotionality surrounding Kennedy's death, along with the fear and distrust of the Soviet Union, the consequences of any official evidence of communist involvement may have been disastrous. Pushing the buttons for launching a nuclear attack on targets within the Soviet Union was within the range of possibility. Hopefully, no evidence of a communist plot would be uncovered.

Those who accepted "the lone-gunman theory" tended to emphasize either social or psychological explanations of the motives of the assassin. Those who saw Oswald as "a social misfit" noted that he had been cheated in the marines, felt he was being persecuted, disliked Kennedy's policies, was discontented with our way of life, and took the president's life for personal vengeance. Such attributions of motives reflected the idea that some individuals have a rough time of finding a satisfactory place for themselves in the modern world. They feel that they have received a raw deal from life and tend to strike back by becoming violent. Oswald's incredible act of violence was thus seen as growing out of the accumulated frustrations of being required to play roles for which his capabilities and interests were limited.

Psychological explanations of Oswald's motives involved several variations on the notion that "he must have been crazy." Here the focus was not on social relationships and social pressures but on the mental state of the assassin. Oswald was described as "a madman," "a crackpot," "a psychotic," "mentally ill," "deranged," "perverted," "muddled up," "irrational," "disturbed," and similar variations. The act was comprehensible only if Oswald was crazy, and many hoped that this was indeed the case. Some who drew on the mental derangement explanation believed that we should administer psychological tests to everyone in order to identify potential killers. Others felt that it clearly demonstrated the need for setting up community psychiatric centers to provide help for those in need of it.

Comparisons were made between Oswald and other known political assassins in America's past. For example, it was noted that the men who killed presidents James Garfield and William McKinley were also lonely, isolated individuals who were drifters without any clear sense of purpose in life. Their excessive personal ambitions had been combined with an intense sense of failure and feelings of self-doubt. Killing the president of the United States, or some other prominent public figure, became a way of being somebody, having a name that people will recognize, achieving a place in history and thus achieving immortality. Notoriety, in whatever form, is then a type of status attainment that is sought through initiating violent acts toward those in positions of power and authority.

While the report of the Warren Commission provided "an official closure" to the case, the issue of who killed JFK failed to go away. The motivations for the assassination remained sufficiently obscure to generate widespread discussion for many years to come. The simple notion that a single individual, acting alone, had killed the president was insufficient for many people who became emotionally involved with the event. The simple explanation did not mesh very well with the complexity of the emotional responses. Something seemed to be missing. The need had been generated to know more about the event than was in fact knowable.

Hundreds of books and magazine articles were written, and are still being written, to offer alternative explanations to the official government investigation. Although there were twenty-six volumes of testimony and exhibits that accompanied the Warren report*, claims were made that the commission had arrived at its conclusions hastily and had failed to take into account all of the relevant information that was available. The basic conclusion of the Warren Commission that Oswald had killed the president was seen as inadequate, incomplete, and possibly a cover-up. Such a response implied a basic distrust of public officials and the political process.

The arguments for alternatives to the Warren report were often based on the assumption that it is important to set the story straight for the historical

---

*The official title is *Report of the President's Commission on the Assassination of President Kennedy*. In practice, however, the references is frequently shortened to "the Warren report" or to the "Warren Commission Report."

record. Accordingly, plausibility arguments were structured in such a fashion as to have the appearance of being believable. Filling in the gaps in the news media coverage and in the Warren report became a widespread preoccupation. The number of bullets fired, the time interval of the firings, where the bullets came from, and the number of people involved received close scrutiny. There were also questions raised about the adequacy of the forensic conduct of the autopsy. The speeches of Kennedy were combed for clues on his agenda for the nation and the policies he planned to implement. The question of who killed Kennedy was being transformed into the question of who would have liked to see Kennedy dead.

One of the conspiracy theories held that a combination of J. Edgar Hoover, the FBI, and the Mafia were implicated. Allegedly, Hoover had known that a Mafia contract had been issued on the life of President Kennedy and had done nothing about it. The security forces that were assigned to protect the president in Dallas had been surprisingly lax. It was generally known that there was animosity between Hoover and the Kennedys. Hoover had used the resources of the FBI to amass personal files on top political leaders and was in a position to use these files as a form of blackmail. Kennedy resented the capacity of the director of the FBI to intimidate the president of the United States and was seriously considering what could be done about it. While there was no evidence of Hoover's direct involvement in the assassination plot, it was believed that he deliberately had decided not to act on the information available to him.

Kennedy's speech at American University received a great deal of attention from those who were looking for motives and evidence in support of a conspiracy. In this address, he announced an agreement with the Soviet Union on a ban on nuclear testing in the atmosphere. Kennedy observed that both the United States and the Soviet Union "hold a mutually deep interest in a just and genuine peace and in halting the arms race." Kennedy went on to say, "For, in the final analysis, our most basic common link is that we all inhabit this small planet. We all breathe the same air. We all cherish our children's future. And we are all mortal." Through having made these comments, it was argued, he was setting a political agenda for the nation. He planned to negotiate a settlement to the cold war, to put a stop to the arms race, and to normalize relationships with the Soviet Union and with Cuba.

In constructing conspiracy theories, it was argued that there were vested interests in the cold war among the military, among business corporations, and among secret agencies within the government. The profitability of many corporations was highly dependent on defense contracts and some of the employees of the CIA would stand to lose if Kennedy's plans for reducing the tensions of the cold war were implemented. Evidence was presented to support plausibility arguments that Kennedy's assassination was plotted by either the CIA or by corporate America. Such arguments were constructed primarily around "motives" for the assassination rather than a concrete demonstration that a plot had occurred.

A variation on the above argument held that the assassination resulted from a conspiratorial plot within the CIA: A group of fanatics in the CIA had been working with Cuban refugees in planning an assassination of Castro and an overthrow of the communist regime in Cuba. Some of the Cuban refugees had participated in the unsuccessful Bay of Pigs invasion and had formed a coalition with a right-wing segment of the CIA. There had been disappointments with Kennedy's failure to follow up the Bay of Pigs invasion with a military assault force. There was also disappointment that Kennedy had negotiated a settlement of the Cuban Missile Crisis with Khruschev, rather than following through with an invasion of Cuba. Kennedy was seen as having turned soft on communism and thus constituted a threat to the free world. The same people who were planning an assassination of Castro turned their attention toward assassinating President Kennedy instead. In this scenario, Oswald was seen as playing only a very small part in either planning or executing the assassination plot.

Conspiracy theorists frequently invited the public to serve as a "jury" to weigh the evidence being presented. In the courtroom metaphor, conspiracy theorists were playing the role of prosecutor. However, the analogy breaks down in an important respect. There was no judge to invoke "the rule of irrelevance." In courtroom proceedings, the judge occupies a central place through his or her authority to decide what is admissible as evidence, to determine what information does or does not have a bearing on the specific case. In the absence of judicial restraint, conspiracy theorists had no limits on the claims that could be made. Some maintained that Kennedy's body was secretly altered in the flight to Washington to disguise the wounds made by a second gunman. Others claimed that Kennedy's body was not in the coffin buried at Arlington, that Kennedy was still alive, although brain dead and kept in protective custody by the Kennedy family.

Concerns for the mystery of Kennedy's death seemed to build upon its own momentum. Whether the interest grew out of a genuine quest for more information or whether it primarily had an entertainment value is a debatable point. Certainly the sadness over the president's death and the loss of a major political leader does not lend itself to indifference. Yet, there seemed to be a macabre quality to the sustained interest in the assassination accounts. Some accounts appeared to be "with tongue in cheek," so to speak, and overladen with the cynicism of a sick joke. Despite pleas to the contrary, the case remained open and surrounded with increasing ambiguity. In the years following the assassination, a diminishing percentage of Americans accepted the basic conclusion of the Warren Commission as valid.

Remembering Kennedy

In remembering Kennedy, the national trauma of his death tends to overshadow his image as a man or the accomplishments of his presidency. Other presidents are remembered on their date of birth. Kennedy is remembered on the date of his death. Remembering Kennedy takes a variety of forms. Assassination buffs hold conventions to read papers and to elaborate on the conditions and explanations of his death. The proposition that "truth will win out in the long run" seems to energize this group. Tourists to Dallas frequently include a visit to the assassination site on their travel agenda. And on November 22 of each year, crowds still converge on "the grassy knoll" and the area surrounding the Texas School Book Depository.

On the anniversary of his death, Kennedy is remembered in television programs, in additional books being published on the Kennedy legacy, and in national news magazines publishing special commemorative issues. The photographs frequently reproduced in these commemorative publications have a vivid place in the memories of Americans. These include photographs of Kennedy walking along the beach, playing football with this brothers at Hyannis Port, and playing with his children. Other well-known photographs include Kennedy in his rocking chair or the empty rocking chair following his death, the picture of Jackie Kennedy taking off her ring and kissing his casket, the military-like salute of the honor guard by John John, the dignitaries marching in the funeral procession, the sad and stoic faces of members of the Kennedy family, and the eternal flame at Arlington Cemetery. Approximately 4 million people make a pilgrimage to his grave each year. Gazing upon the eternal flame, they sometimes offer prayers and listen to tapes of his speeches. The caretakers at Arlington still receive letters addressed to Kennedy in care of the cemetery. The letters frequently express admiration for the president and ask favors of him.

Following his death, there was a widespread interest in preserving and perpetuating the memory of Kennedy. His portrait was implanted on commemorative stamps and coins; the space center at Cape Canaveral was renamed the Kennedy Space Center; the national center for the performing arts was named in his honor; streets, bridges, highways, schools, and libraries were named or renamed to commemorate Kennedy. He had become a valued resource in the nation's memories.

The full scope of Kennedy images, however, was to be shaped by the cultural milieu of the decades that were to follow. The 1960s and the 1970s were not favorable times for heroes. Debunking the great men of the past became a favorite pastime. Traditional patterns of thought were being turned upside down. For example, Abraham Lincoln was now being portrayed less as a powerful leader than as a victim of psychiatric disorders. The criminals Bonnie and Clyde were now being elevated to heroic proportions through cinematic portrayals of their epic robbery of banks during the Great Depression. While Kennedy symbolized the best of us for some, to others his death had revealed that he was a mere mortal, just like the rest of us. In an age of suspicion and distrust, a great deal of attention was directed toward the mortal man in back of the public facade.

Within this context, the Kennedy image became tarnished. Some claimed that he was not the World War II hero he was made out to be; that he may not have actually written the book that won him a Pulitzer Prize; that he did not write his own speeches; that he had insatiable sexual urges; that he cheated on Jackie, even while he occupied the White House; that both he and his brother Bobby had affairs with Marilyn Monroe and may have been implicated in her death; that he was ruthless and an opportunist; and that the success of his political career was a splendid example of impression management. Very few people in recent times have had their personal life exposed to such a high level of public scrutiny.

The extraordinary response of Americans to the images of Kennedy were commensurate with the extraordinary responses to his death. The collective sadness over the slaying of the president had temporarily bound the nation together in a moral community. It was both an intensely integrative experience and an intensely disorganizing experience. Keeping alive the Kennedy memory is meaningful to some and met with cynical indifference by others. Cynics find the recurring attention to Kennedy to be disgusting: "The man is dead, and nothing can be done about that. Whatever happened in Dallas on that fateful day may never be known or knowable, and it really doesn't matter. The time has come to close the case." Others regard Kennedy as the model of a man to emulate. They continue to be intrigued with the mystery of his death and continue to ponder the question of how the world would have been different had he lived.

Bibliography

Bellah, Robert N. 1975. "Civil Religion in America." In *Life Styles Diversity in American Society,* ed. Saul D. Feldman and Gerald W. Thielbar, pp. 16–33. Boston: Little, Brown.
Belin, David W. 1973. *November 22, 1963: You Are the Jury.* New York: Quadrangle.
Brown, Thomas. 1988. *JFK: History of an Image.* Bloomington: Indiana University Press.
Buchanan, Thomas C. 1964. *Who Killed Kennedy?* New York: Putnam.

Canfield, Michael, and Alan J. Weberman. 1975. *Coup d'Etat in America: The CIA and the Assassination of John F. Kennedy.* New York: Third Press.

Epstein, Edward J. 1966. *Inquest: The Warren Commission and the Establishment of Truth.* New York: Bantam.

Evica, George Michael. 1978. *And We Are All Mortal.* West Hartford, CT: University of Hartford Press.

Farlie, Henry. 1973. *The Kennedy Promise: The Politics of Expectation.* Garden City, NY: Doubleday.

Garrison, Jim. 1988. *On the Trail of the Assassins.* New York: Sheridan Square Press.

Greenberg, Bradley, and Edwin Parker, eds. 1965. *The Kennedy Assassination and the American Public.* Stanford: Stanford University Press.

Grunwald, Lisa. 1991. "Why We Still Care." *Life* (December): 34–46.

Halberstam, David. 1972. *The Best and the Brightest.* New York: Random House.

Josten, Joachim. 1964. *Oswald: Assassin or Fall Guy?* New York: Marzani and Munsell.

Kantor, Seth. 1978. *Who Was Jack Ruby?* New York: Everest House.

Katz, Jack. 1975. "Essences as Moral Identities: Verifiability and Responsibility in Imputations of Deviance and Charisma." *American Journal of Sociology* 80: 1369–1390.

Kunhardt, Philip B., Jr. 1988. *Life in Camelot: The Kennedy Years.* New York: Time.

Lammonde, Paris. 1969. *The Kennedy Conspiracy: An Uncommissioned Report on the Jim Garrison Investigation.* New York: Meredith Press.

Lane, Mark. 1966. *Rush to Judgment.* New York: Holt, Rinehart, and Winston.

Life, Anniversary Special, Winter, 1988. *John F. Kennedy Memorial Edition.*

Lifton, Robert J. 1968. "On Death and Death Symbolism." In *The Self in Social Interaction,* ed. Chad Gordon and Kenneth J. Gergen, pp. 251–258. New York: John Wiley.

Manchester, William. 1967. *The Death of a President: November 20–25, 1963.* New York: Harper and Row.

Martin, Ralph G. 1983. *A Hero for Our Time: An Intimate Story of the Kennedy Years.* New York: Macmillan.

Posner, Gerald. 1993. *Case Closed: Lee Harvey Oswald and the Assassination of JFK.* New York: Random House.

Reeves, Thomas C. 1991. *A Question of Character: A Life of John F. Kennedy.* New York: Free Press.

Salinger, Pierre. 1966. *With Kennedy.* Garden City, NY: Doubleday.

Schlesinger, Arthur M. 1971. *A Thousand Days: John F. Kennedy in the White House.* New York: Fawcett.

Schuyler, Michael. 1985. "The Bitter Harvest: Lyndon B. Johnson and the Assassination of John F. Kennedy." *Journal of American Culture* 8: 101–109.

Scott, Peter Dale, Paul L. Hock, and Russell Stetler, eds. 1976. *The Assassinations: Dallas and Beyond.* New York: Vintage Books.

Shils, Edward A. 1965. "Charisma, Order, and Status." *American Sociological Review* 30: 199–213.

Sorensen, Theodore C. 1969. *The Kennedy Legacy.* New York: Macmillan.

Summers, Anthony. 1980. *Conspiracy.* New York: McGraw-Hill.

Thompson, Josiah. 1967. *Six Seconds in Dallas: A Microstudy of the Kennedy Assassination.* New York: Bernard Geis Associates.

United Press International and *American Heritage Magazine.* 1964. *Four Days: The Historical Record of the Death of President Kennedy.*

Warren Commission Report. 1964. *Report of the President's Commission on the Assassination of President John F. Kennedy.* Washington, DC: U.S. Government Printing Office.

Zelizer, Barbie. 1992. *Covering the Body: The Kennedy Assassination, the Media, and the Shaping of Collective Memory.* Chicago: University of Chicago Press.

8 • The Vietnam War

The Vietnam War stands beside the Civil War as one of the longer and more enduring traumas in the nation's history. The trauma of Vietnam had no clear and dramatic beginning, as with the Japanese attack on Pearl Harbor or the Confederate firing on Fort Sumter. There was no single precipitating event; there was no formal declaration of war; and there was no "police action" under the auspices of the United Nations, as there had been in Korea. Instead, the national trauma grew out of an evolving set of conditions that resulted in outcomes that no one intended or really wanted. The cumulative effects of a series of political decisions, each of which seemed reasonable to those who made them, resulted in tragic consequences of epic proportions.

A metaphor for the justification behind our military involvement in Vietnam was provided in a speech delivered by President Dwight Eisenhower on April 7, 1954. In his speech, Eisenhower compared the countries of Southeast Asia to "a row of dominoes." He warned that if Indo-China fell to the communists, the rest of the countries of Southeast Asia would "go over very quickly." Our political leadership had been called into question by the success of communist revolutions in China and Cuba. In Eisenhower's view, we should take a firm stand to prevent the spread of communism to any other country. Through accepting Eisenhower's argument, "the domino" metaphor served as a guiding principle in shaping our foreign policy and provided a justification for our subsequent military involvement in Vietnam.

On August 2, 1961, President Kennedy announced that he was sending several thousand troops to Vietnam as "advisers." The idea was that American military expertise could be drawn upon to suppress communist insurgency in South Vietnam. Kennedy asserted that our troops would be armed and authorized to fire on the enemy. Without a formal declaration of war, we were becoming involved in a military encounter that would have traumatic consequences for both the Vietnamese and the American people. The growing resistance of the Viet Cong resulted in a gradual escalation of the number of troops sent to Vietnam.

Conduct of the War

From a military standpoint, it appeared that the war in Vietnam would be easy to win. It was assumed that because the enemy did not have helicopters, tanks, planes, armed personnel carriers, and other sophisticated weapons of war, they would soon be defeated. The lessons from history pointed toward the conclusion that a technologically advanced war machine could quickly defeat an unsophisticated and primitive one.

The military paradox of Vietnam was that, although we had the sophisticated military technology to win World War III, we did not know how to effectively fight a land-based, guerrilla-type war against a peasant people in the rice paddies and jungles of Southeast Asia. Previous wars were fought primarily by the rules of European warfare, where there were clear battle lines. The good guys were on one side, the bad guys were on the other, and there was "no-man's-land" in between them. Under these conditions military superiority in firepower and manpower could determine the outcome. War had come to basically mean the meeting of mass armies on the field of battle. The military manuals were written disproportionately on the tactics and strategies for fighting a conventional war.

The war in Vietnam was different. There were no clearly defined battle lines, and the enemy could not be clearly identified. Those who engaged in routine activities during the day became warriors at night. A great deal of the fighting was hit-and-run: Strike a military target, blow up an ammunition dump, ambush an infantry patrol, and then vanish into the jungle or the night. The enemy forces comprised not only military personnel but also old men, women, and children who wore no uniforms.

Demonstrating technological superiority first required finding the enemy, and in Vietnam that was difficult. The Viet Cong were dispersed throughout the countryside and were hard to locate. A great deal of the ground action consisted of infantry patrols on "search-and-destroy" missions. The idea was that the patrols could be used to locate the enemy, draw their fire, withdraw, and then send in the bombers and big artillery to finish the job. The idea appeared to be a good one in theory, but failed to work in practice. The Viet Cong were the ones to decide on the time and the place for the military encounter. In combat situations, about 80 percent of the initial fire came from the enemy. They would strike ferociously and then disappear. Hundreds of tunnels had been constructed to shield the Viet Cong and their supplies.

It was decided to use chemical defoliants on jungle areas to make it easier to spot the Viet Cong and military targets. Hundreds of tons of dioxin Agent Orange were dropped on the vegetation in Vietnam. This also turned out to be a strategy that did not work. The destruction of foliage simply made it easier for the Viet Cong to spot infantry patrols sooner and at a greater distance. The health hazards to our troops of exposure to toxic chemicals was denied for a long period of time. It was only long after the war that official recognition was given to health consequences of prolonged exposure to Agent Orange.

Following the Tonkin Gulf Resolution, the air force carried out intense bombing raids on the cities and military installations of North Vietnam. The idea was that the enemy would become demoralized as a result of the vast devastation that could be inflicted upon them. The effects of the bombing raids, however, turned out to be the reverse of what was intended. The bombing raids had a unifying effect on the North Vietnamese people and intensified their determination to continue the war. It was believed in the Pentagon that if we could demonstrate technological superiority, the enemy would recognize that they could not win and would be willing to negotiate a conclusion to the war. Such an assumption turned out to be in error.

The trauma of Vietnam intensified as deep divisions surfaced within the nation over our foreign policy, over perceptions of the immorality of the war, and over the frustration of being involved in a war we could not win. In Vietnam we had "a tiger by the tail," so to speak, and there seemed to be no reasonable way to let go. The frustration of Lyndon Johnson was reflected in his comments: "I can't get out. I can't finish with what I've got. So, what the hell am I going to do?" Johnson's paralysis over what to do mirrored the collective frustration and confusion of the entire nation.

The war dragged on to last several times longer than any previous war in American history. Over the years, several fact-finding groups were sent from Washington to Vietnam to assess the situation and to make recommendations on what was needed to win the war. Repeatedly, the expert opinion from our political and military leadership pointed toward the same conclusion: Send more troops, send more supplies, send more sophisticated military equipment. Acting on these recommendations, the military force in Vietnam grew to enormous proportions, yet we were getting no closer to a decisive victory. By 1969, the United States military personnel in Vietnam had escalated to 541,000 soldiers and marines and nearly 200,000 additional servicemen stationed at air bases within striking distance of military targets in Vietnam. Before the war was over, several million men and women had been on assignment to Vietnam.

As our commitment of personnel and equipment to the war increased, more was needed in the way of accountability. As a gauge of how well we were doing, an emphasis was placed on "the body count" of the enemy dead. The requirement to produce enemy casualties added to the brutality of the war. Both combatants and noncombatants came to be included in the reported number of enemy killed. In operational terms, anyone killed by an American soldier was by definition "an enemy." The number of rounds of ammunition used, the number of bombs dropped, and the number of artillery rounds fired all became measures of the progress we were making militarily. A wide gap was developing between the illusions and the realities of the war. In the absence of clearly identified military targets, bombs, artillery, and ammunition were being used indiscriminately. The civilians in Vietnam constituted a disproportionate number of the casualties of war.

Veterans in Vietnam

There were several features of the war that promoted intense levels of trauma for the men who fought in it. In the absence of clearly defined battle lines, it was difficult to distinguish between Vietnamese civilians and military combatants. The military units comprising the enemy forces were to a very large degree invisible. The problem of not being able to identify the enemy was compounded by generalized feelings of alienation and estrangement from the civilian population in Vietnam. Their culture was not understood, and in any given case, the boundaries between friends and enemies were not clearly defined. Some soldiers came to view all Vietnamese as the enemy. In effect, physical proximity and closeness to other people was accompanied by an intense sense of psychological distance and apartness.

The Vietnam War was disproportionately fought by adolescents. The average age of the American soldier in Vietnam was only 19.1 years, whereas the average age of the soldiers in World War II was 26.5 years. Many had never been away from their homes and families before and lacked adult maturity and judgment. The orderly progression of events in early adulthood had not occurred. A large percentage of them had only a high school education or less, had not yet had time to develop stable relationships with members of the opposite sex, and were unable to emotionally balance and deal with the seeming purposelessness of the war. Some were driven by a hatred of the enemy and by negative perceptions of the Vietnamese people. Killing was experienced by some as excitement that provided an outlet for rage and survivor guilt.

In addition to the selection of the very young for combat assignments, there was also selectivity in terms of race and social class. For example, blacks were significantly overrepresented among those who were drafted into the army, were assigned to Vietnam, served in combat units, and were fatalities in the war. The armed forces placed special emphasis on recruiting racial minorities, in part on the assumption that military service provided a major opportunity for the integration of the underprivileged into the mainstream of American society. But more importantly, the recruitment efforts were directed toward those least prepared to resist the authority of the state in the mobilization of manpower for the war machine.

Most previous wars had permitted a sense of camaraderie to develop among "army buddies." The process of confronting a common enemy and sharing the dangers of exposure to enemy fire typically had a cohesive effect on military units. For example, during World War II the cooperative actions in the pursuit of a joint enterprise resulted in cohesive bonds among the members of military units. However, in Vietnam individuals were sent in as replacements and were thrown in with strangers with whom there had been no shared experiences or ongoing relationships. As a result, the replacements were sent on combat assignments without the opportunity to develop a sense of mutual support with those who had been in their units for a longer period of time. The war became a highly individualized experience.

Levels of conflict among the men in military units ran high. The new replacements encountered practices that were in conflict with their sense of morality and proper conduct in human relationships. Fights frequently broke out among the men, and intense levels of hatred developed. They encountered lizards, snakes, insects, and other animals of a type they had never seen before. The weather was hot, humid, and uncomfortable. They found themselves in dangerous situations that they did not understand. The trauma of the combat assignment was well reflected by the comment of one of the more experienced combat veterans in the movie *Platoon*: "If you are going to get killed in Vietnam, you are lucky if it happens in the first few weeks. That way, you don't have to suffer so much."

In Vietnam the conflicts between the leaders and followers were intense. In the absence of any clear set of military objectives, conduct in the field became problematic. The assigned mission frequently lacked a clear set of instructions and did not make sense to the men who were expected to carry it out. For example, heavy casualties occurred in an assault on a hill occupied by the Viet Cong; subsequently, however, the hill was abandoned because it lacked strategic significance. Such procedures seemed senseless to the men involved. If the hill had no military value, why were the commanders willing to sacrifice so many men in its conquest? Serious doubts were raised about the competence of officers who sheltered themselves from the risks they exposed others to and who gave improper and malevolent orders. In comparison with other wars, the practice of "fragging" was common in Vietnam. Fragging is a practice by which a disliked officer is killed in such a fashion that his death would appear to have resulted from enemy action. As one Vietnam veteran stated the matter: "We did not fight the enemy. We fought ourselves. The enemy was within ourselves."

In addition to the conflicts within units, there was also a sense of entrapment in continuing a war that had no end in sight. The war resembled imprisonment, in that there was no means of escape. The enemy lies ahead, and there is no avenue of withdrawal or retreat. The combat veterans used the acronym REMFs (Rear Echelon Mother Fuckers) to vent their sense of despair. The REMFs included the support personnel on cushy assignments in Vietnam, the military command that extended all the way to the Pentagon, and the politicians in Washington who promoted the continuance of a senseless war. It was generally believed that those in positions of political authority could have stopped the war had they chosen to do so. Instead, the REMFs were indifferent and uncaring about the suffering of combat veterans. The victims of war had become pawns in a game that others were playing.

An article that appeared in the *New York Times* in November 1969 described a massacre that had occurred at the village of My Lai. The newsworthy event reported that under the command of Lieutenant William Calley Jr., a platoon had rounded up all the old men, women, and children in the village of My Lai and shot them. The news was accompanied by responses of shock and disbelief for many Americans. For others, the news came as no surprise. Information had been readily available on American atrocities in Vietnam and the brutal treatment of Vietnamese civilians. The event became highly symbolic of our involvement in Vietnam and provided a mirror by which we could see ourselves and what we were doing. It provided a sufficiently close analogy to the atrocities of Nazi Germany that many Americans were seriously disturbed.

In the subsequent trial and conviction of Calley, he did not deny what had happened at My Lai. He admitted to giving the orders and being immediately responsible for the massacre. However, his defense rested on the claim that he had done "what any good soldier would do," which was to carry out the orders he had received from the higher command. The court martial tribunal found Calley guilty of misconduct and ruled that even in time of war the individual soldier has a moral responsibility to disobey an order if it is improperly given. Thus, responsibility was being placed on individual soldiers, rather than on the broader military system. Many Americans believed that Calley was being used as a scapegoat.

The trauma of Vietnam was increasing in intensity as Americans were becoming aware of the subterfuge and cover-up of military strategies in the conduct of the war. Many suspected that the massacre of noncombatants at My Lai, and at other villages we never heard about, had been authorized by the higher military command. Terrorist tactics had been employed by the Viet Cong, and if we did not use similar tactics, our capacity for winning the war would be limited. We were becoming increasingly frustrated by the stalemate of the war and the lack of any clear evidence of military victory; our objectives were becoming increasingly confused. Whatever idealism we may have had in the initial pursuit of the war was now being called into question.

As it became apparent that we were making little headway toward winning the war, the decision was made to de-escalate our involvement. Opposition to the war was growing both within the general public and among members of Congress. Rather than a further increase of our involvement, there was a gradual reduction of the number of American troops in Vietnam. The American withdrawal was accompanied by a futile attempt to turn the actual fighting of the war over to the South Vietnamese, while we continued to supply military equipment. As the Americans reduced their commitment to the war, the activity of the Viet Cong intensified.

Following a negotiated release of prisoners of war, the last of the American forces were withdrawn from South Vietnam. By this time, the Viet Cong had amassed a large military force for an assault on the city of Saigon. Many Americans still remember the television coverage of the chaos surrounding the evacuation of Saigon by the Americans and the conquest of the city by the communist forces. While a "settlement" of the war had been negotiated, it was clear to Americans that it was a major war we had lost. The Vietnamese who had aligned themselves with the Americans in the war were now being treated as "collaborators" or as "traitors." A sense of despair resulted, and the American evacuation of Saigon was resented.

Following the end of the war, many American families continued to agonize over the 2,266 servicemen who were missing in action. Uncertainty persisted over whether all of the Americans held as prisoners of war had been released or not. Whether those missing in action or held as prisoners of war were alive or dead could not be determined. Uncertainty prevented families from going through the usual type of mourning that permits individuals to cope with the crisis of death and to get on with the business of living. The Pentagon in the late 1970s declared all missing servicemen dead, assuming that this declaration was a humane way of achieving closure on the issue. Yet, reports continued to come out of Southeast Asia on the sighting of Americans who were being held against their will. The inability to achieve definitive closure on the issue resulted in an intense mixture of hope and despair for the families involved. No suitable form of psychological relief from the crisis was available.

Opposition to the War

The Vietnam War was traumatic, not only for those who fought in it but also for those who were strongly opposed to it. There was never any formal declaration of war. The official justification for our involvement was that of coming to the aid of a small country that was in the process of being overrun by communist forces. The vast majority of elected officials supported our foreign policy and our increased involvement in Vietnam. The voices of those opposed to the war fell on deaf ears. Secret government files were kept on the backgrounds and activities of those opposed to the war. Critics of government policy were seen as subversives and as being disloyal to the United States.

The initial critique of the war grew out of a lack of confidence in our political leadership. We had failed to learn from the French experience in Indo-China. It was believed that our political leaders were unable to distinguish adequately between nationalistic movements and movements that were set in motion by an international communist conspiracy. Out of a concern with the spread of communism, we had rejected our own revolutionary past at a time in which movements of liberation from the tyranny of colonialism were emerging in third-world countries. The American Declaration of Independence had clearly laid out the conditions under which a revolution is both necessary and justified. The books distributed by the U.S. Information Agency had excluded materials on our own revolutionary past. As a result, the leaders in third-world countries who wanted to know "how to make a revolution" could not readily find such a book from an American source. Through a rejection of our own revolutionary past, the United States failed to provide an adequate model for many third-world countries to follow. Only the revolutionary rhetoric of Marxism–Leninism remained viable and available. In our national policy, we were assuming that political stability on a worldwide basis was in the best interest of the United States. Such an assumption led to our support of corrupt and tyrannical governments.

Our involvement in Vietnam had become a topic of heated debate by the time of the presidential election of 1964. The conservatives gained control of the Republican Convention and nominated Barry Goldwater for the presidency. Goldwater's campaign reflected the view that we should vigorously pursue our military objectives in Vietnam. In the nation at large, the battle lines were being drawn between "the hawks" and "the doves." The hawks wanted to step up our military operations in Vietnam, while the doves wanted to reduce our military involvement or get out altogether. Goldwater's campaign emphasized taking a direct and forceful approach to winning the war in Vietnam. While Goldwater was defeated in the election, the approach he advocated was subsequently adopted by the Johnson administration.

The major opposition to American involvement in Vietnam originated on college campuses and among the students of the counter-culture generation. The opposition was based largely on a condemnation of the war on moral grounds. Many college students came to believe that the United States was intervening in what was seen as a civil war, was supporting a corrupt and unpopular government, and was using sophisticated military technology against a peasant population in a third-world country. Large-scale demonstrations against the war surfaced at the University of Michigan, the Berkeley campus of the University of California, the University of Wisconsin, and colleges and universities throughout the country. "Teach-ins" were held as a way of arousing opposition to our conduct of the war, marches and demonstrations were staged in major cities and college towns throughout the country, petitions were sent to representatives in Congress, and a series of radical publications emerged to question the legitimacy of public authorities and the militaristic emphasis in American life. The trauma of America's involvement in Vietnam was reflected in the caption on the cover of *Ramparts* magazine in April 1969, which read, "Alienation is when your country is at war and you want the other side to win."

The veterans of World War II were appalled at news reports of American youth burning their draft cards and burning the American flag. Their generation had not questioned the legitimacy of the requirement to serve in the armed forces during times of war. When college students were no longer deferred from military service, several American youth expressed their disenchantment by crossing the border into Canada and renouncing their citizenship. It was not that the students were unwilling to make a personal sacrifice for their country, but instead they perceived it an absurdity to risk making the ultimate sacrifice for a cause they believed to be unjust. Renouncing one's citizenship and going to live permanently in another country is not a step that most Americans are able to take lightly.

Many of the draft-age males who avoided military service were able to do so not because they had moral concerns about the war but because they could take advantage of the system. Very few students at private schools such as Harvard, Yale, or Princeton were among those conscripted into military service. Accepting the terms of compulsory military service was frequently regarded as stupid. Finding the loopholes was defined as the smart thing to do. The families of privileged youth were influential in obtaining deferments and exemptions. They knew how to draw upon legal technicalities and how to select noncombat military alternatives. Requests for exemption on the grounds of being a conscientious objector were frequently denied. Being a conscientious objector to "a specific war" was not regarded as a legitimate ground for avoiding military service.

The nation had become highly polarized by the time of the Democratic Convention in Chicago in 1968. Thousands of protesters from all over the country converged on Chicago to register their opposition to the war. Upon instructions from Mayor Richard J. Daley, the Chicago police were determined to maintain order in the city. On a hot summer night, widespread conflict broke out between the protesters and the police, who used tear gas and clubs in their assaults on the demonstrators. A subsequent presidential commission investigating the violence surrounding the Democratic Convention concluded that "the police had rioted." The nation watched the brutal confrontation on television and were appalled at what they saw.

Opposition to the war mounted in intensity as the scope of the war was extended. Following President Lyndon Johnson's announcement that bombing raids would be conducted against North Vietnam, active opposition to the war increased. Some saw the loss of civilian lives from the bombing raids as a further reflection of the immorality of the war. The opposition to the war reached a peak in early May 1970 with President Nixon's announcement of American plans for conducting bombing raids on Cambodia. The concentration of Viet Cong forces in Cambodia permitted them to strike American targets and then withdraw rapidly to the safety of a "neutral" country. Those opposed to the war regarded the announcement as a statement of intent to broaden the war in Southeast Asia rather than to contain it. Following the announcement, demonstrations erupted on college campuses throughout the country.

At Kent State University in Ohio, students protesting the war had burned down a World War II Quonset hut that housed the ROTC unit on campus. When the demonstrations spilled over into the town of Kent, the Ohio National Guard was called in to restore and maintain order. The National Guard unit was armed, and in response to the tense situation started firing indiscriminately into the students on campus. Four students were killed, and several others were wounded. As the news spread, campuses were disrupted throughout the country. Many colleges and universities were required to suspend normal operations for several days.

The episode at Kent State University became one of the symbolic events of a turbulent decade. It became a symbolic event not only because of its immediate impact on college campuses, but also because of the focus it provided for the issues of war and peace, for the crisis of authority in modern social life, and for the rights of freedom of speech and dissent in an open society. Many of the colleges and universities in the United States became disrupted through student demonstrations and protest. On campuses, the responses were not only to the moral issues of the war, but also to the actions of the police and the National Guard on college campuses. Many of those who opposed the war saw the actions of the Ohio National Guard as a form of criminal conduct. The resources of the state were drawn upon to deny individuals their constitutional rights.

The casualties of the war mounted and the purpose of the war became increasingly unclear. In November 1969 approximately 250,000 protesters marched on Washington, D.C. It was one of the largest demonstrations in the nation's history. The protesters favored immediate withdrawal of American troops from Vietnam. One of the dramatic features of the demonstration involved the veterans who had returned from the war. Several who had been wounded in Vietnam participated in the parades and demonstrations by walking on their crutches or riding in wheel chairs. Some who were decorated for valor in Vietnam took off their medals and threw them over the barrier that had been erected to protect the nation's capital. The veterans were symbolically returning their medals to the leaders of the country that had honored them.

Subsequent opposition to the war in Vietnam was based less on the issues raised by demonstrators and protesters than on a recognition that we were not winning the war. The escalation of military efforts turned out to be unsuccessful, and since the war could not be won easily by stepping up military operations, many people arrived at the conclusion that we should find a way to get out. Many Americans remembered the moving line across Europe as the allies launched their assault on the forces of Nazi Germany. The closer the battle line came to Berlin, the closer we were to winning the war. There were no comparable gauges for assessing how well we were doing in Vietnam. The military had drawn upon the body count as a measure of our progress, but within the general public it was becoming increasingly evident that we were getting no closer to winning the war.

Post-Traumatic Stress Syndrome

The tragedy of the war continued for a long period of time after the war was over. The veterans returned to an ungrateful nation. We had lost the war, and there were deep divisions within the society over whether or not we should have been there in the first place. Americans had grown weary of seeing death and misery each night in the television news broadcasts. Most Americans just wanted the war to end and to forget about it. Many of the returning veterans who had actively participated in the war, however, could not forget about it.

The returning warriors were victimized both by their tragic experiences in Vietnam and by the responses to them of an ungrateful nation. The trauma of the war continued in recurrent nightmares, in the resurgence of intense feelings of sadness, and in an enduring sense of numbness. Psychologically, the veterans were still fighting the Viet Cong and dodging land mines. The veterans were also victimized by returning home to an unsupportive nation and such negative stereotypes as "ruthless baby-killer," "drug addict," and "having fought in an immoral war." There was a lack of appreciation both by the general public and the American government. Nationally, we wanted to put the trauma of the war behind us and get on with the business of restoring normality.

The homecoming for the Vietnam veteran was a highly atomistic event. There were no community ceremonies or rituals, there were no parades or marching bands, there were no cheering crowds, there were no tears of joy, there were no yellow ribbons tied around the trees. The returning veterans were treated casually by others in the community, as if they had been away on vacation. They were expected to behave as if nothing had happened. The nation did not want to be reminded of our disastrous defeat in Vietnam.

The ending of all wars requires some degree of "ritualistic purification" of the returning veteran. The normal guidelines for morality, decency, and humanity become suspended in the war enterprise. Because of what is required in war, the soldier necessarily becomes a changed person. Enduring effects on the individual result from facing death through receiving fire from the enemy, killing someone, seeing someone wounded, or observing gruesome enemy tactics. Such extraordinary experiences fall outside the boundaries of normal life and must be dealt with in some way or another. At the end of World War II, the victory celebrations helped "to purify" the men who had been required to kill other human beings. There were no such communal forms of purification for the veterans returning from Vietnam.

The veterans returning from Vietnam found themselves disproportionately among the unemployed and the underemployed. Many of them had never been in the labor force prior to military service and did not have a job to return to. The skills developed in the service, particularly among combat veterans, lacked transferability to civilian jobs. To a very large degree, they were ignored by their government and stigmatized by potential employers. A former helicopter pilot was requested by a potential employer to take off his coat to see if there was evidence of needle marks from taking drugs; a nurse who served in a medical combat unit in Vietnam was assigned to emptying bedpans in a civilian hospital. Thus, self-fulfilling prophecies about their personal qualifications tended to work against them.

There were no special government provisions for helping veterans find a place for themselves in the civilian labor force.

Many of the veterans returned to their home towns torn and confused about their participation in the war. Uncertainties persisted about what we were doing there and why we did not win. The stress of having participated in the war was expressed in a variety of physical and psychological symptoms. Veterans developed sleep disturbances, including difficulties in getting to sleep, in early morning waking, and in some cases the problem of sleeping too much. Sleep was frequently disrupted by recurrent nightmares in which the veterans saw themselves dodging land mines and booby traps, encountering ambushes, witnessing their buddies die, or witnessing or participating in atrocities. Thus, the war did not end for many of the veterans with their return to civilian life. The problems remained of reconstructing their experiences and their self-identities.

Many of the returning veterans had difficulty in "forgetting" unwanted memories. These included the indelible effects of exploding mortar rounds, which resulted in the tendency in civilian life to overreact to sudden and loud noises; recurring visions of comrades cutting ears off of enemy corpses as trophies of war; and the pungent odors of decaying corpses in the hot jungles of Vietnam. The memories were also vivid of the blunders of war: comrades were killed by "friendly fire," tanks ran over infantrymen, helicopters accidentally crashed, and marines shot other marines by mistake. These and many other types of accidents are the inevitable consequences of arming large numbers of young men with the lethal and complicated weapons of war.

The returning veterans were faced with difficulties in sharing their war experiences with others. They found themselves in physical proximity to others while psychologically feeling that they were far away. Conversations became strained for both those doing the talking and those doing the listening. Many experiences were too painful to talk about, and family members and former friends did not know how to relate to the returning warrior. Either too much or too little was being read into the messages received from each other. The war experiences had been too disconnected from any shared set of social norms or values to permit effective communication. The veterans became psychologically isolated and thrown back on their own fragile resources at the very time they were in need of social support.

The post-traumatic stress syndrome included persistent feelings of sadness or "emptiness," an inability to derive pleasure from everyday activities, difficulty in concentrating or making decisions, feelings of guilt and worthlessness, eating disorders, thoughts of suicide, and chronic aches and pains that did not respond to treatment. The war veterans were disproportionately represented among alcoholics, hospital patients, the divorced, and prison inmates.

The very conditions that had facilitated psychological adjustment to a combat situation interfered with effective reentry into civilian life. For example, coping with the trauma of war is facilitated by what psychiatrists call the process of "psychological numbing." Neutralizing one's emotional responses to the trauma of war serves as a protective mechanism that provides a buffer against being incapacitated by the unfolding of events. While one cannot control the occurrence of gruesome events, one can control one's responses to them through developing a sense of emotional neutrality. But once in civilian life, the process of psychological numbing had lost its usefulness.

Many of the veterans returning from Vietnam had difficulty in forming and sustaining intimate relationships with family members, old friends, and members of the opposite sex. To a very large degree, the difficulties grew out of the loss of a capacity for emotional expressiveness. The basic training in the army and the marine corps required them to extinguish expressions of emotion. Emotionality was seen as a feminine characteristic that had no place in the macho world of the military. As one platoon sergeant put it, "Sentiment is a word in the dictionary somewhere between shit and suicide." Later, in combat situations, emotional attachments to others in one's unit were dysfunctional to the adjustment process. Developing attitudes of emotional neutrality became a protective mechanism by which individual soldiers could develop immunity to the potentially devastating effects of war and destruction.

Feeling guilty about being alive was a frequent response on the part of soldiers who survived combat. Some degree of survivor guilt surfaces in questions such as "Why do some men continue to live while others are killed?" and "Why him and not me?" The guilt grows out of the chaos of war. There appears to be a certain amount of randomness to the casualties of war. Stepping on a land mine or being killed in a fire fight is, to a large degree, a chance occurrence. Who lives and who dies fails to follow any discernible pattern of divine justice or any set of notions about what is right or wrong in human affairs.

In previous wars, concerns for the symptoms of traumatic stress were directed primarily toward the performance of the soldier in a combat situation. Some saw psychiatric disorders as growing out of a lack of discipline, a weak character, inadequate military socialization, or being a coward. Others regarded disorders of the mind as stemming from the physiological effects of war on the human body. In World War I, the term "shell shock" was employed on the assumption that traumatic stress was caused by high air pressure from exploding shells that had affected the brain or caused physical damage to the nervous system. During World War II, the label was changed to "war neurosis" or "combat fatigue." These terms were used to label all psychological disturbances in combat soldiers. Treatment was oriented toward returning soldiers to their units. Very little attention was directed toward the psychological problems of veterans once the war was over.

The war in Vietnam was different. The symptoms of traumatic stress persisted and were widespread for veterans who had returned to the United States. The reported number of psychiatric disorders was greater after the war than during it. Prolonged exposure to feelings of entrapment and danger had enduring consequences. While the veterans of all wars are faced with the problem of integrating their war experiences into their overall life designs, the veterans of Vietnam confronted a special set of difficulties. They had confronted events that were outside the usual range of human experiences as well as outside the usual American experiences with war. They found it difficult to set their mind at ease and to find their place within the normal scheme of everyday life.

The Vietnam Veterans Memorial

The nation wanted to forget about the war, as they had with the Korean conflict, but the men and women who served and their families could not. Some degree of closure to the trauma of Vietnam was needed. Such closure in previous wars had been achieved through raising monuments to celebrate the victories that had been won, to idealize the bravery and heroism of those who served, and to promote the themes of personal sacrifice and moral community. The ending of the Vietnam War was different. We had no major victories to celebrate. We had made a major national commitment to a war that was controversial and morally questionable, to a war we had lost. In the conduct of the war, we had no major accomplishment to celebrate.

Some form of redemption was needed to provide relief for a traumatized nation. There had been deep divisions over the conduct of the war, but there were no disagreements in expressions of sympathy for those who had responded to the call for duty and had died. Some form of recognition was needed for the supreme sacrifices that individuals had made on the fields of battle. Some men and women had voluntarily served out of a sense of duty; others had been coerced into servicing the personnel needs of the war machine. Whatever the case, it was clear that hundreds of thousands had innocently carried out the policies of their elected leaders.

With the dedication of the Vietnam Veterans Memorial in 1982, the nation was finally provided with a form of commemoration to facilitate reflections on the meaning of the war. The memorial itself was designed to be silent and politically neutral on the controversial issues of the war. The responses of those who came were highly emotional and far from being personally subdued or politically neutral. At an emotional moment in the dedication ceremony, the bitter voice of a veteran cried out "What were we fighting for?" No attempt was made to give a satisfactory answer to his question.

The memorial is located on a two-acre plot on the edge of the National Mall and is artistically in alignment with both the Lincoln Memorial and the Washington Monument. The symbolic structure comprises a V-shaped wall with the names engraved in granite of the 53,000 Americans who died in the war. The wall slopes downwardly into the ground, symbolizing death, in contrast to the upward thrust of the other memorials in Washington. The memorial is not a celebration of military victories, heroism, a noble cause, or political idealism. Instead, the symbolism is focused on the grimness and the suffering associated with the casualties of war. Listing the names chronologically by the time of death, rather than alphabetically, intensifies the emotional drama of the wall. Finding a specific name necessarily requires personal effort and evokes an awareness of the thousands of Americans who also made a sacrifice.

Despite the initial criticism of the memorial as "a degrading ditch," "an open urinal," "a gash of shame," or "a wailing wall," it was soon to become a sacred place. No one could have anticipated the emotional impact the wall would have on the millions of visitors who come each year. In the first year alone, approximately two and a half million Americans made a pilgrimage to the wall. Hundreds of thousands came to look for the name of a loved one, a family member, a friend, or an army buddy. The large numbers who came included both those who had actively participated in or supported the war as well as those who had opposed it. They all came and they all wept.

Visitors to the Vietnam Veterans Memorial see their own reflections in the black granite wall. The wall not only reveals the names of the casualties of the war, but also provides a mirrored image of what is taking place among those viewing the wall. Such effects do not lend themselves to indifference. In seeing ourselves in the reflections on the wall, the anger, the hostility, and the ambivalence about the war surface in a therapeutic fashion. Rather than blocking out memories of the war, they are temporarily brought to the surface in a gentle, reflective way. The commemoration thus provides a mechanism for Americans to reflect on the sacrifices that were made through our involvement in a chaotic and meaningless war. It also permits the Vietnam generation to reflect on what they were doing during the war and the part they personally had to play.

Bibliography

Brende, Joel O., and Erwin Parson. 1985. *Vietnam Veterans: The Road to Recovery.* New York: Plenum.

Bryan, C.D.B. 1976. *Friendly Fire.* New York: Putnam.

Caputo, Philip. 1977. *A Rumor of War.* New York: Ballantine Books.

Card, Josefina J. 1983. *Lives After Vietnam.* Lexington, MA: D.C. Heath.

Edelman, Bernard, ed. 1985. *Dear America: Letters Home from Vietnam.* New York: W.W. Norton.

Fiddick, Thomas. 1989. "Beyond the Domino Theory: The Vietnam War and Metaphors of Sport." *Journal of American Culture* 12: 79–88.

Gibson, James William. 1988. *The Perfect War: The War We Couldn't Lose and How We Did.* New York: Vintage Books.

Gitlin, Todd. 1980. *The Whole World Is Watching.* Berkeley: University of California Press.

Hendlin, Herbert, and Ann Pollinger Haas. 1984. *Wounds of War: The Psychological Aftermath of Combat in Vietnam.* New York: Basic Books.

Hendrix, Charles C., and Lisa M. Anneli. 1993. "Impact of Vietnam War Service on Veterans' Perception of Family Life." *Family Relations* 42: 87–92.

Hess, Gary R. 1990. *Vietnam and the United States: Origins and Legacy of War.* Boston: Twayne.

Horowitz, Mardi J., and George F. Solomon. 1975. "A Prediction of Delayed Stress Response Syndromes in Vietnam Veterans." *Journal of Social Issues* 31: 67–80.

Howell-Koehler, Nancy, ed. 1984. *Vietnam: The Battle Comes Home.* New York: Morgan and Morgan.

Karnow, Stanley. 1983. *Vietnam: A History.* New York: Viking Press.

Keegan, John. 1976. *The Face of Battle.* New York: Viking Press.

Kelly, William E., ed. 1985. *Post-Traumatic Stress Disorder and the War Veteran Patient.* New York: Brunner/Mazel.

Kelman, Herbert C., and Lee H. Lawrence. 1972. "Assessment of Responsibility in the Case of Lt. Calley." *Journal of Social Issues* 28, no. 1: 177–212.

Kovic, Ron. 1976. *Born on the Fourth of July.* New York: McGraw-Hill.

Laufer, Robert S., M.S. Gallops, and Ellen Frey-Wouters. 1984. "War Stress and Trauma: The Vietnam Veteran Experience." *Journal of Health and Social Behavior* 25: 65–84.

Lawson, Jacqueline E. 1989. "She's a Pretty Woman . . . for a Gook: The Misogyny of the Vietnam War." *Journal of American Culture* 12: 55–66.

Lewis, Jerry M. 1971. "The Telling of Kent State." *Social Problems* 19: 267–278.

Lifton, Robert J. 1973. *Home from the War.* New York: Simon and Schuster.

Lipset, Seymour Martin, and Philip G. Altback, eds. 1969. *Students in Revolt.* Boston: Beacon Press.

Lipset, Seymour Martin, and Sheldon S. Wolin, eds. 1965. *The Berkeley Student Revolt: Facts and Interpretation.* Garden City, NY: Anchor Books.

MacPherson, Myra. 1985. *Long Time Passing: Vietnam and the Haunted Generation.* New York: Signet.

McNamara, Robert S. 1995. *In Retrospect: The Tragedy and Lessons of Vietnam.* New York: Times Books.

Moskos, Charles C., Jr. 1975. "The American Combat Soldier in Vietnam." *Journal of Social Issues* 31, no. 4: 25–38.

Ochberg, Frank M., ed. 1988. *Post Traumatic Therapy and Victims of Violence.* New York: Brunner/Mazel.

Scott, Grant F. 1990. "Meditations in Black: The Vietnam Veterans Memorial." *Journal of American Culture* 13: 37–40.

Scruggs, Jan C., and Joel L. Swerdlow. 1985. *To Heal a Nation: The Vietnam Veterans Memorial.* New York: Harper and Row.

Shay, Jonathan. 1994. *Achilles in Vietnam: Combat Trauma and the Undoing of Character.* New York: Atheneum.

Sonnenberg, Stephen, Arthur S. Blank Jr., and John A. Talbot. 1985. *The Trauma of War: Stress and Recovery in Vietnam Veterans.* Washington, DC: American Psychiatric Press.

Wagner-Pacifici, Robin, and Barry Schwartz. 1991. "The Vietnam Veterans Memorial: Commemorating a Difficult Past." *American Journal of Sociology* 97: 376–420.

9 • The Assassination of Martin Luther King Jr.

On April 4, 1968, the nation was shocked by the news that Martin Luther King Jr. had been shot by a sniper while he stood talking on the balcony of a motel in Memphis, Tennessee. He died shortly afterward in St. Joseph's Hospital from a wound in the neck. He was only thirty-nine years of age at the time of his death. King had been in Memphis to lend his support to a strike by sanitation workers. As the symbolic leader of the civil rights movement, he had delivered hundreds of speeches and sermons in the quest for social justice. He had succeeded in transforming the politics of social change into a religious responsibility. The trauma of his assassination brought into sharp focus the epic struggle of the quest for racial equality. He had mobilized a large constituency to address the question of how to bring about an end to the blatant forms of racial discrimination in our society. King had taken a direct-action approach by staging large demonstrations and working within the courts and legislatures to bring about changes that had long been needed.

On the eve of his assassination, King delivered his speech, "I Have Seen the Promised Land." This speech, as with several previous ones, contained clear references to a premonition of his own death. He observed: "The nation is sick. Trouble is in the land. Confusion is all around." While noting the desirability of living a long life, he observed, "I am not concerned about that now. . . . I have been to the mountain top," and, "I have seen the promised land." After saying, "I may not get there with you," he noted that as a people, "we will get to the promised land." Moral and spiritual convictions were combined with a strong belief that history would eventually correct the injustices implicit in the maltreatment of American citizens of African descent.

Americans were disturbed as they reflected on the issues of racial justice that had been ignored or glossed over in everyday life. In effect, the civil rights movement held up a mirror through which Americans were able to see themselves, and many did not like what they saw. They saw the ugliness of racial discrimination, and they saw police violence directed toward peaceful demonstrators. What they saw was shocking and incredible. The moral foundation of society was turned upon itself.

As a result of the controversy over civil rights, there were mixed reactions to King's assassination. Black militants saw his murder as a vindication of their view that the strategies of nonviolence were limited in their effectiveness. The assassination was simply another case of the violence directed toward blacks by the white majority. Many whites saw his murder as simply a reflection of the violence that had surrounded King. While he used the rhetoric of nonviolent resistance, the civil rights movement was perceived by some as a violent confrontation between the adversaries involved. In this view, King was seen as having provoked violence and thus it was no surprise that his life had ended in a violent death.

The majority of Americans, however, were shocked and saddened by the death of an American who had received the Nobel Peace Prize for his contribution to human rights and social justice. The assassination of King occurred only a little more than four years after the assassination of President John F. Kennedy. The moral conscience of the nation was brought under examination as Americans reflected on the violence that seemed to be endemic to American life. Comparisons were made between Kennedy and King. Both were seen as martyrs with strong convictions, with idealistic visions for the future of the country, and with personal commitments to the cause of social justice. It became noteworthy and symbolic that King's assassination took place on Good Friday, a day recognized as a day of death for another great religious leader.

James Earl Ray was later captured and convicted of King's murder. As with the Warren Commission report on Kennedy's assassination, serious doubts continued to surface for years afterward about the credibility of the official closure of the case. It was noted, for example, that the personal profile of Ray failed to follow the psychological profile of the political assassin, that he had no personal convictions that had a bearing on the civil rights movement, and that much more was involved than had been publicly revealed. Serious questions were raised about whoever else may have been implicated.

Over the years, the suspicion developed that the FBI may have been involved in the assassination. The size of the FBI file on King was larger than the file for any other single individual. J. Edgar Hoover's preoccupation with the communist menace had led to the belief that the social disruptions surrounding the civil rights movement were communist inspired. While no convincing link with communism was ever made, the belief persisted that the struggle over civil rights was a stigma that the United States could not afford because it reduced our effectiveness in winning the neutral countries of the world to our side in the cold war. Any challenge to the status quo came to be broadly defined as unpatriotic and thus a threat to American national security. The climate of the cold war did not favor examining the contradictions that were inherent in the American system.

Intense feelings of sadness and anger surfaced within the black community. The assassination was seen as bearing a close resemblance to the violent, repressive measures that were deeply embedded in patterns of racial discrimination and exclusion. The anger became sufficiently intense that widespread rioting and looting occurred in metropolitan areas throughout the country. Urban areas became volatile powder kegs as pent-up frustrations were expressed through violent and aggressive outlets. The oppressed were no longer able to endure what they perceived as an unjust system.

The assassination of King marked the end of the civil rights movement. Under his leadership, the strategies of nonviolent resistance had resulted in legislative and judicial action to end the more glaring forms of racial discrimination in the public spheres of our society. The enactment of the Civil Rights Bill guaranteed blacks their civil liberties, and all agencies of the government were directed to put an end to discriminatory practices. King had demonstrated that the development of a strong and cohesive organization for the protection of minority rights can make a difference. King's symbolic leadership in an epic struggle provides a major reference point for Americans to reflect on issues of social justice and political action.

A Fragmented Society

The militancy of the civil rights movement forced Americans to recognize that the United States was a fragmented society. The forms of oppression, exploitation, and physical abuse had produced routine conditions of fear and anger among African Americans. The unwillingness of blacks to further endure the humiliations that had been imposed upon them produced an acute crisis for those committed to upholding the status quo. The nation became traumatized by having to confront its own internal contradictions.

Segregated schools, buses, lunch counters, swimming pools, rest rooms, and drinking fountains were among the many aspects of public life that restricted the freedom of movement of black Americans. Discrimination in voter registration, housing, college admissions, and employment were among the aspects of public life by which blacks were relegated to an inferior status. All of these practices reflected deep-seated racism in American life and contradicted the ideology held by those in positions of power and influence that "America is a land of equal opportunity for all."

In mobilizing a constituency, King drew heavily upon two major documents in the heritage of the nation: the Constitution and the Declaration of Independence. These were central ingredients in shaping the national identity of Americans. King describes these documents as "promissory notes" that guaranteed "the inalienable right to life, liberty, and the pursuit of happiness" for all. In one of his speeches, King declared that America had defaulted on her promissory note to her citizens of color. The words of Jefferson that "we hold these truths to be self-evident, that all men are created equal" was taken seriously and regarded as justifying a call to action.

Within American culture, the notion of social justice holds that rules and standards must be applied impartially to all social groups. The notion of impartiality embraces the principles that equals are to be treated equally and that like cases are to be treated in a like manner. To Americans the overriding rule for specifying equivalency is based on the concept of citizenship. Here the system of justice emphasizes that certain rights and privileges are to be applied universally to those accorded the status of citizen. Equivalency in the rights of citizenship was based on the notion that individual differences by sex, religion, property, and national origin are irrelevant for determining the rights of access to various parts of the social system.

It was the Montgomery Bus Boycott that thrust King into a position of national prominence. On December 1, 1955, Ms. Rosa Parks was ordered by a bus driver to relinquish her seat to a white man. Rosa Parks had spent a hard day at work and was tired. Attempts of the bus driver to intimidate her were unsuccessful and she was arrested. The arrest became a focused event that tapped into the resentments over the preferential treatment of whites and the requirement that blacks sit only in the back seats of buses. Few practices evoked such bitter resentments among blacks as the humiliation of legally sanctioned segregation in public transportation. Jim Crow trains, buses, and streetcars served as a grim reminder to blacks of their inferior status.

The arrest, imprisonment, and conviction of Rosa Parks resulted in meetings of the Montgomery Improvement Association to plan a line of action within the black community. Rather than a compliant acceptance of racial injustice, the decision was made to seek remedial action through a bus boycott. The local chapter of the NAACP selected King to provide leadership for the organized protest.

King was only twenty-six years old at the time and was more a privileged than a deprived member of the African American community. He was selected on the basis of his moral commitments, his education, his intelligence, and his speaking ability. As is often the case, leadership of movements among the oppressed comes from the privileged members of society who identify with the plight of the underprivileged. King's motives were not oriented so much toward promoting self-interests as toward expressing moral indignation over the lack of justice within the social system. His style of commitment derived from a sense of obligation to act on the basis of an inner set of convictions without regard for the consequences of doing so.

King's oratory had an electrifying quality about it, not only because of the relevance of what he had to say but also because of his mode of delivery. Using a style of delivery that was prominent among black clergy, he made extensive use of the repetition of central themes and used a wide range of voice inflections to maximize the effect. While those opposed to King and the civil rights movement saw him as "a dangerous demagogue," his speeches symbolized the hopes and aspirations of his constituents.

The defiance of the Jim Crow laws in Montgomery provoked whites into using terrorist and repressive measures. King was arrested on a trumped-up speeding violation, and a bomb was exploded on the porch of his Montgomery home. The leaders of the bus boycott were charged with being parties to a conspiracy to prevent the operation of a business without "just or legal cause." Attempts were made to terminate car-pooling as an alternative to riding buses. Participants in the boycott were subjected to harassment, and in some cases they lost their jobs. The boycott ended with a decision by the Supreme Court that Alabama's state laws requiring racial segregation on buses was unconstitutional. Federal injunctions were issued to state officials as well as to city and bus company officials in Montgomery.

The conflict between local governments and federal authority was a central ingredient in the struggle for civil rights. A major confrontation occurred in Little Rock when the governor of Arkansas attempted to block nine black students from attending an all-white high school. In response to the defiance of federal authority, President Dwight Eisenhower federalized the Arkansas National Guard to enforce the Supreme Court order for school integration. When James Meredith attempted to enroll at the University of Mississippi, it was necessary for him to be escorted to campus by U.S. marshals. Governor George Wallace stood in the schoolhouse door to block the entrance of black students to the University of Alabama. Wallace removed himself only after President Kennedy federalized the Alabama National Guard to enforce the mandate for school integration. Measures for promoting a racial caste system in the South was in the process of crumbling. Local areas were using stop-gap measures to prop up a repressive and unjust system.

The violence and terror directed toward blacks by the Ku Klux Klan and White Citizens Councils were often ignored by local law enforcement officials. In cases where prosecution did occur, the penalties imposed were insignificant in view of the seriousness of the crimes that were committed. The justice controversy was further intensified through arguments for the rights of states and local communities to enact and enforce discriminatory legislation. In the struggle over civil rights, the issue of authority thus came to occupy center stage.

The chronic crises in the lives of the oppressed came to be seen as amenable to remedial action as "personal troubles" were turned into "public issues." Some attempted to avoid the public issues of injustice by arguing that the confrontations were prompted by "outside agitators" or by communists. Efforts were directed toward using the coercive powers of local law enforcement agencies to suppress the civil rights movement. The issues became sufficiently dramatic, however, that the entire nation watched the confrontations with a sense of alarm and dismay. Americans watched on television as police dogs, fire hoses, and other forms of police violence were directed toward peaceful demonstrators. The millions of television viewers constituted a type of judiciary as attention became focused on issues of racism and social justice. Few Americans were able to remain indifferent to what they were observing. The moral conscience of society was turned upon itself through the nonviolent tactics advocated by King.

The civil rights movement succeeded because it was able to involve the entire nation with issues of social justice. King's leadership was oriented toward building a biracial coalition. He argued that those committed to the principles of social justice can never be satisfied as long as "certain explicit inequalities" concerning African Americans continue to exist. In developing a biracial coalition, King succeeded in winning the support of northern liberals and tapped into the idealism of college students. Through the creation of the Southern Christian Leadership Conference, churches were used as forums for addressing issues of social justice in both the North and the South. King had succeeded in combining religious and spiritual values with a concern for practical politics.

The success of King in building a biracial coalition was evident in the number of people who participated in the civil rights march on Washington. On August 28, 1963, King addressed a crowd of over 200,000 that had come to Washington. Speaking in front of the Lincoln Memorial, King laid out his vision for America. In his "I Have a Dream" speech he emphasized the themes of civil religion. Christian values and spirituality became blended with the ideals of the Declaration of Independence, the Constitution, and the Emancipation Proclamation. He noted that the new militancy of the black community was linked with the destiny of the nation. "Storming the battlements of injustice" was seen as a necessary task for all Americans. He argued that the freedom of black Americans was inextricably linked to freedom for all Americans. He observed that his personal dream was "deeply rooted in the American dream" and that the values being promoted were the values central to the national identity of Americans. He noted, "Injustice anywhere is a threat to justice everywhere."

As the symbolic leader of the civil rights movement, King drew upon his readings in philosophy and on the world's religions. His fundamentalist religious background came to be tempered by his studies of liberal ideologies and the doctrine of the social gospel. All was directed toward serious reflections on the problems of social inequality and repression. It was his conviction that the direction of history was necessarily moving toward a more humane society. In the long run, the moral values of brotherhood would triumph over hatred and oppression.

The credibility of King's arguments were enhanced by his ability to recognize the uncertainty over the outcomes of political protest in any given case. His central theme was that conditions of racism in the South were intolerable. To achieve a sense of personal dignity and pride, it was an obligation to take decisive steps to create a sense of moral community. While organized protest may very well evoke a violent response from the oppressors, it was a risk that was necessary to take. It was clear to his followers that he was asking nothing more of them than he was willing to risk for himself. Imprisonment, death threats, the bombing of his home, and being stabbed were among the forms of intimidation and physical injury that he had personally confronted. A refusal to give in to a sense of fear and despair provided an inspiration for his followers and won a sympathetic response from neutral observers throughout the nation.

The notion that those individuals stigmatized by the color of their skin should be granted equal rights in the public sphere generated intense hostilities and resentments. Those holding positions of power and privilege were unwilling to give up voluntarily their special advantages, and this reluctance provided grounds for widespread confrontations. Bus boycotts, sit-in demonstrations, urban looting, and other forms of social protest were implicated in the quest for social justice on the part of those who believed that they were being treated unfairly. Court proceedings were drawn upon to document the illegality of discriminatory practices. If blacks gained the right to vote, the racial demagoguery that political leaders had previously drawn upon to promote their careers would no longer be a feasible option.

During the last years of his life, King concluded that the problems of racism were inseparable from the problems of poverty and the violence associated with the war in Vietnam. All were interrelated and, in King's view, equally wrong. The blockage of opportunities for social participation and restrictions on freedom of movement were among the class-related aspects of minority status. Racial minorities were disproportionately caught up in lifestyles of deprivation and poverty. King abhorred the institutional violence associated with the Vietnam War and saw minorities and the poor as disproportionately bearing the brunt of the tragedies involved. In his view, equating patriotism with militarism and war was both unwarranted and a dangerous tradition.

The success of public demonstrations in securing passage of civil rights legislation had suggested that pressure from the grass-roots level may be necessary for effectively addressing the problems of poverty and militarism in American life. These were problems that seriously affected all Americans at the lower socioeconomic levels, including whites as well as blacks. Some form of redress was seen as necessary for attenuating the exploitation of some segments of the population for the benefit of others. King had made plans for a "poor people's march" on Washington shortly before his assassination. King hoped the march would develop a recognition of the integrity of the individual personality and increase the opportunities for full participation in a moral community for all Americans, thus enriching American quality of life.

Strategies of Nonviolent Resistance

The goals of the civil rights movement had been clearly established by the early twentieth century. The major issues of disagreement centered around the tactics and strategies for bringing about social change. Earlier, it had been believed that the main avenue for achieving racial equality was through reducing the level of prejudice within the general population. A major breakthrough in the movement came with a recognition that overt discrimination represented the soft spot in the oppressive system. Something can be done about discrimination, while negative stereotypes may be held with impunity as long as they are not overtly expressed within the public sphere.

The significance of King lies to a very large degree in the tactics and strategies he advocated and refined in efforts to bring about social change. His contribution may be summarized around the notion of nonviolent resistance. Drawing upon the writings of Henry David Thoreau and the example set by Mahatma Gandhi in India, King argued for deliberately violating laws and social practices that were unjust and in violation of basic human rights. The injustices of the system could be demonstrated through disturbing the tranquillity of everyday life. Through an appeal to a higher level of morality, the movement underscored and highlighted the underlying defects of the social system. The vision of King's approach was that of full and equal participation of all citizens in the life of the nation.

The events surrounding the Montgomery Bus Boycott had generated a great deal of attention in India, the Soviet Union, and other nations of the world. The country that had been foremost in promoting a policy of human rights in the United Nations was now required to confront its own contradictions. Following an invitation from Prime Minister Jawaharlal Nehru, King spent a month in India talking to top government officials and others about the success of the techniques of passive resistance in toppling the British regime. What King found to be remarkable was the manner by which India had won her independence without bloodshed and without evoking the hostility of the British. Mahatma Gandhi had succeeded in transforming political conflicts into moral and spiritual issues for achieving his objectives.

In his appeal to the oppressed, King emphasized the importance of spiritual values and a demonstration of moral superiority. Warning African Americans about becoming distrustful of all white people, he stated, "The battlement of injustice must be carried forth by a bi-racial army." Rather than developing a hatred of the oppressors, they should be regarded with compassion. King offered his followers hope as an alternative to despair and self-pride as an alternative to the negative imagery provided by racial stereotypes. The central ingredients of the national identity shared by all citizens, black and white, were the ones that would prevail in the long run. A sense of self-authenticity could be achieved through the discipline of placing one's life on the line for a cause believed to be just.

King ran into difficulty in convincing his followers of the effectiveness of the technique of nonviolent resistance. He was arguing for principles that were alien to most Americans. Notions about reciprocity, getting even, retaliation were seen as normal and appropriate responses to one's enemies. The doctrine of "an eye for an eye" was more readily understood than the argument that one should develop a sense of sympathy and brotherhood toward one's oppressors. It is much easier to understand the ways in which rage and violence could grow out of exploitation, oppression, and disenchantment than to understand a doctrine calling for a sense of compassion. In King's view, the oppressed and the oppressors had become intricately linked in promoting an unjust system. A shared sense of connection to a moral community were the ingredients for achieving remedial action.

He succeeded in mobilizing a large following by convincing a large number of African Americans and the more privileged members of the white majority that it was possible to put an end to the system of oppression. The primary obstacles to mobilizing a black constituency grew not so much out of attitudes of apathy as out of patterns of conformity and fear. Becoming actively involved in social protest required modifications of the adaptive mechanisms by which adjustments had been made to a hostile environment. Individuals were well aware of the risks associated with challenges to the white establishment. Becoming an activist was viewed as placing at risk the personal safety of oneself and family members as well as risking the security of one's property and valuables.

In response to the nonviolent strategies employed by the civil rights movement, terrorist measures were used by both law enforcement officials and by members of the white majority who were committed to "keeping blacks in their place." Historically, lynching had been one of the major forms of terror directed toward black males. Self-appointed defenders of racial purity and the status quo had directed incredible forms of violence toward black citizens. The burning of crosses, beatings, stabbings, and other forms of physical abuse, torture, and property destruction had long been used as forms of terror for maintaining the caste system in race relations.

The forms of coercion employed by the Ku Klux Klan and White Citizens Councils had been tolerated and approved by law enforcement agencies. The insidious practices were accompanied by the endorsement and participation of the police themselves. The effectiveness of terror as a form of social control depended to a very large degree on its arbitrary character and its lack of predictability. No black male could rest assured of freedom from victimization from any minor infraction of the unwritten code. Being socialized into minority status included an awareness of color lines that were not to be crossed. As a result, blacks were required to endure in silence many forms of abuse and injustice.

Open confrontation took a particularly violent turn in the voter registration campaign at Selma, Alabama. In Selma, 99 percent of the registered voters were white, while blacks constituted more than half of the population. Literacy tests were used to systematically deny blacks the right to vote, regardless of level of education. Even blacks with a college education were judged to be illiterate by voter registrars. In contrast, the literacy tests were not used in determining the eligibility of whites for voting. When an organized group of blacks marched to the courthouse in Selma to demand the right to vote, they were blocked by law enforcement officials. The demonstrators met with police violence and were forcefully dispersed as television cameras recorded the event for all the world to see. Evidence of police brutality and an institutional system of oppression became apparent.

In response to the failure in Selma, a decision was made to conduct a fifty-mile march from Selma to Montgomery to call national attention to the discriminatory voting laws of Alabama. The nation watched with shock as the peaceful demonstrators were met with violent resistance from the sheriff's department and state police at the bridge leading out of Selma. The police waded into demonstrators with billy clubs, fixed bayonets, and tear gas. While the demonstrators were forcefully turned back and dispersed, plans for the march continued. Out of a sense of indignation over the conduct of the police, hundreds of sympathizers descended on Selma to participate in a continuation of the march. In response to pressures from Washington to provide police protection for the demonstrators, local officials maintained that public safety or protection could not be provided for criminals and agitators. President Kennedy then federalized the National Guard of Alabama to provide protection for the demonstrators in their march to Montgomery. The subsequent passage of the Voting Rights Act put an end to the discriminatory registration practices that had denied blacks the right to participate in the electoral process.

In the campaign to break segregation laws in public transportation, "freedom rides" through the South were organized. The laws prohibiting integration of public transportation were deliberately violated by whites riding in the back of buses and by blacks occupying the front seats. Angry crowds gathered and violence erupted as the freedom buses stopped along the way. The nation became indignant as they watched mob action being directed toward peaceful demonstrators while the police looked on passively. The violence of local citizens was regarded by white segregationist as reasonable and appropriate responses to what they defined as criminal conduct.

The tactics of lunch-counter sit-ins, swimming pool wade-ins, freedom rides, and voter registration campaigns were initiated to call public attention to discriminatory practices. Since each of these actions involved an attack on the existing social order, they became newsworthy events. The television news coverage of these events provided an authenticity to the issues that could not have been attained through other means of communication. Hearing or reading about an event does not have the emotional impact that is provided by the visual materials presented on television. The brutal beatings and the use of tear gas, fire hoses, and police dogs were institutional forms of terror that could not go unnoticed. People were psychologically called to pay attention and to serve as a "public judiciary" for making decisions on the issues in question. Reflective attitudes were generated, and the holders of power were required to examine their own moral conscience.

The civil rights movement called attention to the importance of the role of the police in civil disturbances. The excessive use of violence in attempts at law enforcement frequently had the reverse effect of what was intended. Rather than coercing people into compliance, the scope and intensity of the resolve to resist were increased among the disenchanted. Rather than serving as emblems of legitimate authority, the badge and the uniform became symbols of oppression and injustice. Local law enforcement officials in the South frequently confronted tasks for which they were unprepared. Neither their training nor their previous experiences had prepared them for large-scale confrontations over human rights and political conflicts. A lack of guidelines on police procedures was evident in dealing with the civil rights demonstrators. The primary responsibility in law enforcement came to be defined as the suppression of conflict. In this process, police brutality was reflected in the use of coercive procedures that did not align with societal notions about legitimate conduct.

The participants in organized social protests cannot alone solve the problems of social injustice. They must win sympathy and support for their cause through an appeal to the "mass judiciary" of newspaper readers and television viewers who sit in judgment on the issues in question. The participants in the civil rights movement ran the risk of being labeled as deviants, criminals, or troublemakers. It was also possible that they could win admiration by becoming champions of a heroic cause and by making personal sacrifices for the improvement of social conditions. The extent to which civil disturbances were regarded as legitimate social protest or as criminal conduct depended on the responses of numerous others and on the meaning they gave to these acts. Success or failure in the use of nonviolent resistance rested outside the hands of the participants themselves. The final outcomes resided with public opinion and with the responses of social control agencies.

The historical oppression of blacks and the brutality that had been directed toward them added to the credibility of their appeals. They were addressing grievances that seemed to require ameliorative action. Perceptions of the civil rights movement as legitimate social protest rested on perceptions that their cause was just, that a large number of people had participated, and that the demonstrators represented the basic sentiments of the black community. Moral appeals take on a greater degree of urgency if they are accompanied by threats and if some degree of fear can be generated in the oppressors.

Black-power militants, both within and outside the civil rights movement, became impatient and indignant with the meager results that were being achieved. King was seen as moving too slowly, and they rejected the doctrine of nonviolent resistance. The notion that blacks should remain passive when confronted with physical abuse was regarded as an absurdity. They became extremists, vocalizing hatred of whites and arguing for blacks "to take up the gun" for self-defense. The rhetoric used by the black-power advocates made King appear as a moderate and reasonable leader. Seeing King as a moderate, rather than an extremist, added to the credibility of his moral appeals.

As the level of protest escalated in the civil rights movement, the decision at the higher levels of power was whether to use coercive measures to reduce the level of turmoil or to recognize the claims of a need for a more just system. While segregationists favored using coercive measures to suppress dissent, most Americans recognized the legitimacy of the claim that remedial actions were necessary. When Lyndon Johnson presented his arguments to Congress for civil rights legislation, he ended his address with the words "We Shall Overcome," thus drawing upon the vocabulary of the civil rights movement. National opinion clearly supported ending segregation in the public spheres of life, but fell short in favoring full equality in the nonpublic spheres. The more blatant forms of discrimination had ended by the time of King's assassination, while deep-seated attitudes of racism continued to be held.

The Unfinished Journey

With the subsequent designation of King's birthday as a national holiday, formal recognition was given to the importance of social justice in the life of the nation. On the anniversary of his birth, the news media tap into collective memories by selectively reproducing his speeches and showing photographs of civil rights demonstrations and marches. In reflecting on the issue of race, a good deal of attention is directed toward King's question, "Where do we go from here?" An unfinished task is that of working out a satisfactory resolution to the racial and ethnic diversity of the nation in view of deep-seated resistance, among both minorities and the more privileged sectors of society, to a policy of full assimilation.

One prominent view during the 1940s and 1950s was that racial minorities would eventually become fully assimilated into American society. The assimilationists placed emphasis upon social justice and viewed racism as a carryover from the past that would eventually disappear. Assimilation had been the dominant pattern by which various immigrant groups gave up their separate identities and became blended into the general population. With the reduction of racial prejudice and discrimination, race was expected to decline in importance as a basis for social classification and self-identity.

In King's speech before the Lincoln Memorial, he observed, "I have a dream my four children will one day live in a nation where they will not be judged by the color of their skin but by the content of their character." This implied a hope that the dignity and integrity of individual personalities would be recognized without regard for race, ethnicity, or other social characteristics that are often used to separate people from each other. King's vision was based on the notion that we are all interrelated. The freedoms and opportunities of individuals are intertwined with the forces that bind the nation together into a sense of moral community.

King's vision of a "color-blind" society was challenged by the militancy that surfaced within the black community. Black-power militants argued that obtaining full integration into American life is not a realistic option for most blacks, since the white majority will not voluntarily give up their special privileges. Racism was seen as an integral part of American life with numerous advantages accruing to those who make up the white majority. In their view, the stresses derived from race relations will persist, and overt conflict will continue to emerge on a sporadic basis. As a result, it is important for blacks to develop a separate ethnic heritage and to view race relations as a contested struggle for desired resources.

While the separatist ideology of Stokely Carmichael, H. Rap Brown, Malcolm X, and other black-power advocates never received widespread support among African Americans, their emphasis on "black nationalism" or "black pride" did tap a responsive chord. The emergence of an emphasis on black culture among African Americans derived from the view that a great deal would be lost if blacks aimed for full assimilation into American life. The widespread appeal of Alex Haley's search for his roots and in the social heritage of Africa grew out of the recognition that a sense of history is important for developing self-awareness. Awareness of one's social heritage came to be recognized as an important ingredient for a self-identity. The growing interest in black culture and history constituted a basis for the development of self-pride, which stood in opposition to the racial stereotypes deeply embedded in folk beliefs and history.

With the emergence of African American associations during the late 1960s and early 1970s came an emphasis on black experiences and black culture. Becoming aware of the historical distinctiveness of black experiences and creating an authentic black subculture became important concerns. Black historians elicited recognition of heroic struggles under conditions of slavery and oppression and to the many contributions blacks have made to American life. Such positive elements in black culture form the basis for the emergence of ethnic consciousness among blacks and provide an alternative to the racial stereotypes historically reflected in the folk beliefs of the white majority.

While recognizing that ethnicity emphasizes the positive aspects of a subculture, the parallel emergence of the black-power movement constituted a more direct response to developments in the surrounding society. Black-power militants of the late 1960s advocated the use of force and coercion in dealing with whites and the existing power structure. They assumed that the full assimilation of blacks into the mainstream of American life was not likely to occur and that it was not desirable anyway. They rejected the idea of cultural unity and maintained that the interests of black and white Americans were incompatible. Rather than being viewed as a unified society, the United States came to be viewed as a system designed to represent the interests of those having the upper hand in the power equation. Black-power militants believed it was necessary for blacks to organize and to pursue their own self-interests within the framework of a multigroup society.

While many of the blatant forms of discrimination in the public sphere were ended by the civil rights movement, new and more subtle forms of racism have surfaced in American life. In several respects, the new forms of racism are more insidious because they lie beneath the surface and are seldom brought out into the open for examination. These include arguments that the government has done too much for blacks and minorities in recent years, that opening up job opportunities for minorities is a form of "reverse discrimination," that blacks are genetically inferior and therefore cannot be expected to compete effectively with whites in college performance, and that "truth" in public discourse is subordinated to "political correctness." So the list goes on. While overt behavior can generate a public response when it is offensive or illegal, the more subtle racial attitudes can be held with impunity because they are not directly visible and thus are not subject to public sanction.

A major unfinished task is that of working out a more satisfactory national policy on race and ethnicity. If attitudes of cynical indifference prevail in the public arena, there are likely to be numerous unwanted and unintended consequences. The societal costs will show up in a variety of ways, such as wasted talent, interpersonal violence, property crimes, drug abuse, and other forms of personal pathology. The sporadic occurrences of urban rioting and looting result in a fear of crime and a sense of vulnerability in the residents of urban areas.

The turmoil and rancorous conflicts over issues of ethnicity in other parts of the world serve as a grim reminder of what should be avoided. Whether a policy of assimilation or a policy of cultural pluralism will eventually prevail remains to be determined by the unfolding of historical events. In the meantime, the legacy of Martin Luther King Jr. serves as a valuable reference point for assessing the limitations and prospects of developing a national sense of moral community.

Bibliography

Banerji, Sanjukta. 1987. *Deferred Hopes: Blacks in Contemporary America.* New York: Advent Books.

Barbour, Floyd R. 1968. *The Black Power Revolt.* Boston: Porter Sargent.

Blumberg, Rhoda Lois. 1984. *Civil Rights: The 1960s Freedom Struggle.* Boston: Twayne.

Boxill, Bernard R. 1984. *Blacks and Social Justice.* Totowa, NJ: Rowman and Allanheld.

Branch, Taylor. 1988. *Parting the Waters: America in the King Years 1954–63.* New York: Simon and Schuster.

Cloward, Richard A., and Frances Fox Piven. 1975. *The Politics of Turmoil.* New York: Vintage Books.

Colaiaco, James A. 1993. *Martin Luther King, Jr.: Apostle of Militant Nonviolence.* New York: St. Martin's Press.

Downing, Frederick L. 1986. *To See the Promised Land.* Macon, GA: Mercer University Press.

Dudley, William, ed. 1991. *Racism in America: Opposing Viewpoints.* San Diego: Greenhaven Press.

Friedly, Michael, and David Gallen. 1993. *Martin Luther King Jr.: The FBI File.* New York: Carroll and Graf.

Ginsburg, Morris. 1965. *On Justice in Society.* Ithaca, NY: Cornell University Press.

Grier, William H., and Price M. Cobbs. 1969. *Black Rage.* New York: Bantam Books.

Hoskins, Lotte, ed. 1986. *"I Have a Dream": The Quotations of Martin Luther King, Jr.* New York: Grosset and Dunlap.

Jeffries, Vincent, Ralph H. Turner, and Richard T. Morris. 1971. "The Public Perceptions of the Watts Riot as Social Protest." *American Sociological Review* 36: 443–451.

Killian, Lewis M. 1968. *The Impossible Revolution? Black Power and the American Dream.* New York: Random House.

———. 1972. *"The Significance of Extremism in the Black Revolution."* Social Problems 20: 41–49.

Lerner, Melvin J. 1975. "The Justice Motive in Social Behavior." *Journal of Social Issues* 31: 1–20.

Metzger, L. Paul. 1971. "American Sociology and Black Assimilation: Conflicting Perspectives." *American Journal of Sociology* 76: 627–647.

Oates, Stephen B. 1994. *Let the Trumpet Sound: The Life of Martin Luther King, Jr.* New York: Harper Perennial.

Pepper, William F. 1995. *Orders to Kill: The Truth Behind the Murder of Martin Luther King.* New York: Carroll and Graf.

Pettigrew, Thomas F. 1971. *Racially Separate or Together.* New York: McGraw-Hill.

Powledge, Fred. 1991. *Free at Last? The Civil Rights Movement and the People Who Made It.* New York: Harper Perennial.

Silberman, Charles E. 1978. *Criminal Violence, Criminal Justice.* New York: Random House.

Sitkoff, Harvard. 1981. *The Struggle for Black Equality 1954–1980.* New York: Hill and Wang.

Spencer, Martin E. 1971. "Conflict and the Neutrals." *Sociological Quarterly* 14: 219–231.

Turner, Ralph H. 1969. "The Public Perception of Protest." *American Sociological Review* 34: 815–830.

Wilkinson, Doris Yvonne. 1970. "Tactics of Protest as Media: The Case of the Black Revolution." *Sociological Focus* 3: 13–22.

Wilson, William Julius. 1978. *The Declining Significance of Race.* Chicago: University of Chicago Press.

10 • The Watergate Affair

High crimes and misdemeanors, the obstruction of justice, and the abuse of power were among the charges brought against Richard Nixon during his second presidential administration. Most Americans followed the episodes surrounding the political scandal as though they were watching the unfolding of a detective fiction story or a morality play. The legacy of such presidents as Franklin Roosevelt, Harry Truman, Dwight Eisenhower, and John Kennedy had led to a great deal of respect, even reverence, for the president of the United States. The tale that unfolded seemed fictional, incredible, and unbelievable.

Criminality is usually associated with street crimes in the thinking of most Americans. The notion that the president of the United States was "a criminal" could not be readily comprehended by most Americans. Elements of both belief and disbelief blended in public perceptions. After all, Nixon's campaign had drawn upon the latent fears of Americans about potential criminal victimization through burglary, robbery, and other street crimes. The notion that the man who had waged a "law-and-order" campaign may himself be a criminal was shocking.

The Watergate affair was characterized by a gradual development and a slow beginning. Newspaper reports in June 1972, indicated that burglars had been caught breaking into the Democratic Headquarters that was located in the Watergate apartment–office complex in Washington, D.C. There was nothing unusually noteworthy about this. On a daily basis, newspapers are filled with such stories about minor offenses. Why anyone would want to break into the Democratic Headquarters and what they expected to accomplish were initially questions of only minor concern.

The term "Watergate," however, eventually entered into the American vocabulary as a synonym for scandal and political corruption among government officials. While Watergate, in and of itself, was only a limited affair, it subsequently became symbolic of a broader series of illegal activities. Before the scandal ran its course, such terms as "dirty tricks," "political espionage," "illegal wiretaps," "smoking guns," "stonewalling," "hanging tough," "cover-up," and "hit list" worked their way into everyday vocabularies. It was not the Watergate affair, in and of itself, that produced a national trauma, but the impeachment proceedings against and subsequent resignation of the president of the United States.

The Democrats had attempted to make the break-in a campaign issue, but were unsuccessful in doing so. Democratic presidential candidate George McGovern claimed that tapping phone conversations was a form of political espionage that undermined the democratic process and should not be tolerated. Such a claim, however, was not taken seriously by the voters. It appeared to be a desperate strategy on the part of a man who was far behind in the polls. On election day, McGovern carried only the state of Massachusetts and the District of Columbia.

The plot thickened during the subsequent trial and conviction of the men who had been caught in the burglary, when it was revealed that several of the men had served with the CIA and the FBI. The skills these men exhibited for engaging in criminal activities, such as unlawful entry and wiretapping, were not skills that had been learned casually or accidentally; they were as refined and elaborate as those of the men who engaged in the covert activities of our national security system. What were the motives of these men? Why did they do it? Who were they working for? Whose orders were being followed? In effect, suspicions developed that the Watergate break-in represented only the tip of an iceberg. Much more had to be involved.

The staff at the *Washington Post* recognized that there was an important story that needed to be told. Accordingly, two reporters, Bob Woodward and Carl Bernstein, were assigned to investigate the episode on a full-time basis. Their phone calls and interviews with government employees revealed evidence of a vast cover-up of illegal activities at the center of power, evidence suggesting that the Watergate burglary was not an isolated event. It turned out to be only a small part of the illegal activities that had surrounded Nixon's reelection campaign.

Woodward and Bernstein encountered a great deal of resistance in their attempts to interview government employees. A tense atmosphere prevailed in Washington, and a large number of government employees were afraid to reveal what they knew. Jobs were at stake and individual employees ran the risk of personal humiliation. A break in the case came with the release of information by a single informant, to whom the reporters gave the code name "Deep Throat." Their informant occupied a central position in the White House branch of the government. As a man or woman of integrity, the informant was uneasy about what was going on and held the personal conviction that the nation had a right to know. Despite the significant role of their informant in uncovering the Watergate scandal, his or her identity has not yet been revealed. Woodward and Bernstein are pledged not to reveal their informant's identity until after his or her death.

In the tale that unfolded, it was revealed that subversive activities were used during the Democratic primaries to discredit and humiliate Senator Muskie of Maine, who was seen as a formidable candidate in the upcoming election. It was also discovered that corporations receiving defense contracts had been surreptitiously pressured into making large contributions to Nixon's campaign, that Nixon's campaign committee had spent large amounts of cash without any formal accounting procedures, that secret files were being kept on members of Congress and on individuals designated as enemies of the White House, and that various other illegal activities had undermined the democratic process.

It became clear at the headquarters of the Committee to Reelect the President, designated by the acronym CREEP, that a serious problem had developed. The best-laid plans of mice and men often go astray. Serious attempts to stonewall and cover up were initiated almost immediately. Many records and written documents were shredded to minimize the risk of someone establishing a link between the Watergate burglary and the campaign to reelect the president.

In the thinking of Richard Nixon and his associates, the metaphor of "war" had been applied to the political campaign. The domestic "enemies" in the war consisted of all those opposed to Nixon's leadership or his policies. In the White House, an elaborate plan was devised for dealing with those whose names made the "enemies list." Men from the CIA and Nixon's immediate circle of advisers elaborated strategies for conducting covert operations, labeled as "dirty tricks." The plans included infiltrating the headquarters of each of the Democratic contenders, tapping their phones, stealing their stationery, forging signatures, and making photocopies of their written documents. Further plans included the use of the IRS for harassment and leaking information to the press that would discredit specific individuals, including unwarranted allegations about drunk driving and sexual misconduct.

The domestic foes included not only leaders of the political opposition, but also employees of the government who leaked information to the press about questionable government operations. Foremost among these was Daniel Ellsberg who "leaked" the Pentagon Papers to the *New York Times*. The Pentagon Papers revealed that many forms of deception and misrepresentation had been employed both by military and political officials to cover up blunders during the Vietnam War. President Nixon was outraged. Loyalty to his administration was seen as a primary responsibility by all government employees. Anything that would reflect negatively upon government policies was seen as subversive. Accordingly, a unit designated as "the plumbers" was created to prevent the leak of information to the press about government operations. Special efforts were made to embarrass and discredit Ellsberg; for example, his psychiatrist's office was broken into to uncover information about him that would be personally damaging.

Several critical events unfolded to establish links between the White House and the Watergate burglary. The first came with an announcement from Judge John J. Sirica that he had received a letter from James McCord, one of the men convicted of the Watergate break-in. McCord's letter indicated that the defendants had been paid to maintain their silence, that perjury had been committed, and that numerous participants in the episode had not yet been identified. Before the case ran its course, McCord and several others expressed concern about becoming scapegoats in efforts to conceal the involvement of top government officials. Serious crimes had been detected, and now someone would have to pay the price by becoming "the sacrificial lamb."

Successful leaders frequently are able to remain aloof from the unsavory work that is required in politics. The dirty work may be delegated to subordinates who are less visible and thus able to work in an underhanded way without being detected. While denying any White House involvement in the Watergate affair, the president attempted to use the CIA to circumvent an investigation by the FBI that was initiated by the federal judiciary. In effect, he was using one agency of the government to prevent another agency from doing its job. Such an attempt at the obstruction of justice suggested desperate efforts at concealment and cover-up. Eventually, it was Nixon's persistence in concealment and cover-up that resulted in the charge of obstruction of justice in the articles of impeachment.

After the evidence became clear that members of the White House staff were involved in attempts to cover up the Watergate affair, the Senate initiated its own investigation. Public opinion polls were indicating a rapid erosion of public trust in Nixon's leadership. In televised hearings, a member of the White House staff, John Dean, had been granted immunity to tell the Senate Watergate Committee what he knew about the cover-up. In a lengthy prepared statement, Dean testified that both the president and his aides had participated in attempts to stonewall the Watergate investigation. As Dean's testimony unfolded, the nation responded with astonishment. Both those who voted for Nixon and those who voted against him felt betrayed.

Divided opinion was reflected in the interpersonal debates that took place throughout the country. Stalwart supporters of Nixon could not believe the accusations that were made against him. Americans have the freedom to criticize the president of the United States in any way they wish, but the level of discourse was seen by some as sinking to new levels. Some of the Republicans on the Senate Watergate Committee took extreme measures to discredit Dean's testimony. Each question and each answer was closely monitored within an adversarial context. Dean was a ready-made target as the first high-ranking official to reveal his own illegal activities and those of other members of the White House staff. There was a great deal of uneasiness both within the government and within the general public. The substantive issues on Nixon's complicity were far from being settled.

Determining what the president knew and when he knew it were foremost in the minds of many people. Dean's allegations stood in sharp contrast to Nixon's persistent denials. The president had previously announced publicly that an investigation from his office indicated that no member of the White House staff was involved. Whom should one believe, Dean or Nixon? An answer came through the testimony of Alexander Butterfield, a former White House aide. Butterfield revealed that a sophisticated recording system had been installed in the White House early in 1971 for recording all conversations and phone calls. Certainly, the recording of all conversations in the White House would indicate one way or the other whether or not the president was involved. The tapes potentially contained the "smoking gun" for implicating the president.

Both the special prosecutor, Archibald Cox, and the Senate Watergate Committee issued a subpoena for the White House tapes. It was the first time a subpoena had been issued to the president of the United States since the administration of Thomas Jefferson. Nixon refused to comply on the ground of "executive privilege." He maintained that the tapes were confidential and the exclusive property of the president. When Cox insisted, Nixon ordered Attorney General Eliot Richardson to fire him. The refusal of Richardson to do so resulted in what came to be called the "Saturday-night massacre." Nixon removed from office both Richardson and his deputy William Ruckelshaus, who also had refused to fire Cox. Solicitor General Robert Bork carried out Nixon's order by firing Cox and sealing the records in the special prosecutor's office. The outrage at this abuse of power resulted in further demands that Nixon release the tapes and that a new Watergate prosecutor be appointed.

As the pressure for the release of the tapes mounted, the impasse was resolved by placing the case before the Supreme Court. As a last-ditch effort, Nixon was convinced that the court would rule in favor of the principle of "executive privilege." The court did not. In a unanimous decision, the court ruled that Nixon must turn over the tapes as requested by the special Watergate prosecutor and by the Senate committee. Nixon responded by agreeing to release a transcript of the tapes, with only irrelevancies deleted, but not the tapes themselves. The proposal of releasing only an edited transcript was rejected by the judiciary. Nothing short of a release of the tapes themselves would be acceptable. Even the president of the United States must comply with an order issued by the Supreme Court.

When the tapes were finally released, eighteen minutes of a conversation, taped shortly after the Watergate burglary, had been erased. However, the tapes clearly indicated that the president had knowledge of the attempted cover-up from the very beginning and had participated in it. The nation was shocked at the vulgarity of the conversations among those in the inner circle at the White House and by what they were talking about. Clearly those at the center of power saw themselves as standing above the law as they planned clandestine operations against individuals and against other agencies of the government. The evidence was now clear that Nixon had participated in an obstruction of justice and thus had violated his oath of office.

The nation was shocked in the midst of the Watergate scandal to hear that an investigation had uncovered evidence that Spiro Agnew, the vice president of the United States, had been implicated in criminal activity during the course of his political career. The evidence seemed clear that Agnew had violated public positions of trust by accepting kickbacks from contractors and by accepting bribes from corporations while he was governor of Maryland. Further, there was evidence that he had failed to report and pay income tax on the funds he had received. Agnew resigned as vice president, pleaded no contest to income tax evasion, and received a three-year suspended prison term. The former attorney general, John Mitchell, who served as chair of the Committee to Re-Elect the President, was revealed to be a man who lacked scruples and was subsequently convicted of perjury and sent to prison. Before the Watergate affair was over, twenty-five of Nixon's aides and confidants were charged and convicted of criminal conduct, including three of his former cabinet members.

Those having a serious interest in American politics quickly saw a threat to the American system of government. The crimes of the Nixon administration had been exposed, and if they were ignored, all future presidents could consider themselves free to arbitrarily abuse the power that was inherent in the office. A failure to act when action was necessary would set a precedent for transforming the American system of government. Either the president would have to resign or he would have to be impeached and forcefully removed from office.

The move to impeach a president is a serious undertaking. Prior to the impeachment proceedings against Nixon, only one other attempt had been made to impeach a president in the history of the nation. In 1868, impeachment proceedings were brought against President Andrew Johnson. Historians now agree that the charges brought against Johnson were politically motivated and based on shameful and unwarranted allegations. Andrew Johnson had been seen as overly conciliatory in his attitudes toward the South and in his plans for reconstruction following the carnage of the Civil War. Several members of the House Judiciary Committee were fearful that history was about to repeat itself. The charges brought against Nixon seemed unbelievable and lacking in credibility. Many believed the enemies of Richard Nixon were out to get him.

Following the release of the tapes, support for the president eroded rapidly, even among many who previously had been loyal to him. Calls for his resignation were issued by newspapers, by Republican leaders in the Senate, and by influential people throughout the country. The trauma to the nation was of sufficient severity that prolonging the agony seemed unnecessary. All members of the House Judiciary Committee were now in favor of impeachment. Prior indecision evaporated as the high drama recorded in the White House tapes was revealed. Very few people in Congress, in the federal judiciary, or in the public at large desired to have Nixon remain in office. Consensus had now been reached that either Nixon would resign or be impeached and convicted of the crimes he had committed. The reasonable options available to the president were diminishing very rapidly.

Full impeachment proceedings in the House and subsequent trial and conviction in the Senate would be a long, drawn-out affair that very few, if anyone, really wanted. The time had come to abandon ship, so to speak, and only a small number of stalwarts were willing to further support the president. The two-thirds vote in the Senate that was needed for his conviction now seemed a certainty. Yet, Nixon tenaciously held on to the office. After all, he had been duly elected as president of the United States, and in his view, his actions were fully in the best interests of the nation.

There was concern about what Nixon might actually do out of a sense of desperation. As president, he was the commander-in-chief of the armed forces and had final control over the use of nuclear weapons. Out of a concern from what might happen under the circumstances, Defense Secretary James Schlesinger issued a directive to all military commanders that no direct order from the White House would be carried out without his counter-signature. The dangers inherent in the situation seemed to warrant such precautions.

The personal despair and anguish of Nixon was preventing him from attending to the affairs of state. With some degree of uneasiness, the president's assistant Alexander Haig had for some time been doing most of the routine work that was needed for the continuity of the office. There was also a concern among some of those close to the president that he might commit suicide. Personal appeals were cautiously made to Nixon for him to cut his losses and to resign with dignity. It was no longer in his own best interest or in the best interest of the nation for him to continue.

On August 8, 1974, the nation encountered one of the more emotional moments in its history when the thirty-seventh president of the United States went on television and announced to the world, "I shall resign the presidency effective at noon tomorrow." The drama of his resignation has often been described as having the ingredients of a Greek tragedy. The agony of recent events was rapidly coming to a close. The following day, the nation watched as Nixon gave his farewell to the White House staff and boarded a military helicopter for his move into exile. With mixed emotions, the nation sighed with relief.

Gerald Ford, as the new president, issued a pardon one month later for any of the crimes Nixon may have committed while in office. Prior to Ford's pardon, plans were being made on Capitol Hill for the trial and conviction of Nixon. Now the case was officially closed; Nixon could not be convicted and sent to prison. However, serious questions about the secrecy surrounding government operations continued to surface and resurface in the concerns of many Americans. The majority of Americans disapproved of the pardon and believed that the same rules of conduct that are applied to others should also be applied to the president of the United States. Many were relieved by the closure of the Watergate affair, while others were convinced that an easy way out had been provided for our criminal president.

The Morality of Power

The Watergate affair confirmed the worst suspicions of Americans about the immorality of public officials. Politics has always been regarded as "a dirty business" by many Americans. Yet, drawing upon the imagery of such presidents as George Washington, Abraham Lincoln, and Harry Truman, Americans also expect their presidents to be men of integrity and to stand above the dirty work that is involved in the political process. The Nixon scandal was traumatic to the nation. Extraordinary forms of political deviance get a lot of attention in the daily press, but when the extraordinary deviance implicates the president of the United States the effects are electrifying.

Historically, Americans have agreed with Lord Acton's dictum that "power corrupts, and absolute power corrupts absolutely." It was for this reason that the framers of the Constitution built checks and balances into the system and deliberately limited the powers of the presidency. Certain forms of authority were delegated to the Congress; other forms of authority were delegated to the executive branch of government; and yet other forms of authority were delegated to the judiciary. Limiting the powers of the president was a way of preventing absolute power from corrupting absolutely. The rules binding the conduct of public officials are well known to any man or woman who achieves a top position of authority in our society.

Public response to the Watergate affair became divided along the lines of perceptions of the man and perceptions of the office. Was the conduct of Nixon an aberration that reflected the moral character of the man, or were "high crimes and misdemeanors" symptomatic of the way the political system works? Some thought the issue of morality was primarily a system problem.

Some believed that no man who had come so far so fast in American politics could have done so without acquiring a blunted sense of moral responsibility. The ideology of America as the land of opportunity lends itself to schemers and manipulators who evaluate the quality of their character on the basis of the outcomes they achieve. Bending the rules is looked upon as acceptable if it achieves the results that are intended. Insofar as morality was seen as a system problem, Nixon was regarded as "one of us," but perhaps "not the best of us" because he got caught.

Some who emphasized the problems with the system saw Nixon as a product of the cold-war mentality. He was foremost among those promoting the fear and hatred of communism, foremost among those who were hostile toward antiwar activists, and foremost among those who believed that domestic enemies had infiltrated our government and were working to undermine the American way of life. Nixon drew upon the darker side of the American consciousness and was willing to circumvent the democratic process if it was seen as a threat to national security. Nixon's career had largely been built around the image of forcefully standing up to the communists. Patriotic sentiments became linked with support of cold-war initiatives. Nixon's efforts at concealment and cover-up were simply a spin-off from the widespread use of misrepresentation and deception during the course of the Vietnam War.

Sociologists have argued that if deviancy did not exist, there are circumstances in which it would have to be created. It is through specific cases that moral boundaries are drawn and the rules binding conduct are confirmed. What constitutes political sophistication and what constitutes criminal conduct frequently cannot be determined until the courts have spoken. Penalties and sanctions must be imposed in specific cases to establish the rules and guiding principles that are binding on the conduct of public officials.

The Watergate affair may very well have been necessary for establishing limits to the abuse of power. Certainly other presidents have abused the power of their office in a variety of ways. Some Americans remembered the attempts of Franklin Roosevelt to pack the Supreme Court, that the Teapot Dome affair scandalized Warren Harding's administration, and that John F. Kennedy had been implicated in the Bay of Pigs fiasco and may have been implicated in a plot to assassinate Castro. There was no historical precedent, however, similar to the scope of the blatant abuses of power during the Nixon administration. Accordingly, many believed that there was nothing wrong with the system, that it worked well, and that the problem was simply that of Nixon's morality.

What manner of man would engage in such nefarious practices while holding the position of president of the United States? The answer was sought in the character flaws of Nixon. The term "tricky Dick" had been widely used by Nixon critics who perceived him as a devious character. He was seen as a little man with big political ambitions and a lack of moral scruples.

It was noted that Nixon's early career was boosted substantially by the tenacity with which he sought to expose "hidden communists." His paranoia about the communist menace was subsequently extended to the belief that other people were out to get him, including political opponents, anti-war activists, the press, and liberal intellectuals. The only way you can win in this type of situation, he apparently believed, was "to give them the sword." Politics was seen as resembling war in that anything goes in the attempt to incapacitate or neutralize the opposition. Personal strength and political efficacy is determined by whose will prevails in the face of opposition and conflict.

For Nixon the prize of the political game was personal power and what he personally saw as being in the best interests of the country. Regardless of the scandals of Watergate and his forced resignation, Nixon apparently believed that history would look favorably upon his administration. In his view, it is the political accomplishments of the man that really matter, rather than the means he employed in attaining them. Those who stand in opposition to "national interests" have to be dealt with in a heavy-handed way. Civil liberties and due process must be suspended if they interfere with "national security" concerns.

The autobiographical writings of former presidents, in some way or another, address the issue of a differential between the experience "of power" and the experience "with power." Lyndon Johnson, for example, was a man who had a reputation for arm-twisting; however, he was not able to set the national agenda he wished to promote. The emerging issues that require the attention of the president are frequently not of his own choosing. Further, the personal power of the president is limited by the many constituencies that he has to confront and deal with in some way or another. Harry Truman wrote about the loneliness of the office that grows out of the monumental decisions that the president alone must make and for which he alone must accept responsibility. Presiding over a nation thus involves much more than the personal desires and wishes of the man who holds the office.

The special case of Richard Nixon was one in which he regarded his election as a personal mandate. The sense of power that accompanied the office was translated into a sense of personal invulnerability. He felt free to do whatever he wanted to do as long as it was concealed from the public. To avoid the loneliness described by Truman, he surrounded himself with like-minded individuals. A primary criterion for the selection of subordinates was total loyalty and dedication to his leadership. The ideology of "national interests" and "national security" was drawn upon to justify the use of unethical procedures.

Some believed the forced resignation of Nixon confirmed the integrity of the political process. All of the major branches of government played a key role in the removal of Nixon from office. There were men of integrity who chose to resign rather than carry out Nixon's orders, which were improperly given. Even the Nixon supporters within his own party came to feel betrayed and decided that nothing short of Nixon's resignation was acceptable. The abuse of power became an insult to the men and women of integrity who had devoted their lives to public service.

The Legacy of Watergate

The primary legacy of Watergate was to confirm the importance of constitutional authority. The American system is one of governing by laws rather than the whims and actions of individual men and women. Individual presidents may come and go, but the integrity of the system remains. All future presidents will be aware of the risks involved in an obstruction of justice and the abuse of political power. Whether the precedent actually serves as a deterrent to misconduct is a debatable point. However, it is clear that the machinery for dealing with misconduct in office is now firmly in place. The Constitution has not been changed, but the meaning it has for the conduct of public affairs has been clarified. Nixon's resignation confirmed that under a constitutional government, even the most powerful man in American politics can be forcefully removed from office.

We now know of the intensity of the trauma that is involved in an effort to impeach the president of the United States. The matter was not taken lightly in Nixon's case, nor will the issue of impeachment be taken lightly in the future. Political disagreements with a president are not grounds for impeachment, but a serious violation of the oath of office is. Some degree of leeway in personal style must necessarily be given to political leaders, but at the same time it is clear that the resources of the office are not to be used primarily to serve personal ends.

There was nothing inevitable about the downfall of President Nixon. It is not the behavior of the man in office that generates a cry of moral indignation, but the public disclosure of what he had done. The more successful crimes are those that are never detected and thus are never brought forward for public scrutiny and reaction. Getting caught represents ineptness and carelessness in the area of crime itself. Ineptness in the Watergate affair was reflected in the activities of the former CIA agents who were supposed to be experts in covert activities. Nixon's ineptness was reflected in the fact that he had "bugged himself" in the elaborate recording system that had been installed in the White House. Apparently, Nixon regarded "the president" as being invulnerable and believed that the power inherent in the office was his personal power to use as he wished.

Had there not been ineptness on the part of the Watergate burglars and had there not been an attempt to conceal White House involvement, the high crimes and misdemeanors of Richard Nixon might never have seen the light of day. The atmosphere in Washington during the Nixon administration was sufficiently tense that government employees who knew what was happening preferred to remain silent, rather than to risk their jobs or personal humiliation. Certainly, Woodward and Bernstein encountered a great deal of resistance from many of the government employees they attempted to interview.

The investigative reporting of Woodward and Bernstein confirmed the importance of freedom of the press and elevated the stature of the news media in American life. Through efforts to inform the nation about consequential events, the news media play an increasingly important role in the political process. Political leaders have a high degree of visibility, and all aspects of their personal and public lives have become fair game for public scrutiny. The Watergate affair helped to send important messages to future generations about the parameters of acceptable behavior for the occupant of a political office.

Those convicted of street crimes, such as burglary or armed robbery, tend to receive stiff prison sentences if they are caught. Crimes committed by those who hold high positions of status and power, tend to receive relatively light sentences. The conspirators in the Watergate affair spent only a short time in prison, and the prisons where they served their time were more like country clubs than maximum-security institutions. A cynical view held that justice did not prevail. The combination of the seriousness of the crimes they committed with the relatively light sentences they received confirmed the view that "we do not live in a just world." The social consequences of an armed robbery are small in comparison to those crimes that undermine the basic values and ideals of the democratic process.

Rather than express guilt and remorse, the coconspirators attempted to justify themselves. For example, G. Gordon Liddy clearly stated that he had no regrets about what had been done but only regretted that they had been caught. At no time did President Nixon express regrets about his conduct in office or apologize to the nation. Instead, he spent a great deal of time over the next twenty years extolling the accomplishments of his presidency, his political competence, and the value of the political advice he had to give to the nation.

Part of the legacy of Watergate was a confirmation of the cynical view that "crime pays." Americans apparently had an interest in knowing more about the Watergate affair than had been reported in the news media or in judicial and legislative reports. "The high crimes and misdemeanors" mentioned in the House impeachment proceedings against Nixon were never fully investigated because of Nixon's resignation and his subsequent pardon. In effect, Nixon became only "an unindicted co-conspirator." Liddy, Dean, Halderman, Ehrlichman, Colson, Hunt, and others who were implicated in criminal conduct became wealthy men from the royalties on their books. Nixon also profited greatly from the sales of his memoirs and other books that he wrote in an attempt to vindicate his tenure in office, to establish himself as a senior statesman, and to become a noteworthy commentator on political affairs.

The role of secrecy in government temporarily became an issue following Watergate. Many believed there was too much concealment and cover-up of what was going on in Washington. Americans had been shocked by the scope of the covert activities that had become a standard part of government operations. Particular dismay was expressed over the lack of accountability by the FBI and the CIA. However, in reflections on secrecy, a distinction needs to be made between the backstage routines that are necessary in the government process and those covert activities that are designed as domestic espionage. Indignation arises at the thought that techniques that were refined in our espionage operations overseas might be employed to embarrass, humiliate, and incapacitate individuals who were believed to be enemies of the party in power.

The "war" metaphor is misleading as a guiding principle in the conduct of a political campaign. Indeed, the primary objective of a national political party is to win an election and to supply the nation with the personnel to run the government. However, attempts to morally discredit men and women of integrity and to prevent them from waging a political campaign goes beyond the pale of common decency. The purpose of the American political party is to put together a coalition that is broadly supported in public opinion for setting the agenda of the nation. The democratic process calls for debates to test out the validity of ideas and to permit the electorate to assess the relative qualifications of candidates. These ideals are undermined when the goal is defined as "winning the election by whatever means are necessary." Clearly, the use of personnel from national security agencies to circumvent the electoral process should not be tolerated.

There is a widespread belief that the presidency tends to promote the personal growth and development of the man who holds the office. Americans remembered Harry Truman as a man who had grown with the office and had made monumental decisions that went far beyond the capabilities expected of him when he was inaugurated as president. The case of Richard Nixon, however, suggested no evidence of such growth and development as a result of holding the office.

A new generation has grown up since the time in which the Watergate affair commanded the attention of the nation. Naming the president who resigned to avoid removal from office has fallen into the game of trivial pursuits. A national survey of high school students revealed that the majority neither knew the name of the president who resigned nor when that event occurred. Apparently, the Watergate affair, but not the term itself, has receded in American consciousness. Yet, the legacy of Watergate is still with us today. The distrust of government and the lack of confidence in political leaders is evident in the attitudes of the new generation. Even if the sources of these attitudes are not evident to this new generation, it is clear that Watergate played a part in their development.

There was very little about Watergate that seems worthy of enduring attention. Most Americans responded as spectators, rather than as active participants. A large viewing audience had watched the television coverage of the hearings of the Senate Watergate Committee and the proceedings of the House Judiciary Committee. However, there were no shared collective sentiments that bound the viewers together. Most people responded with curiosity over what would happen next, rather than any shared sense of moral indignation and outrage. As detached observers, most Americans were in effect serving as a collective "judiciary." As the evidence mounted and the facts became "perfectly clear," to use one of

Nixon's favorite phrases, most Americans simply wanted to see the man removed from office.

In the absence of any noteworthy heroic deeds or grim personal sacrifices, there was little about Watergate that seemed worth remembering. The lessons of Watergate resemble stories that have been told and retold in various forms over the past 2,000 years or more. Unrestrained ambition can result in the destruction of an individual, and violations of the basic rules of social order must necessarily result in punishment. The drama resembled a morality play in which the lessons seemed simple enough.

At the funeral of Richard Nixon on April 27, 1994, few references were made to the disgrace of his conduct in office. In the eulogies delivered, an emphasis was placed on his great political leadership and accomplishments. These included references to how Nixon had opened relationships with China, how he had pursued detente with the Soviet Union, and how the Vietnam War had ended during his tenure in office. Reverend Billy Graham described him as "one of the most misunderstood men" and "one of the greatest men of the century." Former president Ronald Reagan observed that "his foreign policy accomplishments will secure his exalted place in history." Former president George Bush noted, "The difficulties he encountered in office may have diminished his presidency, but what should be remembered are his many outstanding achievements, both foreign and domestic."

National responses to the televised funeral were surrounded with ambivalent emotions. Some regarded his personal conduct as no worse than that of other presidents, while others had a sickened reaction to the praise directed toward Nixon and his leadership. As a nation, Americans have not yet recovered the trust they had in their presidents prior to Nixon. Following Watergate, close scrutiny has been given to the character and personal qualities of top political leaders. This is in part due to Bernstein and Woodward serving as role models for investigative reporting. It is also partly due to public concerns with the moral dimension of political leadership.

Bibliography

Bernstein, Carl, and Bob Woodward. 1974. *All the President's Men*. New York: Simon and Schuster.

Bok, Sissela. 1979. *Lying: Moral Choice in Public and Private Life*. New York: Vintage Books.

Chafe, William H. 1986. "Bringing Us Together." In *The Unfinished Journey*, pp. 381–429. New York: Oxford University Press.

Ervin, Sam J., Jr. 1980. *The Whole Truth: The Watergate Conspiracy*. New York: Random House.

Fields, Howard. 1978. *High Crimes and Misdemeanors.* New York: W.W. Norton.

Frost, David. *"I Gave Them a Sword": Behind the Scenes of the Nixon Interviews.* New York: Ballantine Books.

Hamilton, V. Lee. 1978. "Who Is Responsible? Toward a Social Psychology of Attribution." *Social Psychology* 41: 316–327.

Katz, Jack. 1977. "Cover-Up and Collective Integrity: On the Natural Antagonism of Authority Internal and External to Organizations." *Social Problems* 25: 3–17.

Kutler, Stanley I. 1990. *The Wars of Watergate: The Last Crisis of Richard Nixon.* New York: Alfred A. Knopf.

Lurie, Leonard. 1973. *The Impeachment of Richard Nixon.* New York: Berkeley Medallion Books.

Mankiewicz, Frank. 1975. *U.S. v. Richard M. Nixon: The Final Crisis.* New York: Quadrangle.

Mills, C. Wright. 1956. "The Higher Immorality." In *The Power Elite*, pp. 343–361. New York: Oxford University Press.

Molotch, Harvey L., and Deirdre Boden. 1985. "Talking Social Structure: Discourse, Domination and the Watergate Hearings." *American Sociological Review* 50: 273–288.

Robinson, Douglas. 1985. "Nixon in Crisis-Land: The Rhetoric of 'Six Crises'." *Journal of American Culture* 8: 79–86.

Schudson, Michael. 1992. *Watergate in American Memory: How We Remember, Forget, and Reconstruct the Past.* New York: Basic Books.

Sirica, John J. 1979. *To Set the Record Straight: The Break-in, the Tapes, the Conspirators, the Pardon.* New York: Signet Books.

Sussman, Barry. 1992. *The Great Cover-up: Nixon and the Scandal of Watergate.* Arlington, VA: Steven Locks Press.

Thompson, Dennis F. 1980. "Moral Responsibility of Public Officials: The Problem of Many Hands." *American Political Science Review* 74: 905–916.

White, Theodore H. 1975. *Breach of Faith: The Fall of Richard Nixon.* New York: Athenaeum.

———. 1973. *The Making of the President 1972.* New York: Bantam Books.

Wicker, Tom. 1991. *One of Us: Richard Nixon and the American Dream.* New York: Random House.

Woods, John R. 1985. *Watergate Revisited.* Secaucus, NJ: Citadel Press.

Woodward, Bob, and Carl Bernstein. 1976. *The Final Days.* New York: Touchstone.

11 • Technological Accidents

Advances in sophisticated technology are foremost among the spectacular achievements of the twentieth century. We have split the atom, landed a man on the moon, traveled beyond the speed of sound, and eradicated smallpox on a worldwide basis. Such spectacular achievements in technology have provided us with new images of ourselves and of the world in which we live. The central message seems to be that there are many more possibilities for the human condition than previous generations could have recognized.

Our technological emphasis is oriented toward an active mastery of the world, and according to some it is the capacity for developing technology that sets humans apart from others in the animal kingdom. While developing sophisticated systems of technology may be the crowning human accomplishment, there are also grounds for uneasiness. Solutions to identifiable problems frequently have consequences that are unexpected and unintended. We become aware of the unintended consequences of technology when airplanes crash, when ships sink, when dams break, when bridges collapse, and when nuclear reactors explode.

A casual inventory of technological disasters during the course of the twentieth century includes a variety of mishaps and failures, such as the sinking of the *Titanic* in 1912, after it had been publicized as an unsinkable, state-of-the-art ship; the crash of the *Hindenburg* at Lakehurst, New Jersey, in 1937, at a time when there was widespread optimism about the efficiency of dirigibles as a means of international travel; the nuclear mishap at Three Mile Island in 1979, at a time when many people had faith in nuclear power as a means of meeting the growing energy needs of the nation; and the explosion of the space shuttle *Challenger* in 1986, at a time when the excitement about human explorations of outer space was pervasive. Such episodes generated traumatic responses throughout the nation because of the dangers they suggested for the world in which we live. Unscheduled, unplanned, and unintended events cause shock waves that humans have to deal with in a manner and at a time that are not of their own choosing.

The *Challenger* Explosion

While technological catastrophes raise anxiety levels in the general population, spectacular achievements in the use of technology inspires a great deal of the idealism of the modern world. This idealism was well expressed in the speech delivered by President John F. Kennedy at Rice University in 1962 in which he announced the importance of space exploration as a national priority. Kennedy laid out the specific objective of sending a man to the moon and bring him back again "before this decade is over." In announcing an acceleration of expenditures on the space program, Kennedy noted that "it is one of the great adventures of all times" and that "space can be explored and mastered."

The subsequent technological display of landing a man on the moon did indeed serve as a way of announcing to the world the American capability for technological development. The moon landing was presented by the news media as emblematic of the cultural supremacy of the United States. The spectacular episode confirmed the wisdom and courage of its political leaders, the intelligence of its scientific and technological personnel, and the superiority of the American political system. The television coverage of the moon landing was one of the proudest moments in the history of the nation.

Comparisons were made between the trip to the moon and the voyage of Columbus and the expedition of Lewis and Clark. Each involved travel into uncharted territory, a sense of adventure, and a courageous undertaking. The trip to the moon, however, involved risks that went beyond any earth-bound activity. There was the possibility that our sophisticated technology might fail to work in a new and unknown environment. There was also a concern about what the astronauts might bring back from the moon; it was not actually known whether there were biogenic agents on the moon to which we had no immunity. After the splashdown, the astronauts were placed in isolation for extensive examination to determine the presence of any new or novel form of contamination.

The astronaut emerged as a new type of hero in a world in which heroes were becoming increasingly scarce. Space flights captured the imagination of the American public, and such names as John Glenn, Chuck Yeager, and Neil Armstrong became familiar to most Americans. The astronaut was seen as intelligent, honest, competent, physically fit, cool, and courageous. As the title of a book that was subsequently made into a movie suggested, the astronaut was an American hero with "the right stuff." They were recognized as exceptionally gifted individuals who epitomized cultural values and ideals.

The initial astronauts were selected from a cadre of test pilots. The competition was stiff, and those selected became the envy of others. Acceptance of danger was a necessary ingredient for their flight assignments. The rockets they would take into outer space were, in effect, launched by the explosion of a "controlled bomb." The probability of death was part of the folklore of test pilots and astronauts. Commitment to flying was at the risk of the loss of one's life.

Many problems developed in the elaboration of the sophisticated technology for space travel. Most Americans were aware of the spectacular accomplishments in space, but not of the blunders and mishaps, nor of the intense conflicts among the personnel at NASA. The scientific and technical personnel were under intense pressure from management to solve complicated problems under deadlines from Washington. As a result, there was a great deal of risk-taking in many flights that had been launched prematurely. Even the initial moon flight came close to a disaster. In Houston, it took about four hours to calibrate the liftoff from the moon for a rendezvous with the spacecraft in orbit for the return to earth. Any further delay would likely have had catastrophic results because there was only ten seconds of fuel left in the craft that had lifted off the moon.

Following the initial moon landing, public interest in the space program weakened. We had clearly demonstrated to the world that American space technology was superior to that of the Russians. About 600 million people around the world watched television coverage of Neil Armstrong and Buzz Aldrin walking on the moon. Relatively few people followed with interest subsequent moon flights. The mystery of the possibility of traveling to the moon and exploring its surface had been solved. The moon turned out to be a relatively uninteresting place for most people. The turbulence of the times seemed to require a focus of attention on more immediate and urgent problems, such as the war in Vietnam, the civil rights movement, and the civil disorders in metropolitan areas.

Now that we were ahead of the Russians, the continuance of prior levels of funding for space research was no longer assured. Some believed the engineering feats performed in outer space had only a limited use here on earth and were not worthy of the claims that were being made on a stressed federal budget. NASA also came under attack for its criteria in the selection of astronauts. It was argued that test pilots were not actually needed, because the maneuverability of the spacecraft was largely under the guidance of computers from the Mission Control Center. There were doubts about whether astronauts were even necessary aboard a spacecraft. Social pressure was put on NASA to recruit women, minorities, and civilians for the cadre of astronauts.

To reverse the declining interest of Americans in space research, a special flight of the space shuttle *Challenger* was planned for early 1986. The notion that space travel could be made available to ordinary people was being promoted. In the flight design, the seven crew members were to include two members of minority groups and two women. A high level of excitement was generated through national competition in selecting a public school teacher for the space flight. The success of previous flights had generated enough confidence to include civilians along with military personnel in *Challenger*'s crew. Several astronauts disagreed with the decision and believed that only test pilots had the expertise that might be required for dealing with emergencies in outer space.

United Airlines provided free travel to the Kennedy space center for the two finalists from each state in the competition for the teacher-in-space venture. Hundreds of friends and relatives had gathered at hotels in the area. Millions of students in schools throughout the country were glued to television sets to watch the astronauts enter the space shuttle for their historic adventure. Christa McAuliffe, the school teacher from New Hampshire, was prepared to conduct experiments for classrooms that would be broadcasted from outer space. Teaching from outer space was expected to provide a powerful role model and would revitalize basic American values and ideals.

One of the more traumatic moments in the history of the nation was on the verge of unfolding. The launch of the *Challenger* seemed to go smoothly enough, but only seventy-three seconds after liftoff, a huge explosion occurred. Initially, there was uncertainty about what was actually happening, but soon it became evident that a major disaster had occurred. There was no chance of survival for any of the seven crew members aboard. The nation was in a state of shock as the television coverage played and replayed the tragic event.

Millions of school children throughout the nation were traumatized by their experience. They had encountered the reality of death, some for the first time, and were required to deal with it. Seeing a major role model obliterated on live television was shocking. Several students quickly changed their minds about wanting to become an astronaut when they grew up. Teachers set aside time in the classroom for students to express their concerns. Clinical psychologists and psychiatrists gave advice to parents on how to deal with nightmares and other stress responses of children. At McAuliffe's high school in Concord, New Hampshire, psychological counseling was made available for any student who wanted or needed it. Many adults saw a resemblance between the sadness of the event and the sadness they had experienced with the death of President Kennedy.

An investigation into the *Challenger* explosion revealed that the accident was caused by the failure of an "O"-ring, a synthetic rubber ring designed to ensure that the separate sections of the booster rocket held together. Problems with the "O"-ring had been noted in technical reports, but these reports remained hidden in administrative files. Engineers at the space center were well aware of recurrent technical problems with the space shuttle. The failure to coordinate the expertise of the many specialists in the space program was regarded by some as evidence of incompetence on the part of the agency that had successfully landed a man on the moon.

Some blamed the political pressure to launch the flight prior to President Ronald Reagan's State of the Union message. Reagan apparently wanted to mention the success of the *Challenger* flight to embellish his address to the nation. As a result of the pressure to prematurely launch the flight, the weather conditions at Cape Canaveral were not properly taken into account. There had been icicles on the launch pad that morning, and no previous shuttle flight had been launched at such a low temperature.

Several retrospective judgments were expressed in response to the tragedy. Technicians in the space program felt that there was a need to resist politically motivated timetables for the deployment of exotic and high-risk technologies. Racing with the Russians, or meeting the timetable set by politicians, requires a willingness to sacrifice lives and to take risks that are unwarranted. Some held the view that because of the risks in the use of exotic technologies, each mission should be regarded as an experimental launch, and there should be no civilians aboard unless they have important scientific missions to perform.

Students of popular culture have noted that in the first few months after the accident, a large number of "dirty *Challenger* jokes" surfaced around the country. Many of them were focused on McAuliffe and expressed underlying disenchantment with public education, the mass media, and the emphasis on the space program. The following jokes are representative:

What color were Christa McAuliffe's eyes?
  Blue. One blew this way and one blew that way.

What was the last thing Christa McAuliffe said to her husband?
  You feed the dog and I'll feed the fish.

How do we know that Christa McAuliffe was a good teacher?
  She only blew up once in front of her class.

What do you call seven astronauts at the bottom of the ocean?
A good beginning.

Although the jokes seemed to express belligerent cruelty, they served the function of releasing some of the tension stemming from the tragedy. Telling *Challenger* jokes was a way of side-stepping awareness of one's own mortality and the fragility of the technological environments upon which we increasingly depend. Humor provided a symbolic way of expressing ambivalent attitudes toward the many forms of technology in the lives of individuals—technologies designed to make life easier, but over which individuals sensed a lack of personal control.

Travel Accidents

Travel several times the speed of sound in a rocket launched into outer space is beyond the direct experience of all but a few Americans. Yet, using less complex technologies than those of space travel, the speed and efficiency of travel over the surface of the earth are very much a part of experiences in the modern world. The lifetime travel of the average person prior to the twentieth century was limited to a radius of a few miles from the place of birth. As public transportation became cheaper, faster, and safer, long-distance travel for business and pleasure became possible. Indeed, the development of sophisticated systems of both land-based and airborne travel contributed greatly to the economic, political, and social integration of the nation. Being able to cross continents and oceans in a few hours has greatly altered the human condition. The popularity of long-distance travel is evident in the fact that several of the largest airlines now carry more than 200 million passengers each year.

Despite their popularity, people fly in airplanes and drive in automobiles without knowing much about the technical principles by which they operate. There are mysterious and magic-like qualities to the technologies that have become a central part of the modern landscape. The devices used for rapid transit involve ingredients of both excitement and danger. Some degree of uneasiness grows out of dependency on technologies that are little understood by those who use and benefit from them. The risks embedded in our systems of transportation have recurrently surfaced in collective consciousness with the unfolding of extraordinary tragedies and disasters.

Shortly before midnight on April 14, 1912, one of the more tragic episodes in travel history occurred with the sinking of the *Titanic* in the North Atlantic. The *Titanic* was designed as a luxury ship that would beat out all competition in transatlantic travel. The ship was 11 stories tall, 883 feet long, and 91 feet wide, and weighed 46,000 tons. It was designed to be the largest, the most luxurious, and the most powerful ship ever built. Nothing was spared in providing luxury accommodations. The passenger list for the magnificent "floating luxury hotel" included many rich and famous Americans on their way home from travel in Europe.

Through designing the ship with sixteen watertight compartments, its builders and promoters thought the ship would be "unsinkable." If water ever entered any of the compartments, an automatic switch could close doors to adjacent compartments and keep the ship afloat; however, there were flaws in the design of the compartments. The ship would remain afloat only if no more than two of the compartments were flooded at the same time. After all, how often does an automobile have more than two flats at the same time? Further problems in design stemmed from the fact that all the compartments were located above the waterline on the assumption that any accident would stem from a frontal collision. About forty-eight hours after being launched on its maiden voyage, the claims for the ship were put to an empirical test. The *Titanic* struck an iceberg that ripped the underside of the ship, shearing a series of gashes and flooding six of the compartments. The ship was traveling about twenty-two nautical miles an hour in an attempt to set a new record for a transatlantic crossing.

Within minutes after striking the iceberg, it was clear that the ship would sink and that a serious state of emergency existed. The ship carried only sixteen lifeboats, and these had been regarded as unnecessary for an "unsinkable" ship. Following a basic rule of the sea, the decision was made to limit the lifeboats to women and children. Husbands were separated from their wives; fathers were separated from their children. Shortly after the lifeboats were launched, the ship tilted almost vertically, and plunged nose down into 13,000 feet of icy water. More than 1,500 passengers went down with the ship. What had started out as an exciting and memorable trip ended up as an extraordinary tragedy. The nation was shocked.

The loss of lives among the rich and famous is an especially newsworthy event. The names of both the survivors and the fatalities, along with selective biographical sketches, were listed in newspapers across the country. Accounts of the tragedy provided the raw materials for many documentaries, novels, movies, and other forms of popular culture. Eighty years after the event, the story of the sinking of the *Titanic* continued to capture the imagination of Americans. It was not just the tragedy of the deaths of the rich and the famous that produced the trauma for the nation. Instead, the trauma was embedded in perceptions of the qualifications of experts and the dangers inherent in long-distance travel.

Despite the vague dangers associated with long-distance travel, the increased efficiency and comfort of travel added to the excitement of the times. The solo flight of Charles Lindbergh across the Atlantic in 1927 created a new national hero from the vicarious thrills of adventure and travel. The world was becoming more interdependent, and excitement was generated over the prospect of having direct experiences with events and places that were far removed from the mundane character of everyday life.

The new technologies in transportation, however, were accompanied by several extraordinary tragedies. In 1937, the world watched with interest as Amelia Earhart embarked on an around-the-world flight. Her flight ended with the disappearance of her plane over the South Pacific. What happened in the course of her flight remains a mystery and continues to provoke a great deal of speculation. The Amelia Earhart episode holds a prominent place in the collective memories of the nation about the triumphs and trage-dies of the transportation technologies.

New and innovative forms of commercial travel across the Atlantic con-tinued to capture the imagination of Americans in a century of rapid techno-logical advancement. In 1936, regular flights were scheduled on lighter-than-air dirigibles flying from Europe to the United States. On its first flight to the United States from Germany, the dirigible *Hindenburg* carried fifty-one passengers and fifty-six crew members. The dirigible also carried a gas volume of 7,300,000 cubic feet, which gave it a gross lifting capacity of 418,000 pounds. On its initial voyage, the craft elegantly soared upwardly at Friedrichschafen, Germany, and was pointed westward for a 4,000-mile journey.

In its ten transatlantic crossings during the first year, the craft carried more than 1,000 people. The passenger list included many dignitaries from Europe and America. Amazed at the new sight, on May 6, 1937, a crowd of thousands gathered in Times Square to cheer as the dirigible flew over New York City. Minutes later, the dirigible *Hindenburg* crashed and burned as it approached its landing site at Lakehurst, New Jersey. The lighter-than-air gasses that kept the craft afloat were highly flammable and explosive. Sparks from the engine, or perhaps even static electricity, were believed to have ignited the hydrogen gas aboard. Doubts about the desirability of gas-powered crafts for long-distance travel became widespread.

Such tragedies as the sinking of the *Titanic* and the explosion of the *Hindenburg* call into question the technical competence of the many spe-cialists and experts upon which we increasingly depend. As individuals we do not possess the knowledge that is necessary for assessing the claim that a given ship is "unsinkable" or that a trip across the Atlantic in a dirigible is "safe." The choices we make in our personal lives are dependent to a very large degree on trust. We expect the designers and producers of sophisticated systems of technology to be competent, and we expect those who promote those technologies to be committed to communal values and to hold an ethic of social responsibility. Without making such assumptions, the social world would become disorderly and individuals would have difficulty achieving their goals.

Today, commercial airlines promote the notion that traveling by air is one of the safest forms of travel over long distances. The available statistics seem to bear out this claim. For passengers on commercial flights, there is now an average of less than two fatalities for each 100 million miles flown. What is not mentioned is the large number of near misses each day as an increasing number of airplanes weave their way across a crowded sky. Many commercial planes have been in service for a long time and are beginning to develop metal fatigue, hairline cracks due to erosion, damaged turbine blades, and other problems that go along with extensively used and worn equipment.

Most people accept the claim that flying on commercial airlines is a safe and efficient way to travel. At the same time, there are millions of Americans who have a fear of flying, including those who fly on commercial planes as well as those who do not. In part, the fear of flying grows out of a recognition that humans evolved as land-based creatures, and flying through the air at high speeds is not something humans do naturally. The use of technology to enhance human capabilities involves a great deal of risk and danger.

While commercial airlines generally do provide safe and efficient forms of travel, there are occasions when serious accidents do occur. Planes sometimes lose their wings or propellers, run out of fuel, collide into each other, and crash into rivers, bridges, or mountains. There is no way we can have highly sophisticated technologies for rapid transit that are completely free of risk. Newspapers give a great deal of coverage to airplane crashes but very little to automobile fatalities, highlighting the sense of vulnerability and potential trauma that is connected with commercial aviation.

The fear of flying goes beyond a concern for pilot error or mechanical failure. Notions about the vulnerability of commercial flights to acts of terrorism are confirmed as passengers are exposed to close scrutiny at security checkpoints in airports. During the Gulf War, concerns with security intensified and passengers sensed the tense atmosphere that prevailed. With only limited resources, terrorists have the ability to commandeer a plane, take the crew and passengers hostage, change the destination of the flight, and seek major political concessions. The apparent helplessness of passengers adds to the darker side of being placed in a position of personal vulnerability.

On December 21, 1988, a Pan Am flight bringing Americans home from Europe crashed over the town of Lockerbie in Scotland. All 258 aboard the plane and 18 people on the ground were killed. A bomb had been placed on the plane by terrorists as a form of revenge for the downing of an Iranian airliner from an American ship. The security check at Frankfort had failed to detect a small plastic bomb that had been placed aboard the plane in a suitcase. The newly developed bombs that are small, highly explosive, and nonmetallic are not likely to be detected, despite the precautions that are taken by airports in their security checks. A plastic bomb no larger than a pack of cigarettes can have an explosive capacity that is sufficient to bring down a commercial airliner.

Despite mechanical failures, collisions, crashes, and acts of terrorism, commercial air travel continues to increase in popularity. The crowded airports confirm the public appeal of commercial flights as a form of travel. The acceptance of some degree of risk and uncertainty is necessary for an adaptive response to the conditions that prevail in our time and place. Those who refrain from flying out of a sense of fear are responding to a basic need for order, predictability, and security in their personal lives. But if humans have a basic need for safety and security, they also have a basic need for excitement and adventure. The fear of flying has a hemming-in effect and precludes individuals from having some of the pleasures and experiences that are valued by others in modern social life.

Three Mile Island

Attitudes of ambivalence toward sophisticated technologies were reflected in the heated debates and controversy in the United States over the use of nuclear power plants. The optimistic view of using nuclear energy for the betterment of the human condition collided with pessimistic views about the dire consequences of producing a highly radioactive environment. Commercial and political ideologies clashed with underlying anxieties and fears among individuals about the risks of exposure to nuclear contamination.

Following World War II, the general sentiment of the nation favored finding new and innovative uses for nuclear energy. Some nuclear experts were optimistic about the prospects of harnessing the recently discovered source of energy for generating electricity. Just as Elias Howe's sewing machine replaced the needle and Cyrus McCormick's reaper replaced the sickle, nuclear power could replace fossil fuels in meeting the energy needs of the nation.

In President Dwight Eisenhower's speech on "atoms for peace," he set the agenda for the further development of nuclear technology for civilian and commercial purposes. Emphasizing peaceful uses of nuclear power, his speech had the effect of muting the negative imagery surrounding Hiroshima and Nagasaki. Nuclear power was being packaged around the link between technology and human progress. Nuclear power was promoted as clean, safe, efficient, and essential. Some optimists believed that the generation of electricity would become so efficient in the future that it would not be necessary to monitor its use or charge for it.

Initially, there was widespread public support for the development of nuclear power plants. The population was increasing rapidly, and there was a growing consumer demand for electricity. But while there was an emphasis on atoms for peace, there was also an escalation of research on nuclear weapons. The effects of testing nuclear devices in the atmosphere became a major public concern. Increased levels of radiation from testing nuclear weapons showed up in the polar ice caps, in the grasslands of Wisconsin, and in the cow's milk consumed by babies. Insidious health hazards had shown up in dramatic and unexpected ways. It was partially from such concerns that the United States and the Soviet Union negotiated a ban on nuclear testing in the atmosphere.

Opposition to nuclear power plants increased with the growing concerns for the environment. Fears were expressed about the accidental leakage of radioactive materials into the atmosphere. The tide of public opinion was moving in a negative direction by the time of "the nuclear accident" at Three Mile Island near Harrisburg, Pennsylvania, in March 1979. A leak of radioactive steam from a nuclear generator set off an intense national controversy over the risks and benefits of nuclear power plants. The emerging controversy over the use of nuclear power not only tapped concerns about the technical problems in generating electricity, but also strengthened general attitudes about the dangers and hazards created by modern industry and technology.

The media coverage of the Three Mile Island accident was dramatic, and for an extended period of time the episode remained the lead item in the news. Anxieties were raised about the potential hazards of increased radioactivity in the surrounding area and about the prospects for a nuclear explosion. A mishap of potentially catastrophic proportions was building up in the nuclear reactor. The valves for regulating the flow of water through pipes for cooling the nuclear reactor failed to work properly. Following the failure of a series of backup systems, a hydrogen bubble developed in the containment building, and there was the risk of a major explosion. From the heat that continued to build in the reactor, there was the risk of a nuclear meltdown. Deep public fears grew out of the uncertainty over what was happening and over what was going to happen next.

Despite pronouncements by the utility company that everything was under control, the governor of Pennsylvania advised pregnant women and those with pre-school children to evacuate the area if they lived within a five-mile radius of the damaged reactor. Confusion mounted as the police went from door to door instructing people to remain inside, to close all windows, and to turn off their air conditioners. During the first few days of the accident, over 150,000 people living within a fifteen-mile radius of the damaged reactor either evacuated the area or had a member of their family evacuated. Many of the thousands who left the area did so with the feeling that they might never see their homes again. Several who remained in the area did so with a sense of uneasiness. Work obligations and other daily responsibilities kept them from leaving. One of the bars in the nearby area tapped into attitudes of resignation and fatalism by holding "an end-of-the-world party."

Initially, guidelines from government committees on the location of nuclear reactors emphasized the importance of keeping them as far from densely populated areas as possible. The intent was to minimize the dangers of exposing a large number of people to any serious release of radioactivity from an accident with a nuclear reactor. The initial precautions, however, were subsequently set aside as an increasing number of electric utility companies developed nuclear power plants. There were few remote sites available in areas where the commercial needs for electricity were greatest. Remote sites would increase the costs of power transmission and would be less convenient for those who manage and operate the plants. The Three Mile Island plant was located on a long and narrow strip in the Susquehanna River, only eleven miles from the center of the Harrisburg metropolitan area.

According to some estimates, the nuclear reactor at Three Mile Island came within thirty to forty-five seconds of a complete meltdown before it was brought under control. The problems of the aftermath were of a type and a magnitude that neither the utility company nor government regulatory agencies were prepared to handle. Some means had to be found for disposing of the thousands of gallons of radioactive water in the containment building. We have never had any satisfactory way of disposing of large amounts of radioactive waste materials. Moving radioactive waste materials from one location to another does not fully solve the problem.

Despite assurances from the utility company and government officials that the crisis was over, many people remained doubtful. Millions of Americans watched on television as radiation detectors were used to check people and food supplies for possible contamination. To alleviate anxieties, President Jimmy Carter visited the damaged power plant, and officials reported that his exposure to radiation was less than that which occurs any day of the year in Denver, Colorado, or at the altitudes flown by jet airplanes.

Ample evidence was available to suggest that several mishaps had already occurred at nuclear power plants in other parts of the country. Some of the troubles grew out of flaws in design and shoddy construction. Others grew out of ineptitude in working with sophisticated systems of technology that were not well understood by anyone. Additional problems stemmed from having a large number of valves and pipes that could become defective and wear out at unexpected times. It was revealed that the Diablo Canyon nuclear power plant was located near an earthquake fault. Another nuclear power plant was located within the flight pattern of a landing strip at a metropolitan airport. Images of what might happen if a jet plane crashed into a nuclear power plant were terrifying. Some thought of Murphy's law, which held that "what can go wrong, will go wrong, and at the least opportune time."

While Three Mile Island became the major symbol in the controversy over nuclear power, a more serious accident had occurred previously at the Fermi demonstration reactor located on Lake Erie, south of Detroit. In October 1966, a nuclear meltdown occurred in the core assembly during an experiment for achieving the power goal that had been set by the company. The heat built up faster than expected, and the automatic safety devices for the cooling system failed to work. Following several terrifying months and a series of complicated decisions, the fuel assemblies were removed with great difficulty, cut into pieces, and cooled for months in huge pools of water. It took more than three years to remove the radioactive materials from the plant and seal them in steel drums for storage. Throughout, there was serious risk to the health and safety of several hundred thousand people. As the title of a study about the accident put it, "We Almost Lost Detroit."

Following the Three Mile Island episode, concerns were registered in public demonstrations throughout the country, and a hastily organized rally in Washington, D.C. drew a crowd of about 100,000. At the antinuclear rallies, anger was directed toward both utility companies and regulatory agencies. Electrical utilities were seen as being compulsive in their pursuit of profits and negligent in their disregard for the health and safety of people living in surrounding communities. Government regulations were seen as ineffective because the regulatory agencies were committed to promoting the use of nuclear energy. The controversy over nuclear power commanded the attention of the nation and tapped into attitudes toward the costs and benefits of modern technology and industry.

Prior to the Three Mile Island episode, many Americans had already become doubtful about claims for the safety of nuclear power plants. Anxieties had been intensified by a movie, *The China Syndrome*, starring Jane Fonda as an investigative reporter for a television news program. The movie conveyed the image that nuclear power plants were unsafe, that attempts had been made to cover up defects in the design and construction of a nuclear power plant, and that employees who attempted to talk to news reporters or to investigative committees met with violent and mysterious deaths. In effect, the message was conveyed that a technological failure of catastrophic proportions was on the verge of happening. The metaphor of "the China syndrome" expressed the notion that a nuclear meltdown would start a chain reaction that would continue until it burned a hole through the entire earth.

Folklore metaphors and analogies were drawn upon to express fears and concerns with the development of nuclear technologies: The nuclear power plant was seen as "a time bomb waiting to be exploded," "a Frankenstein monster that would turn on its creator," and "a powerful genie that, once released from the bottle, could not be put back in again." Humans were seen as "playing God with the fundamental forces of the universe." Such descriptions were ways of placing unknown dangers within a framework that could be understood. The concern was that technology would become uncontrollable. Radiation is invisible and we may be exposed to lethal doses without actually knowing it; the many harmful effects of radiation may not show up until some time later. Such fears frequently tapped into perceptions of danger and feelings of fatalism.

At the time of the Three Mile Island episode, many Americans still believed that the development of nuclear power plants was a good idea. However, those living within a several-mile radius of a nuclear power plant frequently expressed the view that they would prefer to have the plant located someplace else. The minority opposed to nuclear power plants held their opinions with a high level of intensity. They were willing to back up their attitudes with action. Nuclear power plants throughout the country were surrounded by picket lines and active protest against the use of nuclear power. Those who reported being in favor of nuclear power plants did not hold their attitudes with a high level of conviction; even experts could not agree on the feasibility, safety, and efficiency of nuclear power plants.

Some of the worst fears about nuclear power plants were confirmed by the nuclear accident at Chernobyl in the Soviet Union in April 1986. An explosion occurred within seconds after the beginning of a test of the backup electrical system. A rapid acceleration of the reactor generated intense levels of heat and an explosion resulted. A roof weighing about 1,000 tons was blown off the reactor, and radioactive isotopes were sent about half a mile into the atmosphere. An intense fire started and burned for several days. Many of the workers at the plant were killed by the explosion and several of the fire-fighters died from exposure to radioactivity while putting out the fire.

Clouds carrying radioactive isotopes contaminated several hundred square miles of the Soviet Union and generated conditions that made a large land area uninhabitable. Initial attempts to cover up the accident resulted in delayed evacuation of the area and hence a prolonged exposure of thousands of people to radioactive contamination. Approximately 80,000 people had to be evacuated from the surrounding area. Several thousand people died from the accident, and several thousand more were expected to die prematurely from cancers caused by radiation.

The accident at Chernobyl confirmed the view of antinuclear activists that there is no ideal location for a nuclear power plant. Radioactive clouds were carried from Chernobyl across several countries in Eastern Europe, contaminating a large land area. Thousands of tons of vegetables were condemned as unsafe to eat as far away as Italy, and children in Eastern Europe were advised not to drink milk. Reindeer herds as far away as Lapland were decimated by the effects of the contamination. The costs in human life and suffering were of a serious magnitude.

By the time of the Chernobyl incident, public opinion in the United States had solidified around the basic position of the antinuclear activists. A national survey in 1986 revealed that 70 percent of the American population were now opposed to nuclear power plants. Earlier claims for nuclear power plants as safe and efficient were rejected. From an economic standpoint, it was becoming increasingly evident that nuclear power plants were not cost effective. Risks to the personal safety of workers, risks to the health of people living in the surrounding area, and risks to the environment were seen as risks not worth taking. Public sentiment coalesced around the notion of "no more nuclear power plants."

Calamities to Come

For thousands of years, religious prophecies have been directed toward a cataclysmic destruction of the world. According to the sacred texts, the apocalypse would result from the wrath of an angry God who would seek retribution for human sinfulness and moral decay. Today, our visions of the apocalypse have become more secular in character. Visions of the end are more typically directed toward accelerated technological changes that will result in disastrous consequences for the physical environment. The more serious of the human sins and evil were not the violations of conventional forms of morality, but the technological accomplishments that had been associated with the doctrine of progress.

While predictions about the future have been notoriously off base in the past, it is reasonable to direct attention to some of the major predictions that segments of the population are making about the calamities that are to come. The very nature of a national trauma is that it cannot be predicted in advance. While most traumas take the form of "a bolt out of the blue," there are also traumas that gradually evolve over long periods of time, build in intensity, and result in serious unwanted consequences. In the apocalyptic visions of the future, it is the environmental and health concerns that are foremost in the underlying anxieties of the modern age.

The majority of Americans believe that environmental dangers to the average person's health and safety have increased in recent years. If the environmentalists are correct, some of the worst technological accidents are yet to come. A new vocabulary has emerged to describe some of the consequences of our technologically oriented lifestyles. Modern vocabularies include "acid rain," "endangered species," "radioactive waste materials," "environmental degradation," "destruction of the ozone layer," and "the greenhouse effect." Underlying these new terms are concerns about whether social life as it is presently known and understood can be extended into the future. Serious reflections are also expressed about the type of world we will be leaving to future generations.

Throughout most of the past, our waste materials were primarily organic in character and thus biodegradable within a relatively short period of time. The waste materials of modern civilization are of a different order. The metallic, chemical, and radioactive qualities of our current waste materials are much more toxic and have much more enduring effects. Several decades have passed since the launching of the nuclear age, but we still lack an adequate solution to the problem of disposing of radioactive waste materials. It is only in recent years that we have even located and inventoried the hazardous waste dumps of the past. Apparently many industries disposed of chemical waste materials in a socially irresponsible manner.

Concerns with the greenhouse effect are focused on the consequences of human activities for the atmosphere surrounding the earth's surface. The fossil fuels used in the pursuit of everyday activities has increased the level of carbon dioxide and other man-made gasses in the atmosphere. Because these gasses serve as an atmospheric shield, the heat radiated at the earth's surface cannot escape back into space. The effect is a potential warming trend on a worldwide basis. Global warming could have the effect of melting the polar ice caps, which in turn would raise the sea level along coastal areas and flood a great deal of Florida, Louisiana, and other lowlands throughout the world. The suitability of many areas of the world for agriculture would be altered, and many dramatic changes could occur in climate and weather conditions.

Through the use of medical technology, vaccines and antibiotics were developed for the treatment of communicable diseases. The use of these procedures have permitted a larger part of the population to survive many of the debilitating illnesses of the past. Nevertheless, some see serious catastrophes lurking in the background. Microorganisms are now evolving that are immune to antibiotics. Further, new forms of disease are disseminated much more rapidly as a result of international travel. Diseases originating anywhere in the world may be transmitted to the United State at the end of a transcontinental flight.

We know from the AIDS epidemic that viruses may develop for which we have no immunity. The concern about a major calamity grows out of the possibility that a lethal virus will surface for which we will not be able to develop an immunity fast enough. We are now aware that the European conquest of Native Americans was facilitated not so much by their superior weapons as by the diseases they brought with them for which there was no native immunity. We also know that about 30 million people around the world lost their lives with the influenza epidemic of 1918–1919. While health concerns are foremost among the overriding anxieties of Americans, we have no reasonable basis for assessing whether these are realistic or neurotic responses to a future that is unpredictable.

The modern preoccupation with technology derives from the recognition that humans shape their destinies and that they do so from the information they have at their disposal, however incomplete or inadequate that information may be. It is through acting on the basis of information that humans have the capacity within limits to shape their own destinies. While the scope of these limits may be very broad, they may be more restricted than we currently imagine. If we have little doubt about our capacity to build a better world, it is only because we have not adequately confronted the complexities of our lifestyles and the complexities of the world in which we live.

Bibliography

Bach, Julie S., and Lynn Hall, eds. 1986. *The Environmental Crisis: Opposing Viewpoints.* St. Paul, MN: Greenhaven Press.

Brown, Harrison. 1954. *The Challenge of Man's Future.* New York: Viking Press.

Clarke, Lee. 1989. *Acceptable Risk? Making Decisions in a Toxic Environment.* Berkeley: University of California Press.

Douglas, Mary, and Aaron Wildavsky. *Risk and Culture: An Essay on the Selection of Technical and Environmental Dangers.* Berkeley: University of California Press.

Freudenburg, William R., and Susan K. Pastor. 1992. "Public Responses to Technological Risks." *Sociological Quarterly* 33: 389–412.

Fuller, John G. 1975. *We Almost Lost Detroit.* New York: Reader's Digest Press.

Gale, Robert Peter, and Thomas Hauser. 1988. *Final Warning: The Legacy of Chernobyl.* New York: Warner Books.

Gamson, William A., and Andre Modigliani. 1989. "Media Discourse and Public Opinion on Nuclear Power." *American Journal of Sociology* 95: 80–95.

Goldberg, M. Hirsh. 1984. *The Blunder Book: Colossal Errors, Minor Mistakes, and Surprising Slipups That Have Changed the Course of History.* New York: William Morrow.

Keylin, Arleen, and Gene Brown, eds. 1976. "Hindenburg Burns in Lakehurst Crash." In *Disasters: From the Pages of the New York Times,* pp. 106–107. New York: Arno Press.

King, Margaret J. 1984. "Fear of Flying: Marketing Research and the Jet Crisis." *Journal of American Culture* 7: 122–127.

Lawless, Edward W. 1977. *Technology and Social Shock.* New Brunswick, NJ: Rutgers University Press.

Morone, Joseph G., and Edward J. Woodhouse. 1986. *Averting Catastrophe: Strategies for Regulating Risky Technologies.* Berkeley: University of California Press.

Morrow, Patrick D. 1987. "Those Sick Challenger Jokes." *Journal of Popular Culture* 20 (spring): 175–184.

Norman, Donald A. 1988. *The Psychology of Everyday Things.* New York: Basic Books.

Perrow, Charles. 1984. *Normal Accidents: Living with High-Risk Technologies.* New York: Basic Books.

Sojka, Gregory S. 1984. "The Astronaut: An American Hero with 'The Right Stuff.' " *Journal of American Culture* 7, no. 2: 118–121.

Stanley, Manford. 1978. *The Technological Conscience: Survival and Dignity in an Age of Expertise.* Chicago: University of Chicago Press.

Vaughn, Diane. 1996. *The Challenger Launch Decision: Risky Technology, Culture, and Deviance at NASA.* Chicago: University of Chicago Press.

Walsh, Edward J. 1981. "Resource Mobilization and Citizen Protest in Communities Around Three Mile Island." *Social Problems* 29: 1–21.

Walsh, Edward J., and Rex H. Warland. 1983. "Social Movement Involvement in the Wake of a Nuclear Accident: Activists and Free Riders in the TMI Area." *American Sociological Review* 48: 764–780.

Washington Post. (Staff). 1986. *Challengers: The Inspiring Life Stories of the Seven Brave Astronauts of Shuttle Mission 51–L.* New York: Pocket Books.

Westrum, Ron. 1991. *Technologies and Society: The Shaping of People and Things.* Belmont, CA: Wadsworth.

Zamora, Lois Parkinson. 1982. *The Apocalyptic Vision in America.* Bowling Green, OH: Bowling Green University Popular Press.

Part III

Epilogue

12 • Collective Memory

One of the basic lessons from a review of national traumas is a recognition that the social order is fragile and subject to disruptions in unexpected ways. We may desire stability and coherence in the world around us, but at the same time we are required to cope with unwanted events of an extraordinary magnitude. Both triumphs and tragedies are inherent in social living. The triumphs verify the assumption that plans can be made and implemented, while the traumas remind us that hopes and intentions have their limits.

Superimposed on the lifestyles of the twentieth century were troubles of a serious magnitude. Extremes were evident in the shifts from economic abundance to severe economic hardships, from military unpreparedness to the capacity for annihilating all human life on this planet, from an intense fear of communism to political indifference toward the communist label, from the sanctification of political leaders to regarding them as criminals, and from landing a man on the moon to witnessing the explosion of the space shuttle *Challenger*. Sharp contrasts thus surfaced in the experiences of Americans and in the attitudes they held about their recent past. Some reflected on past accomplishments and developed a sense of pride in their country; others focused on traumas, assumed that there will be historical repetitions, and became pessimistic about the future.

The social significance of traumatic events stems from collective debates over the causes, conditions, and consequences of the chaotic forces that impinge upon our consciousness. In the trauma phase of an event, basic questions are raised, such as "how did it happen," "why did it happen," and "what is going to happen next." With the passing of time, however, the boundaries around specific events weaken as they are placed within the general fabric of social life. In telling and retelling the stories of our past, the events in question become stereotyped and selectively distorted as they become embedded in collective memories.

We usually think of memory as reflected in the retrieval of information that is stored in the brains of individuals. However, in the final analysis, memory is a collective phenomenon. The human brain is certainly central to what we associate with being human. After all, it is the complexity and the sophistication of the human brain that sets us apart from all other animals. In the final analysis, however, the contents of the human brain are primarily social in character. It is through the use of language and other symbols, and through our interactions with others, that we construct the possibilities and the limits of the world around us. Images of ourselves and of our external environment are shaped by memories that are passed on by legions of men and women we have never known and never shall meet.

Prior to the printing press and the widespread use of the written word, collective memories were transmitted primarily by means of oral history. Through the myth-making process, group experiences were passed on from one generation to the next. Stories were told about heroic times and the moral foundations of society. Some degree of social continuity was provided by oral traditions in which narratives were often embellished in order to have more dramatic effects on listeners. New generations were provided with frames of reference for deciding what to do, or what not to do, in given situations. Then as now, mythical accounts provided the ingredients for shaping a collective identity. The sacred and the secular became inseparable.

Today, we have newspapers, formal documents, photographs, computers, and other sophisticated devices for storing information that may be retrieved when the need arises. Recorded history provides us with access to information about the problems of the past, how attempts were made to solve those problems, and the outcomes that resulted. Collective memories thus serve as a storehouse of knowledge that goes far beyond the information that is directly stored in the brains of living men and women. The importance of the data from the past, however, is not self-evident. It must be interpreted, given credibility, and constructed along lines that give it applicability to present concerns.

Humans thus take an active part in determining what their collective memories will be. Events are fashioned through a filtering of experiences. Some experiences are dismissed, while others are elaborated and given high levels of significance. Selective inattention and forgetting is a way of minimizing the risk of cluttering memories with information that is perceived to be trivial or irrelevant. In contrast, we tend to remember what we sense is important for us to remember. Individually and collectively we seek to repeat those activities that were rewarding to us in the past and to avoid those activities that were associated with pain and suffering. Memories of how a social system was damaged by a traumatic event serve as a reminder of what to avoid in the future.

In publicly held attitudes and in the decisions of policy makers, national traumas frequently serve as negative frames of reference. The stories of these traumas serve as reminders of our mistakes and how they may be avoided in the future. These stories include accounts of the lack of responsiveness of government officials to the intensifying hardships of the Great Depression, how Americans were unwilling to prepare for war at a time when advance preparations were necessary, how we were caught off-guard at Pearl Harbor, how close we came to nuclear war during the Cuban Missile Crisis, how we got caught in the quagmire of Vietnam without any satisfactory way out, and how the misuse of power led to the forced resignation of a president. Dramatic messages are received from the past and may help the nation to avoid or to minimize such problems in the future.

Collective memories may be thought of as a storehouse of information on how problems were confronted and solved in the past. For example, the mobilization of resources to develop the atomic bomb became a grandiose model of what is possible when there is a concerted effort to solve some identifiable problem. Landing a man on the moon and eradicating smallpox on a worldwide basis were additional spectacular accomplishments that are recorded among recent memories. Collective memories thus incorporate not only the tragedies of the past, but also extraordinary heroic accomplishments. Identifiable problems are seen as amenable to solution through collective action.

National traumas also provide the raw material for shaping national identities and revitalizing values for promoting the collective good. To provide some assurance that the past will be remembered properly, acts of commemoration are directed toward the creation of national shrines, monuments, memorials, and holidays. These creations build upon echoes from the past and facilitate the memory process for current and future generations. To give them a proper place in the fabric of social life, traumatic events need to be selectively remembered. Those aspects of the past that were embarrassing to the nation or lacked relevancy for the moral foundations of society tend to be ignored.

National traumas provide the raw material for a vast amount of cultural elaboration. The hundreds, even thousands, of books, movies, and television productions devoted to national traumas reflect the many ways in which Americans remember their past. Like all other societies, our society must pass its heritage from one generation to the next and prepare people for the challenge of changing conditions. The expanding scope of the entertainment industries in serving this function is evident. Collective memories are drawn upon to tap a responsive chord in mass audiences. The self-attitudes, emotions, and predispositions of the viewers and readers shape and refine the contents and the entertainment value of the productions.

As new generations confront the problems of their time and place, the inventory of data from the past is reevaluated. Some experiences from the past become embellished and elaborated in attempts to give them contemporary relevance. Other experiences are relegated to the dustbin of history because they are no longer perceived as useful. It is perhaps because of the human life cycle that societies retain their innovative potential. New members are added to a social system and older members die. Through the replacement of members, societies take on dynamic qualities reflected in the opportunities provided for new beginnings.

Generational Effects

The members of a generation are influenced disproportionately by what was happening historically during their formative years. While we cannot say with precision what the boundaries are for the formative years, they would seem to be primarily the years of late adolescence and early adulthood. These are the years in which major life decisions are made at the individual level about continuing one's education, selecting a career, entering the labor force, getting married, and becoming a parent. The large number of decisions in early adulthood place individuals in a position of hyper-receptivity to the events that are occurring in their communities and in the nation. Personal encounters with national traumas during the formative years tend to have a disproportionate effect on any given generational unit.

Sociologists have observed that for an event to have a generational effect it must have an enduring place in the memories of those who experienced it during their formative years. The emotional impact of the event must be of a sufficient magnitude that it is remembered in a similar way by a large number of people. Further, the event must generate a sufficient level of public attention that people feel a pressing need to develop attitudes and beliefs about it. Using these criteria, the historical events of the twentieth century that have had the more enduring effects on generational memories include the Great Depression of the 1930s, the epic struggles of World War II, the assassination of President John F. Kennedy, the civil rights movement, and the collective frustrations of the Vietnam War. Other traumas had intense emotional effects on the nation, but were of shorter duration and had less lasting effects in collective memories.

Drawing on a national sample, a University of Michigan study found generational effects in perceptions of the most important events of the past fifty years. The events most frequently mentioned were those that had occurred during the subject's early adulthood. Americans in their fifties and sixties more frequently mentioned the Great Depression and World War II, while Americans in their thirties and forties more frequently mentioned the Vietnam War and the assassination of President Kennedy. Perceptions of consequential historical events are thus more likely to include events that occurred during an individual's impressionable years.

Those entering into early adulthood during the Great Depression had direct experiences with high rates of unemployment and economic hardships. Through knowing what scarcities were like, they became disproportionately oriented toward saving, investment, and the accumulation of assets. The economic prosperity of the post–World War II era was not taken for granted but was seen as an opportunity to increase an individual's sense of economic security. An increase in income level was seen as an opportunity to prepare for the lean years that might lie ahead. Swings in the business cycle were recurrent concerns, since there was no way of knowing in any given case how far the recessionary swing would go. Building assets became associated with both a perception of personal accomplishment and a sense of economic safety and security. For many of the post–World War II generation, savings were seen not so much as a means for accumulating assets in order to enjoy the good life later on, but as a meaningful goal in itself. Perhaps more than previous generations, there was an interest in building assets in order to achieve personal financial security and to pass on assets to the next generation to provide for the financial security of children and grandchildren.

In contrast, the generation entering early adulthood during the 1950s and 1960s had direct experiences with economic abundance and tended to take access to the good life for granted. They tended to see the older generation as overly materialistic and money oriented. They were more concerned with following impulse tendencies, seeking self-actualization, and making free use of consumer credit. "Spend now and pay later" became an accepted point of view for this privileged generation. Self-actualization became a more prevalent concern, and hedonistic behavior tended to take priority over long-range financial planning.

Collective memories frequently are drawn upon to support a political position or to document the urgency of avoiding a particular line of action. For example, the debates in the U.S. Senate over the Gulf War reflected generational effects. Older members of the Senate drew upon their experiences with World War II, saw a similarity between Saddam Hussein and Adolph Hitler, and argued against any form of compromise or appeasement. Nothing short of a direct forceful military response to Iraq's invasion of Kuwait was seen as adequate. In contrast, Vietnam veterans in the Senate were concerned about the long-range implications of our involvement, predicted heavy American casualties, and maintained that we lacked any set of guidelines on how to withdraw. Memories of both World War II and the Vietnam War were thus implicated in the debates over contemporary policy options and alternatives. Some subsequently saw the use of American military might against Iraq as a demonstration of how we should have fought the war in Vietnam. In this respect, the significance of collective memories lie less in their accuracy than in the meanings they have for their adherents.

The emotional impact of generational experiences became evident in interviews with veterans on the fiftieth anniversary of the D-Day invasion of Europe. The event was humanized by placing emphasis on individual soldiers who had played in the historic invasion of Normandy, a major turning point of World War II. Stories about the tenacity of the fighting, the scope of the fatalities, and the trauma of war were openly expressed in newspaper and television reports. On this ceremonial occasion, tragedies in the personal lives of individuals were linked with the historical encounter. The anniversary commemoration permitted veterans to express pent-up emotions and to remind new generations of the sacrifices made by those who preceded them in a time of serious troubles.

The significance of the divisions along generational lines has been intensified as a result of the fact that people live longer and many dramatic changes have occurred. For example, during the course of the twentieth century, fertility declined, life expectancy at birth increased by more than twenty-five years, and the median age of the population increased. As a result, dramatic changes sharpened the contrasts in generational experiences and intensified the fragmentation of the social realm.

The more recent generations are notorious in their disregard for the long reach of their historical past. Henry Ford's comment that "history is bunk" is a sentiment shared by many young adults. There is a sense of comfort in putting bad times behind us and thinking positively about both the present and the future. One college student spoke for her generation when she said: "All this talk about the American institution of slavery and other atrocities in American history just makes me feel sad. I was not alive then and did not have anything to do with such practices. Besides, we don't do that kind of thing anymore. I would prefer not to hear about it."

Depressive disturbances persist for those individuals who are exposed directly to traumatic events. When a trauma becomes national in scope, however, both the needs of individuals and the needs of the social system must be addressed. At the level of the social system, there is a need to give some form of enduring recognition to traumatic events. This tends to take the form of finding some higher level of meaning for the tragedies that were suffered, thus enhancing collective values and ideals. The needs of the social system are addressed through such forms of commemoration as the creation of monuments, memorials, sacred shrines, and holidays.

Commemoration

The act of commemoration is a formal means of giving recognition to the importance of past events and designating them as worthy of collective remembrance. Symbolic representations of past events are designed to give special recognition to great men and women, to heroic undertakings, and to personal sacrifices for the benefit of the nation. The act of commemoration is essentially a means of rejuvenating cultural values and promoting images of society as a moral community. For this reason, the commemoration of public events endows them with sacred meanings and results in a blending of national sentiments with religious ideologies.

In the process of commemoration, a mixture of selective recall and selective distortion tends to operate. War monuments and memorials, for example, are forms of commemoration that typically gloss over the tragedies and horrors of war. The urge to find some higher meaning for war experiences leads to justifications for the sacrifice and the loss. The horror of war is displaced by an emphasis on its glory. Encounters with death and destruction are camouflaged by an emphasis on the sacred task of defending the nation. The speeches at sacred shrines on Memorial Day, the Fourth of July, and Veterans Day are all designed to enhance patriotic values through the glorification of war. Emphasis is placed upon the men and women who "voluntarily" sacrificed their lives for their country. The underlying message seems to be that Americans should be willing to make personal sacrifices for promoting the collective good.

In contrast to previous wars, notions about the proper way to remember the Vietnam War was problematic for Americans. The casualties and atrocities of the war and the errors in political judgment were sufficiently painful that most Americans simply wanted to forget about it and move on. Yet, the trauma of the war was sufficiently intense that it could not be swept aside. Forgetting about it, or denying that it occurred, was not a reasonable option. The mistakes of the war had become a part of the American experience. It was the pressure from the veterans themselves that resulted in the creation of the Vietnam Veterans Memorial. The subtle symbolism of the memorial captures the trauma of the war and permits the millions who visit the wall each year to reflect in their own way on the lessons and meanings of war.

Memories of World War II and the Vietnam War are still vivid in American consciousness, while the Korean War has been described as "the forgotten war." It may be that we remember the wars that provided us with glorious victories or embarrassing defeats, but a war that provides us with a stalemate is hardly worth remembering. When the Korean War ended, the boundaries were drawn at about the same place they had been drawn when it started. The war was not looked upon as "a real war," but only as "a police action" under the auspices of the United Nations. Despite the fierce battles of the war and the 50,000 American fatalities, the Korean war never became a trauma to the nation. Thus, it is not the objective consequences of an event in terms of pain and suffering that makes an event worth remembering, but its impact on the institutional structure of society. During the Korean War, we were neither threatened by an external invasion nor did the war grow out of deep divisions within the nation. It was a war that provided very little to celebrate or to memorialize.

National monuments and memorials are experienced as sacred places by the millions of Americans who visit them each year. The Vietnam Veterans Memorial, Kennedy's gravesite at Arlington Cemetery, the Tomb of the Unknown Soldier, the Lincoln Memorial, Civil War battlegrounds, Pearl Harbor, and the Little Big Horn are among the more frequently visited tourist attractions each year. While by purely objective criteria, these are mundane places and there is nothing particularly special about them, the meanings imputed to them are of a different order. For example, studies of tourists at the Vietnam Veterans Memorial indicate that most of the visitors have an intensely emotional reaction resembling a sacred or religious experience. They see themselves in the mirrored reflections on the wall, and whether they opposed or supported the war, they are not able to remain indifferent or unaffected.

Only a small percentage of Americans make a deliberate pilgrimage to national shrines. More often, a visit to a sacred shrine is a bonus to a trip or to a vacation. Visiting a monument, memorial, shrine, or museum becomes something to do when convenient. If one is driving across Interstate 90, a side trip to Mount Rushmore, to the saloon where Wild Bill Hickock was killed, or to the Custer battleground at the Little Big Horn becomes simply a way of breaking up the monotony of the trip; however, beneath the superficiality of these visits, there are important latent meanings that are evoked.

The meanings assigned to the Little Big Horn, for example, are richly varied for the many tourists who stop there. For some, the Custer battleground evokes reflection on what is perceived as an American policy of genocide toward an indigenous people; for others, it elicits images of Custer as a hero or as a villain; for yet others, it is seen as a major military victory against native Americans who were attempting to protect their tribal lands. In some cases, the reflections may be as specific as imagining the stench of the decayed corpses that were encountered by those assigned to the burial detail. Linking personal lives with historical events is thus a selective process.

We may ask, why go through the inconvenience of long-distance travel to experience memorials in remote places? We could learn about historical places and events by reading about them, by watching videos, movies, or television programs, or by surfing the Internet. Why travel rather than use other forms of information-seeking behavior? A partial answer is that being there provides more of an authentic experience than can be derived from reading a book or watching television. Books are abstract, and the television experience is vicarious and illusory in a way in which direct encounters are not. While television is much more than moving dots on an electronic screen, it provides only an incomplete experience.

The quest for authentic experiences and knowledge bears an affinity to the religious pilgrimages and the sacred journeys that were prominent in other times and places. The pilgrimages of the past, as well as those of today, offer opportunities for establishing a sense of personal connection with a set of ultimate values. The sacred journey facilitates separating the genuine from the spurious, the illusion from the reality, and the authentic from the inauthentic. People need to actively participate in a meaningful cosmos. Both the needs of the soul and the needs of the body must be satisfied.

At the conscious level, we have rejected the sacred and mythical nature of the world we live in. In doing so, however, something is missing. The human spirit requires more than work schedules and the materialistic consumption of consumer goods. The world is becoming increasingly interdependent, and if we are to find an adequate sense of meaning within it, we must extend our awareness of places and events that are geographically separated from the mundane aspects of everyday life.

In contrast to the travel required in visiting monuments and shrines, the commemoration of historical events by people dispersed throughout the country is promoted through the creation of national holidays. Not only does a holiday permit commemoration throughout the nation, it also provides a structure for selectively remembering the traumas and glories of the past. Dwelling routinely on tragic events would reflect a morbid form of anxiety and would be regarded as pathological. Yet, those events that had an extraordinary emotional impact on the society cannot be easily dismissed or completely ignored. For this reason, special anniversaries are set aside as times for reflection on the events in question. Reflection is especially necessary for those events that remain unsettled or incomplete.

The designation of Martin Luther King's birthday as a national holiday, for example, was a way of giving formal recognition to the importance of social justice in the life of the nation. The personal charisma of King came to be associated with a willingness to die for a broader social cause if it becomes necessary. On the anniversary of his birth, the news media selectively reproduce his speeches, show photographs of civil rights demonstrations and marches, and reflect on contemporary issues of social justice. In this respect, the holiday is also a holy day as Americans reflect on the dominant values of their society and the contradictions inherent in modern social living.

In contrast to remembering King on the date of his birth, President John F. Kennedy is remembered on the date of his death. Aside from commemorating his accomplishments, remembering Kennedy is more about reflecting on his unfulfilled potential. Perceptions of his youthfulness and his idealism promote speculation on how the world would have been different had he lived. Freed from the realities of practical politics, the imagery of Kennedy has a dream-like quality about it. As a central public figure of the twentieth century, Kennedy provides a model that enables individuals to reflect on their own hopes and aspirations. The imagery evokes human emotions, which intensify and gain concrete focus. Some believe Kennedy would have circumvented the quagmire of the Vietnam War, would have negotiated a settlement of the arms race with the Soviet Union, would have normalized relationships with Cuba, and would have advanced the cause of civil rights. Remembering Kennedy thus taps into personal hopes for a better world.

The national preoccupation with Kennedy, however, goes far beyond the loss of his leadership potential. While the collective quest for a resolution of the mystery of his death has somewhat of a morbid quality about it, there appears to be a genuine national interest in knowing more about the circumstances surrounding his assassination. Americans who accepted the conclusions of the Warren Commission that Lee Harvey Oswald acted alone in killing the president have been able to complete the mourning process, to bury the event deep in the their generational memories, and to put the event behind them. Americans who reject the report of the Warren Commission, however, still suffer from some degree of trauma. The six seconds in Dallas are replayed over and over in their memories. The excavation of new evidence and the creation of new explanations only serve to reinforce and perpetuate feelings of disturbance and uneasiness. These concerns are likely to dissipate only after the death of the generation that was so deeply moved by the emotional trauma of his death.

The past is a time that has vanished; we visit there only intermittently, and we generally do not wish to linger there for very long. Nevertheless, news-gathering agencies always seem to remember anniversaries of traumatic events. From only a casual review of newspapers, it becomes evident that anniversaries are important to Americans as a time for reflection on traumatic events. Newspaper accounts not only provide a brief description of the trauma on its anniversary but also reproduce photographic images of the event and publish comments made by those who had direct experiences with the event in question. The emphasis is not so much on the lessons learned by the trauma as continuing to give recognition to the emotional impact it had and to the place it selectively holds in the memories of individual men and women.

Popular Culture and Mass Entertainment

In popular culture and mass entertainment, collective memories are reflected in the many ways stories are told to new generations about their historical past. In movies, television programs, and fictional writings, storytelling takes an embellished form. Whatever events occurred in the past are now immobilized, and those who tell stories about them are free to shape them as they wish. The constraints surrounding events as they unfolded no longer apply. Plausibility to the reading and viewing audience is of more concern than historical accuracy.

Through seeking both to entertain and to inform, previous events are reconstructed and selectively brought into focus; the missing gaps are filled in; they are humanized and embellished with extraordinary forms of drama. In mass entertainment, specific imagery becomes highly focused and events are experienced as only fragmentary. The raw materials that may be drawn upon are infinitely variable.

The scope of events and the range of activities that can become objects of interest are substantially greater than they used to be. Remote places and happenings intrude into consciousness with increased frequency, and accordingly the activities of everyday life become refocused and extended. In this process, memories of traumatic events permit a blending of fact with fiction, illusion with reality, and appearances with facades. The public displays that bombard our senses on an everyday basis serve as models of what to do, how to live, and what is possible. The trivial and the incredible tend to be dramatized, and the search for a collective identity becomes a never-ending quest.

In the realm of mass entertainment, the past becomes a form of constructed memory, since the factual details of what actually happened in history are often neither known nor knowable. We may never know in a definitive sense why we were caught so disastrously unprepared at Pearl Harbor, what actual circumstances surrounded the assassination of President Kennedy, or how close we came to nuclear war during the Cuban Missile Crisis. Through the use of imagination and through drawing upon the predispositions of reading or viewing audiences, collective memories are elaborated and embellished. Historical events are treated both as symbolic events and as pseudo-events that reflect on the problems and challenges of contemporary living. Under these circumstances history becomes a form of remembering in which the mixture of fact and fiction is of less concern than the stimulus and entertainment value of the production.

The intent of mass entertainment is not to provide a message, as communication is usually understood, but to trigger a response in the viewing audience. In a successful production, the viewers are drawn into the performances as they identify with the characters portrayed and the situations created. In this process the realities of the technology by which television is produced is of little concern or interest to most of the viewers. The script writing, the rehearsals, the stage props, the photography, and the moving dots of light on an electronic screen recede into the background as viewers become engrossed in the symbolic events portrayed. The self-attitudes, emotions, and predispositions of the viewers shape and refine the contents and the entertainment value of television productions.

The large pool of moviegoers and television watchers judge the entertainment value of cultural productions. The decisions made by millions of people acting as individuals and out of self-interest determine the kinds of entertainment made available. A veto power over television productions may be exercised by simply switching to another channel or by deciding not to watch television at all.

Mass entertainment dramatizes personal troubles, historical events, and social conflicts. Through dramatizing events, television entertainment becomes a type of collective mirror that reflects the individual's self-image and the image of society. From the mirroring of multiple aspects of social life, we may conclude that we live in a hazardous environment, that people sin and suffer from it, that heroic undertakings have successful outcomes for some and are disastrous for others, and that our personal problems are small compared to the problems of others at other times.

While our language separates time into past, present, and future, our experiences tend to unify them as we reflect on the character of symbolic events. The realities of the past take on special meanings through our current perceptions of them, and the future becomes a mixture of present fears and aspirations. In media entertainment, the audience experience of the time dimension may be described as "everywhen." There were certain events that happened in the past, can still happen today, and can happen again in the future. The time dimension becomes blurred, a form of eternal dream

time in which individuals travel psychologically to remote places and respond to the activity of people who represent both the living and the dead.

The traumas of the past provide reference points for assessing the quality
of life in the present. While the emotional impact of the traumas of the past
can only be experienced vicariously by more recent generations, they do
provide cognitive frameworks in stereotypic form for shaping what is perceived as the dangers and the opportunities of the human condition. A sense
of comfort may develop through recognizing that contemporary troubles
may be small in comparison to the difficulties people faced in the past. In
this respect, collective memories provide individuals with frameworks for
locating their present lifestyles along a continuum somewhere between "the
best possible" and the "worst possible" of all social worlds.

Historians are frequently appalled by the inaccuracies and distortions in
the portrayal of past events in mass entertainment. After all, historians are
professionals who have been given the responsibility of constructing accurate records of past events and thus keeping the nation informed about
itself. The historian is necessarily concerned with the accuracy of the story
that is told in a way in which others are not. They are the keepers of
"authentic" and "official" versions of the past. Their professional code of
ethics requires objectivity and accuracy, and their work is subjected to
professional scrutiny and evaluated by peers.

Trusteeship over the official versions of history properly falls within the
jurisdiction of professional historians. But even here, it is evident that we do
not live in a world of "solid fact." The rewriting of history stems less from
new forms of evidence than from attempts to develop new perspectives and
new understandings of past events. The lessons from history are never
direct and self-evident. Their meanings must be constructed anew by each
generation as they confront the changing circumstances of their time and
place. While the actual occurrences of historical events may be frozen in the
past, the new meanings they are given become a part of the dynamics of any
given society. The rewriting of history is often an attempt to place past
events within the living framework of contemporary concerns.

Who are the keepers of collective memories? In the final analysis, we all
are. The intersection of personal biography with historical events is crucial
to the many aspects of knowing who we are and what we are to become.
Determining where we are, how we got to where we are, and where we are
headed as we move into the future is basic to personal and collective identities. The task of the individual is that of finding his or her place within the
broader scheme of human affairs. In this process, some see themselves as
being located at the center of what is happening in their time and place.
Others see themselves as being located on the periphery of the consequen-

tial events of their society. Some seek to become active participants in shaping the social and political climate of their society; others prefer to remain politically apathetic and to pursue their own self-interests.

Links Between the Past and the Future

The human predicament is that we are caught up in a contemporary setting that is necessarily fragmented from both the past and the future. The future is unknowable, and the past in all of its many details and nuances is lost to us. Yet, we attempt to reduce the uncertainty of past events by drawing upon historical fragments that are embellished and taken out of context. Our sense of certainty about what happened in the past can only rest on incomplete information. The immutable character of the past precludes altering the course of events that did occur. We cannot rerun the Civil War, the Japanese attack on Pearl Harbor, or the Cuban Missile Crisis. We can only modify these events through using our imagination and speculating on what might have been. Prominent among such speculations are notions about how the outcomes would have changed had the decisions of key participants been different.

The selectivity of historians in their narratives of the past have been of special concern to subgroups of the population whose experiences have been ignored or downplayed. The modern consciousness of African Americans has called for a new look at the ways in which history has been written in the past. Traditional narratives by professional historians focused disproportionately on the experiences of the dominant group and were designed to reinforce the interests of the ruling class. For example, very little attention was given to the brutality of the institution of slavery from the vantage point of the victims. The rewriting of history is designed to give explicit recognition to the noteworthy accomplishments of African Americans. Historical corrections are necessary to set the record straight and to provide a basis for appreciating the black heritage within the context of a pluralistic society.

Collective memories have also been of recent concern to feminists who maintain that women are seriously disadvantaged by the ways in which history has been reported. While women constitute more than half of the population, their experiences have been underrepresented in historical accounts. To correct the selectivity of historical reporting, there has been an explosion of publications about the part women have played in the historical process. Rather than seeing women as subordinate to men in a patriarchal society, attention is now being given to the important roles women have played in societal development. The new consciousness of women grows out of the quest for social justice, out of an interest in broadening the scope of historical analysis, and out of an interest in promoting the opportunities for women to participate in the political and economic life of the nation.

In the final analysis, collective memories may be understood as forms of myth-making. Their significance lies less in their accuracy than in the meanings they have for adherents. From an objective standpoint, there is a wide gap between "the pictures in our heads" and "the world outside." There will always remain an external world that exists independently of our perceptions of it. We construct the world into systems of meaning that can be drawn upon when the need arises. The creation of myth is pragmatic as accounts of tragic events are drawn upon for self-serving purposes. Myths are useful in sustaining personal identities and commitments as well as in supporting a political policy or in documenting the urgency of avoiding a particular line of action. As forms of myth, however, collective memories also become endowed with sacred meanings as they are drawn upon to embellish perceptions of society as moral community.

Bibliography

Appleby, Joyce, Lynn Hunt, and Margaret Jacob. 1994. *Telling the Truth About History.* New York: W.W. Norton.
Bengston, Vern L. 1970. "The Generation Gap: A Review and Typology of Social Psychological Perspectives." *Youth and Society* 2: 7–32.
Bennett, W. Lance, and Martha S. Feldman. 1981. *Reconstructing Reality in the Courtroom.* New Brunswick, NJ: Rutgers University Press.
Berger, Peter, Brigitte Berger, and Hansfried Kellner. 1974. *The Homeless Mind: Modernization and Consciousness.* New York: Vintage Books.
Boorstin, Daniel J. 1961. *The Image: A Guide to Pseudo-Events in America.* New York: Harper Colophon Books.
Brown, Roger, and James Kulik. 1977. "Flashbulb Memories." *Cognition* 5: 73–99.
Cantril, Hadley. 1965. *The Pattern of Human Concerns.* New Brunswick, NJ: Rutgers University Press.
Casey, Edward S. 1987. *Remembering: A Phenomenological Study.* Bloomington: Indiana University Press.
Chomsky, Noam. 1989. *Necessary Illusions: Thought Control in Democratic Societies.* Boston: South End Press.
Duncan, Hugh Dalziel. 1968. *Symbols in Society.* New York: Oxford University Press.
Elder, Glen H., Jr. 1974. *Children of the Great Depression.* Chicago: University of Chicago Press.
Fehrenbach, T.R. 1963. *This Kind of War.* New York: Macmillan.
Feurer, Lewis S. 1969. *The Conflict of Generations.* New York: Basic Books.
Halbwachs, Maurice. 1992. *On Collective Memory,* ed. Lewis A. Coser. Chicago: University of Chicago Press.
Huber, Joan, ed. 1991. *Macro-Micro Linkages in Sociology.* Newbury Park, CA: Sage.
Kertzer, David L. 1983. "Generation as a Sociological Problem." *Annual Review of Sociology* 9: 125–149.

Kuiken, Don, ed. 1991. *Mood and Memory*. Newbury Park, CA: Sage.

Lowenthal, David. 1985. *The Past Is a Foreign Country*. New York: Cambridge University Press.

MacCannell, Dean. 1976. *The Tourist: A New Theory of the Leisure Class*. New York: Schocken Books.

Mannheim, Karl. [1928] 1952. "The Problem of Generations." In *Essays on the Sociology of Knowledge*, pp. 276–322. London: Routledge and Kegan Paul.

Mico, Ted, John Miller-Monzon, and David Rubel, eds. 1995. *Past Imperfect: History According to the Movies*. New York: Henry Holt.

Mosse, George L. 1990. *Fallen Soldiers: Reshaping the Memory of the World Wars*. New York: Oxford University Press.

Rissover, Fredric, and David C. Birch. 1977. *Mass Media and the Popular Arts*. New York: McGraw-Hill.

Schudson, Michael. 1992. *Watergate in American Memory: How We Remember, Forget, and Reconstruct the Past*. New York: Basic Books.

Schuman, Howard, and Jacqueline Scott. 1989. "Generations and Collective Memories." *American Sociological Review* 54: 359–381.

Schuman, Howard, and Cheryl Rieger. 1992. "Historical Analogies, Generational Effects, and Attitudes Toward War." *American Sociological Review* 57: 315–326.

Schwartz, Barry. 1982. "The Social Context of Commemoration: A Study in Collective Memory." *Social Forces* 61: 374–402.

Simon, William, and John H. Gagnon. 1976. "The Anomie of Affluence." *American Journal of Sociology* 82: 356–378.

Wagner-Pacifici, Robin, and Barry Schwartz. 1991. "The Vietnam Veterans Memorial: Commemorating a Difficult Past." *American Journal of Sociology* 97: 376–420.

Ware, Susan. 1982. *Holding Their Own: American Women in the 1930s*. Boston: Twayne.

Index

About the Author

Arthur G. Neal, formerly a Distinguished University Professor of Sociology at Bowling Green State University, recently joined the Center for Population Research and Census at Portland State University. He is the author or coauthor of nearly twenty books and research monographs and numerous research articles. He has taught a wide variety of graduate seminars in sociology and in American culture studies. Presently he is serving as consultant in mentoring programs for junior faculty at both Portland State University in Oregon and Bowling Green State University in Ohio.